Frank Buckland

Notes and Jottings from Animal Life

Second Edition

Frank Buckland

Notes and Jottings from Animal Life
Second Edition

ISBN/EAN: 9783337058531

Printed in Europe, USA, Canada, Australia, Japan

Cover: Foto ©ninafisch / pixelio.de

More available books at **www.hansebooks.com**

NOTES AND JOTTINGS

FROM

ANIMAL LIFE

BY THE LATE

FRANK BUCKLAND, M.A.

H.M. INSPECTOR OF FISHERIES

AUTHOR OF 'CURIOSITIES OF NATURAL HISTORY' ETC. ETC.

With Illustrations

SECOND EDITION

LONDON

SMITH, ELDER, & CO., 15 WATERLOO PLACE

1886

PREFACE

THESE PAPERS were selected and arranged by FRANK BUCKLAND, shortly before his death, with a view to their early publication. The substance of them had appeared in 'Land and Water,' whence the illustrations (except that of Jemmy the Suricate and the last sketch of the whale) are, by permission, reproduced. Jemmy's portrait is inserted, by permission, from the 'Leisure Hour.' The articles will recall to many the vivid and original power of observation and illustration, and the earnest love of nature, with which their author was gifted.

Some papers remain for future publication.

G. C. BOMPAS.

LONDON : *April* 1882.

CONTENTS

	PAGE
CHRISTMAS DAY WITH MY MONKEYS	1
MR. PONGO, THE GORILLA	7
JOE THE CHIMPANZEE	14
THE RAT, AND JUDY THE MARMOSET	17
MY SURICATE, JEMMY THE THIRD; JOE, THE TAME HARE; AND MY JACKASS	24
CARLISLE CATTLE MARKET	38
AN ELEPHANT IN ALBANY STREET	50
SALMON EGG COLLECTING FOR AUSTRALIA	55
SALMON EGG COLLECTING FOR NEW ZEALAND	67
JOHN HUNTER'S CHAIR—EAT AND BE EATEN	80
TALKING-FISH, EYES OF MUMMY, ANTIQUITIES FROM PERU	92
MY TAME OTTERS	96
MY OTTER TOMMY	100
THE COSTERMONGERS' AND POOR MAN'S MARKET	113
RELICS IN THE ASHMOLEAN MUSEUM, OXFORD	120
CURFEW AND CHARTER HORNS	124
PRE-ADAMITE LITTLE MEN, BEASTS, BIRDS, AND FISHES	136
THE CRUISE OF THE 'JACKAL'	142
NOTES FROM SCOTLAND	174
NOTES FROM YARMOUTH	185

viii CONTENTS.

	PAGE
London Birdcatchers	210
Sir Walter Scott's Home at Abbotsford	230
Sale of Manders' Menagerie at the Agricultural Hall, Islington	237
Playground for the Lions and Tigers at the Zoological Gardens	243
Tiger Fight at the Zoological Gardens	252
Polar Bear Cubs	254
Descent of the Lion from Northumberland House	266
Lord Bute's Beavers	270
Remarkable Accident to a Red Deer in Windsor Park	290
Lecompte, the Seals' Friend	299
Structure and Habits of Whales	313
The White Whale at Westminster Aquarium	341
Natural History of the Arctic Narwhal	350
Uncle Tom, the Alligator, at the Southport Aquarium	356
The Waxworks in Westminster Abbey	361
The Jews' Fish-Market in London	372
The Manatee	376
The Great Sea-Serpent	384

LIST OF ILLUSTRATIONS

PORTRAIT OF FRANK BUCKLAND . . . *Frontispiece*

FIGURE   PAGE

1. JEMMY THE SURICATE 25

2. ACCIDENT TO A STAG IN WINDSOR PARK . . 291

3. FORE-LEG OF THE STAG CAUGHT BY FORKED BRANCHES
    OF A THORN TREE 293

4. THE SEA-BEAR AT THE ZOOLOGICAL GARDENS . . . 300

5. THE SEA-LIONS AT THE BRIGHTON AQUARIUM . . 306

6. THE WALRUS 311

7. POSITION OF WHALEBONE WITH MOUTH OPEN . . 315

8. POSITION OF WHALEBONE WITH MOUTH SHUT . . . 317

9. SECTION OF WHALE'S MOUTH SHUT 318

10. SECTION OF WHALE'S MOUTH OPEN 319

11. WHALEBONE WHALE OF THE GREENLAND SEAS . . 320

12. (A) 'RIDGE OF FINS' AS SEEN BY THE OFFICERS OF H.M.
    YACHT 'OSBORNE' 386

13. (B) ANIMAL SEEN THROUGH A TELESCOPE, IN THE ACT
    OF SWIMMING AWAY 387

14. SEA-SERPENT AS SEEN IN THE HIGHLAND LOCH IN 1872 . 402

15. BASKING SHARK WITH FINS PROJECTING ABOVE THE
    WATER 406

16. GREENLAND WHALE SWIMMING AWAY . . . 410

NOTES AND JOTTINGS

FROM

ANIMAL LIFE.

—◆◇◆—

CHRISTMAS DAY WITH MY MONKEYS.

LITTLE Jack began the row ; I know he did, because I saw
him do it.

But who is Little Jack, and what was the row about ?

It was Christmas Day, a very cold Christmas Day, so I
made a good fire, and let out the monkeys for a run.

My family at that time consisted of four monkeys :
Little Jack, Tiny, Carroty Jane, and Jenny.

In the ' Monkey Room,' as the servants called my studio,
lived also the rat, Judy the marmoset, Joe the tame hare,
Jemmy the suricate, the laughing jackass, and the old
grey parrot.

Little Jack is the fun of the whole cage, and at the
same time he is the plague and torment of the inhabitants
thereof. When I bought him I was told he would grow
into a big monkey, instead of which he has grown into a
little monkey. A lady was anxious to have a monkey, and

B

I undertook to get her one. There are monkeys and monkeys; no two are alike in disposition and education. My friend Jamrach had nothing to suit, but Mr. Davy, the bird dealer, knew of one, so I sent to him for the monkey 'on sale or return,' and the result was the appearance of Little Jack sitting on Davy's shoulder. My young friend had not yet been educated. He looked scared, cold, and half starved, and his manners were by no means elegant. He was therefore not fit to go into a lady's drawing-room before he had been 'learnt,' as the Londoners say. He is about as large as a half-grown cat, and though quite a baby he has the face of an old man. He is a Rhesus, the Bhunder, or sacred monkey of India. He is as active as a cat, and flies about the cage with the agility of a big flea. His eyes are like diamonds, full of intelligence, and as quick as a hawk. He is a regular Paul Pry, and intrudes himself just wherever he is not wanted. Thus, when Tiny and Jenny have nestled themselves in a corner Little Jack jumps right into the middle of the group, and does his best to upset the party. Like all little people he has a great idea of his own consequence, and he thinks that I, his master, am terribly afraid of him, for he makes the most hideous faces at me, and chatters in such a manner, that one would think he was at least a big gorilla; perhaps he is in his own estimation. He can't bear being laughed at, and if I laugh at him he gets perfectly savage.

Jenny is a monkey I bought simply to keep Tiny company when the Old Hag died. Jenny is the biggest humbug I ever knew. She can be clever if she likes, but she very seldom likes. Her mind is given entirely to eating, drinking, and grumbling. I have seen her with her two cheek-pouches perfectly crammed with potatoes at her one o'clock dinner, yet when my luncheon comes up she will begin to tremble and shake, and whine just like an old beggar at a street corner. It is very amusing to give her more than her pouches, and her two hands and two feet can hold; she is so terribly greedy that she will try not to let the other monkeys have a bit.

Jenny has the power of pricking her ears a little when angry; she makes a threatening face, and grunts out, ' Haw, haw.' I have discovered Jenny's weak point by accident; she is in mortal terror of the house-broom. I have only to put the broom round the corner of the door, and she cries 'kik, kik,' until it is gone. Such is her fear of this unknown object, that she is incessantly looking round the corner, expecting it to appear. The broom is of great use to me to stop a fight. She has lately taken to carry Little Jack about between her teeth, caring not a bit for his screams; directly she sees the broom she drops Little Jack, who begins to tease her again.

Carroty Jane goes upon three legs, and her face has the aspect of a very old beggar woman. She is so thin that you might almost call her a living skeleton, and yet she is eating the best of food all day long—potatoes, carrots, boiled rice and treacle, nuts, grapes, and raw meat. She is an awful beggar, and when the luncheon comes up, she hobbles across the room, climbs up on to the table, and whines most piteously until she gets something or other. She is as good as a timepiece. A quarter of an hour before her feeding-time, which is always at a stated hour, she begins to shiver and shake, and keep looking towards the corner for John with the potatoes. I cannot think what makes her so thin. I have heard it stated that if cats take to eating flies they always get thin, but what truth there is in it I do not know. Certainly Carroty Jane is a great fly-eater. In the warm weather, when the flies are about, she manages to climb up on to the window-sill, and holding on by one hand, catches flies with the other. She is exceedingly adroit at this work: I don't think I ever saw her miss a fly. She is generally running loose about the room, but when in her cage she is continually watching for flies, and if one is fool enough to settle on the bars, Carroty Jane is sure to have him. She munches up the flies with a genuine gusto. I have known her to eat twenty to thirty flies a day.

She is also very fond of sprats. When I was working at the Scotch herring report I used to receive sprats (Scotice, garvies) and young herrings nearly every morning. These I used to broil for luncheon, and the monkeys used to steal them off the gridiron. The monkeys all but Little Jack would also drink beer; when Tiny wanted beer she crossed her hands in a devotional attitude, and looked in a supplicating manner first at the glass and then at me.

Jane lives on the top of the monkeys' cage, her round stand and pole being placed thereon. Little Jack cannot therefore see her, as the top of the cage intervenes. It is his daily and hourly amusement to watch for the appearance of Jane's tail. This is not much of a tail; it is very 'ratty' in appearance, but yet long enough for Little Jack to grasp occasionally.

Jane had spent the London season on the top of a pole

in a drawing-room in Portland Place, and as she was very ill I had taken her into hospital while her master and mistress were abroad.

When the dinner of boiled potatoes is brought up, the three monkeys sit round the plate, each one eating as fast as he can. Most monkeys have cheek pouches, and I am sure the reason why they have pouches is as follows. Their natural habitat is in trees. They come down on the ground for insects. My monkeys are particularly fond of meal worms. They collect their food on the ground, and put it in their pockets, that is pouches, and go up into the trees again to finish their dinner. When, therefore, the potatoes arrive, my monkeys set to work eating as hard as they can, and fill their pouches at the same time. Little Jack has very large pouches : no trace of them can be seen at ordinary times ; but at dinner-time he fills his pouches to such an extent that the two of them put together are nearly as big as his whole head.

Well, on this Christmas Day the two elderly monkeys were sitting on the perch in the cage, finishing off the contents of their pouches, and their tails were hanging straight down from the perch. What must rascally Little Jack do, but take Tiny's tail in one hand, and Jenny's tail in the other, and give both at the same moment a tremendous pull! This brought the two beauties on to the floor of the cage in an instant. They were both furious at being thus interrupted at dinner-time ; they asked no questions, but each thinking the other had insulted her, began to fight in a most lively manner. They grappled, and rolled over and over like an animated ball. They don't hurt one another when fighting ; their teeth are not big enough ; and I can always stop them by throwing cold water on them. While they were fighting, Little Jack kept jumping down upon them to keep them going, as it were. The rascal was much too active ever to get caught. The noise of the combat brought up Jemmy the suricate from the kitchen below. He always turns up when a monkey fight is going on, and as usual, up my gentleman comes, tail erect, and fur all bristled up, to make himself look big. It so happened that during this fight Tiny's tail projected through the bars. Jemmy immediately bit it with his sharp teeth. Tiny thought it was Little Jack that had done this, so she turned and hunted him all over the cage, but she could not catch him. Little Jack kept popping in and out of the sleeping-box, and then Jenny joined in the hunt, and the three of them scampered all about the cage, like the row we see in the Punch and Judy shows. Jemmy kept guard outside the cage, and bit anybody's tail as their tails happened to come out from the bars. Altogether there was a nice row, and Little Jack, as usual, was at the bottom of it.

WHEN Mr. Pongo, the gorilla, arrived in the year 1877, I had several interviews with him, and I made the following observations on his structure and habits. Mr. Pongo sits nearly always on the floor with his legs tucked under him, in a tailor-like manner. I do not think he is very arboreal in his habits, but that when at home he would probably live in a cave. His face certainly cannot be called ugly, but at the same time it cannot be called intelligent. The nose is much depressed into the face; the lips are even with the nose, and pink inside. He cannot smile, but he grins like a dog. He will snatch and pull away anything put near him. He took a pocket handkerchief from a lady's pocket, put it round his neck, and afterwards wiped his nose with it. This, I am inclined to think, was not imitation, but an accident. He is apparently not right-handed, but uses both hands equally.

One distinctive point between man and the gorilla is in the conformation of the hands. The thumb is exceedingly short, and cannot be used with anything like the same facility as in the human subject.

In the human hand the three bones forming the finger spring direct from the palm of the hand. In the gorilla, the spaces from the knuckles to the first joint of the fingers are united by a membrane, and become practically a continuation of the palm of the hand.

The gorilla uses his hand as a foot much more than as a hand. When walking the fingers are bent inward on to their first joint, thus forming a sort of pad on which the animal walks. The fore-arms and hands form, as it were, supports for the rest of the body; in fact, the gorilla's gait may be likened to a dwarf going on crutches. The hind legs are comparatively small and much bowed outwards like the legs of a baby. The thumb of the foot has great powers of prehension; indeed, it may be said that the thumb proper is carried on the foot.

It is to be remarked that the gorilla has no calf to the leg and no biceps in the fore-arm. According to my observation, he cannot stand upright without supporting himself by means of some object. I have frequently seen human beings acting a part as monkeys. It will be remarked that in this case the moment the man is able to relax his performance he stands instantly upright; the gorilla, on the contrary, the instant he possibly can do so, drops on all fours on the ground. This is entirely in accord with the definition of 'Man' as contrasted with the brute given by the poet of old—

Os homini sublime dedit cœlumque tueri.

As the gorilla walks, it will be seen that his back is almost square, somewhat after the form of the back of a prize cow, or the flat saddle used in horsemanship at a circus. I have ascertained that this great breadth of back is given by the ribs, which are broad and very strong.

In the human subject a space of about a hand's breadth intervenes between the bottom of the ribs and the top of the pelvis or hip-bone. In the gorilla the ribs come close down on to the top of the hip-bone. The hip-bones themselves are not spread out laterally to support the weight of the body as in man, but are narrowed as in many running animals.

The gorilla has apparently no more voice than a roughish guttural sound. I never saw Pongo in a rage. Under these conditions it is just possible he may make a great noise. I have put my finger into his mouth, and have ascertained that he has no pouch nor anything like a pouch. He puts everything he can get hold of into his mouth, and on all occasions his mouth and teeth are used as weapons of offence and defence.

In this one fact alone there is a vast difference between human beings and gorillas. When men quarrel they always use their hands, and in very exceptional instances their teeth.

All monkeys seem to know intuitively that their great teeth are their safeguard. Mr. Bartlett of the Zoological Gardens tells me that he once brought a large ape with tremendous tusks into a room where there were others of the same species. These rascals took no further notice of the arrival than by immediately beginning to yawn, thus showing the whole extent of their terrible tusks. This meant quite plainly 'Oh yes, Mr. Stranger, you have fine long canine teeth, no doubt, but so have we (yawn); just look!'

This gorilla, as far as ascertained, does not use a stick for the purpose of striking, nor has he ever been observed to strike with his hands; it is however most remarkable that he frequently claps his hands; in doing this his right hand

is always uppermost.   I do not think this is the result of
imitation, or that he has been taught it; it is, I think, a
natural action.   I gave him my hat, he placed it before him
upon the floor, and began immediately to drum upon it.

I am afraid the disciples of Darwin will be greatly dis-
comfited by the advent of this gorilla.   If the reader will
kindly put his or her hand to the ear, he or she will find
a very slight little hard knob on the external edge of the
fold of each ear, about a quarter of an inch from its highest
part.   The presence of this knob, according to Darwin, indicates 'the descent' of you and me, my friends, 'from a
hairy quadruped, furnished with a tail and pointed ears,
probably arboreal in its habits, and an inhabitant of the
Old World.'

I was especially careful to examine the gorilla's ear, and
I discovered that he *does not wear a knob on his ear.*[1]

Pongo is but three and a half years old, and therefore
quite a baby.   I was most interested to see how his infantine
instinct is more in accord with the human infantile rather
than with the adult mind.   He is respectful, grave, and
towards adult ladies and gentlemen somewhat distant.   A

[1] There is a point to which I think attention has not been
sufficiently called in the examination of the comparative anatomy of
the man and the monkey.   I mean the presence in the human brain of
that curious body which feels to the fingers like a grit of sand.   This
is called in anthropotomy (i.e. human anatomy) the 'pineal body.'   I
have often examined this pineal body, and wondered what the meaning
of its presence in the human brain could possibly be.   It is composed
of phosphate and carbonate of lime, and is found only in subjects after
seven years of age.

The object of the pineal body is very imperfectly known, and although
its office has been a theme for some of the wildest speculators in physio-
logical theories, we are still in the dark respecting it.

Now, has the gorilla a pineal body in his brain, or has he not?

little boy and girl came in to see him while I was present. After a while they both began to play with Pongo. Gradually they fraternised, and began to play together after the manner of little children. Not being a child, I cannot enter into their funny sayings and doings about nothing at all. So these three, the little boy and girl and the gorilla, played together after their own childish fashion for nearly half an hour, and I made the children experiment on him with ornaments, handkerchiefs, &c.; but no—the ape's brain could not understand the human. Pongo put everything in his mouth, and tried to bite it up.

When the two humans and the gorilla were sitting at play on the floor I could not help seeing the amazing difference between the countenances of the gorilla and of the children; the one decidedly and purely monkey, the others decidedly human. I could not in fact help seeing what a vast line the Creator had drawn between a man and a monkey.

Moreover the human lips are made for speaking, not so the gorilla's. They are the lips of a beast. Humans have hair on their heads; Pongo's hair is not hair in our sense of the word, but simply a kind of fur continuous with the other covering of the body.

Finally, Pongo's structure and manners confirm my conviction that Darwin's theory is here at fault, and that we are *not* descended from monkeys. In actual structure we resemble them somewhat, just as a watch that will wind up, as sold in the streets for a penny, resembles the finest chronometer ever tested at Greenwich by the Astronomer Royal. No, human beings are not monkeys.

Why not rest satisfied with the origin of our race thus revealed to us by the great Creator Himself? 'So God created man in His own image, in the image of God created He him ; male and female created He them.'

For centuries past this has been, and for centuries to come it will be, the standpoint of human intellect and faith.

Having lived with monkeys in my sitting-room for so many years, one thing I have learnt for certain is that monkeys will not intelligently imitate the actions of men ; their sense of hearing, smelling, and sight, far surpasses that of ordinary civilised human beings, but their brain is not sufficiently developed to imitate intelligently.

For instance, a monkey will sit before a fire till it goes out, but the monkey will never put a bit of wood or coal on the fire to keep it alight. I have tried this over and over again with my monkey the Old Hag, who was my constant companion at the fireside for so many years. I have placed a stick in her hand and guided her hand towards the fire, but her brain could not see the connection between the burning stick and the warmth produced therefrom. Now I believe a half-grown baby would put a stick on a fire that was fast burning away, and for the simple reason that the human brain would enable it to appreciate the connection between the lighted stick and the heat.

If the monkey's brain does not enable it to imitate the actions of men, yet the tables can be turned, as shown by the following story.

I saw when inspecting the Coquet in Northumberland, a remarkably strong, active, intelligent boy between four and five years old, playing about the salmon weir. His father told me a very curious story about the child. At Christmas he had been taken to see a pantomime in which monkeys performed a great part. The scene so impressed the child's mind, that the next morning he imagined himself to be a monkey. He would not speak, and no kindness or threats would make him speak a single word. He would not sit at table with his brothers and sisters at meals, but would only eat out of a plate placed on the ground, out of which he ate his food, being on all-fours. If anything to eat was presented to him, he always put it to his nose and smelt it, just as a monkey does, before eating it. He was continually climbing up trees and throwing down boughs, and grinning at the people below, like the monkeys in the cocoa-nut trees in the pantomime. When his father tried to correct him, the little fellow ran after him and bit him on the leg. He would serve his brothers and sisters the same if they teased him. This curious monkey fit lasted several weeks, but the idea gradually passed out of his head.

JOE THE CHIMPANZEE.

MANY of my readers will recollect Joe, the chimpanzee, who 'flourished' (as the school-books have it) at the Zoo in 1866, and for about three years after.

I should like to record the way Mr. Bartlett used to catch his chimpanzee, 'Joe.' Exercise was indispensable for his health, so every fine morning in the summer Joe was let out of his private room, and allowed to scamper loose all about the Monkey room. There he had a game of play with the other monkeys. As he wandered about the cages on the outside they followed him on the inside, thereby playing up what we used to call at school 'Meg's diversion.'

Joe was particularly fond of crawling about on the very top of his cage, out of the reach of Sutton, the keeper of the monkeys. The time at last arrived when visitors began to come into the Gardens. It was then necessary that Joe should be caught and put into his own apartment. It was apparently impossible to catch him either by fair or foul means. No amount of bribery of fruit or sweets would cause him to descend from his perch. To what passion of the monkey's mind could therefore an appeal be made ? and in what form was that appeal to be presented ?

Mr. Bartlett discovered that Joe's weak points were *curiosity* and *cowardice*. He therefore worked upon Joe's failings in the following admirable manner. He went to the keeper, and touching him gently on the shoulder, directed in a mysterious manner his attention to the dark passage underneath the gas-pipe which traverses the house, pretending to point out to Sutton some horrible unknown creature; using an energetic manner, but saying nothing except words to this effect : ' Look out, there he is, there he is.' At the same time the two men would peer into the dark place under the gas-pipe.

Master Joe, who was watching them from the top of the cage, saw the two best friends he had in the world apparently alarmed at some unknown object ; his attention, therefore, became at once fixed and riveted on their movements. He could hear and see nothing except the alarm of his friends at this unknown and fearful object in the dark ; he therefore thought that if his friends (so much superior to him in strength and intellect) were alarmed, surely he also had a right to be frightened. He began to pucker up his face, and gradually to descend in a frightened manner to the floor of the monkey-house. Keeping at a safe distance, he began to pout out his lips to crow, and titter out his loud cry of alarm. Gradually his curiosity induced him to come and see what there really was in the dark place under the gas-pipe. When he was near to the supposed point of danger, Mr. Bartlett and Sutton would simultaneously shout out, ' He's coming out ! he's coming out !' They fled instantly with the greatest alarm as from some object that they pretended was emerging from the darkness towards the room occupied by Mr. Joe. Mr. Joe, seeing that it was a case of *sauve qui peut*, was determined not to be behindhand in the flight; he therefore chattered his loudest, bristled up his hair so as to make him look double his natural size, and bolted instantly with his greatest speed towards the door of his house. Generally he was so anxious to get into a place of safety that he outstripped both of his friends, even sometimes jumping leap-frog fashion over their heads, and won the race, getting into his room some steps in advance of Sutton, who at once closed the door upon my gentleman, and Master Joe's wanderings were over for that day.

It is a curious fact that Joe never seemed to profit by experience; for whenever he was let out for his morning's airing on the top of the monkey cage, this clever plan of Bartlett's of appealing to his failings—curiosity and cowardice—never failed to succeed.

THE RAT, AND JUDY THE MARMOSET.

I OWE a great deal to rats. When a student at St. George's Hospital I wrote an article on rats, which I sent to a magazine, and to my great amazement the publishers sent me a cheque for it. From that moment I have taken a great liking to my first patrons in literature, viz. ' Rats,' and I always somehow connect them in my memory with publishers.

I have for the last twenty years never been without a tame rat. The ' Monkey room ' is the general refuge for the sick animals belonging to my friends, and lucky are those animals who come into this hospital. I almost forget where the rat I am writing about came from. I believe he was one I rescued from an untimely end by being swallowed by the ant-eater at the Zoological Gardens.

It is not generally known what excellent eating young rats are; almost all the carnivorous beasts and birds at the Gardens will eat young rats. I have a great mind in these hard times to try young rats myself; anyhow, to many creatures at the Gardens, especially to invalid snakes, young rats are as turtle soup or whitebait. Our excellent friend Mr. Bartlett, therefore, has set up a rattery, and in this rattery he breeds a great number of rats, thereby saving a considerable sum in the commissariat of the Gardens.

The rattery is managed in this wise. There is a huge box like a large corn-bin. On opening the box it will be seen that its sides are divided into nice, comfortable pigeon-holes, and to the entrance of each pigeon-hole is fixed a ladder, so that rats can come down to feed in a common dining-hall or refectory, where a daily *table d'hôte* breakfast, dinner, and supper are provided. Meals over, the rats go up the ladders to their private apartments, each of which is generally found to contain a nest of blind, squeaking baby rats. When rats are wanted for food purposes the keeper lifts up the door of one of the pigeon-holes and takes out what rats he requires. I recollect when the ant-eater first came to the Gardens, there was a capital caricature in *Punch* of a powdered-headed servant bringing a basket to Mr. Bartlett, from an old lady sitting in a brougham, with these words : ' Please, sir, the missus 'ave sent some new-laid ants' eggs for the Jew-Beater' (*Mermycophaga jubata*). Since that time it has been discovered that the ant-eater will eat young rats. The ant-eater has no teeth, and a very little mouth; hence his American name Bocca chica. When a young rat is presented to him he coils his long, whip-like tongue round the victim and swallows him like a pill. My rat would, some four years ago, have gone straight down the ant-eater's throat if I had not caught hold of his tail, pulled him out of the ant-eater's mouth, and carried him home in my hat. He has now lived for four years and longer in a squirrel's cage at one end of the mantelpiece, while the other end is ornamented by a corresponding squirrel's cage,

containing a sick marmoset, which answers to the name
of Judy. Both Judy and the rat, being nocturnal animals,
remain all day long coiled up in their respective cages.
When the gas is lighted at night Judy comes out of her
cage and bows to the rat, while the rat comes out of his
cage, and lifting his white nose in the air, nods in a
supercilious manner to Judy. The maxim, immortalised
by Horace in the Ode which begins 'Qui fit Mæcenas ut
nemo quam sibi sortem,' applies equally to Judy and the
rat. Judy crawls as well as she can over to the rat's cage,
goes in at the door, and steals the rat's food. The rat, on
the other hand, sneaks into Judy's cage, and picks up the
tit-bits there, which generally consist of grapes, sugar-
plums, meal worms, &c., as Judy is very delicate, and has
to be tempted with luxuries. One day the rat returned
home and caught Judy stealing. He pitched into Judy,
who screamed murder in a most terrible way, and he would
have injured her unless I had interfered.

Judy is a great climber, and spends hours suspended
in a sloth-like manner from the gas-bracket. Every now
and then she whisks her tail into the burning gas, but very
quickly whisks it out again. The consequence of this
process having been often repeated is that Judy's tail is
as hairless as a leather boot-lace. She has very sharp
claws, and spends much of her time hanging on the angle
of the cage nearest the fire. She has free run of the
mantelshelf and the writing-table. She does no mischief,
and being so very light does not upset anything. If
I catch her, or attempt to touch her, she begins her
rattle like a watch which has its spring suddenly broken.
The three monkeys in the cage when they hear this noise

come to her rescue. Tiny shakes at the bars of the cage with her feet and hands, and makes the most wonderful faces I ever saw ; she makes her eyes glare, and screws up her face so that I may be afraid of her.

The marmoset's ordinary note is a very high squeaky plaintive sound, like that of a bat. She has also another note which I cannot describe ; it is of anger or fear. I heard it for the first time when a gentleman brought in a live mouse in a trap for the laughing jackass. The trap was wrapped in paper, and the marmoset bristled up all the hair she had, and that was not very much, and scratched at the trap till she had pulled all the paper off. When she found what the mouse was she seemed much afraid of it, and danced round the cage crying out in her own language, 'There is something alive, there's something alive—look out.'

The rat has the bump of curiosity strongly developed, and nothing pleases him so much as to make an inspection of my writing-table. He creeps cautiously about, and examines everything, his object being to steal. What he likes best is lump sugar. My sugar-basin originally cost a penny ; like the Portland vase, it has been smashed and broken so often that it is impossible to estimate its present value. The cause of these numerous fractures is the rat, who, when he wants a bit of sugar, stands up on his hind legs, supporting himself with his tail in a tripod-like fashion, and upsets the sugar-basin, then, selecting a lump, he bolts with it. It is a remarkable fact that the rat never eats in the open ; he takes all he steals back to his house. In order to do this he has to get on to the mantelpiece, which is about eighteen inches above the writing-table.

To enable him to accomplish this, I have put up for him a rat ladder built somewhat on the lines of a salmon ladder. After I had shown him once or twice how to get up this ladder he very soon learnt what he had to do. I have known him scramble up his ladder with objects which for a rat must be of considerable weight. One day I saw him steal a whole red herring. Having tried the best way to carry it, he ultimately picked it up at the right point where it balanced. When he arrived at the round hole which leads to the sleeping compartment of the squirrel's cage, he was pulled up short by the herring, which was crossways in his mouth. I was curious to see what he would do. He dropped the herring, and seemed to consider. Having quickly made up his mind, he adopted the following plan. Leaving the herring outside, he went into the hole, and turning short round, seized it by the head, and hauled it in with the greatest ease. The muscles about the neck of the rat are very strong, giving him great power to use his wedge-shaped head, whether for boring or carrying. He uses his tail to steer himself, and when climbing, works it as a rope-dancer works his balancing pole.

The rat is a great stealer of bits of paper, and any loose pieces he can find he carries away. When the post comes in in the morning, therefore, the rat has the envelopes as a perquisite. These he tears into little bits, and makes a very comfortable nest with them.

The rat agreed very well with the monkeys, but his greatest ally was Jamrach. Here is the history of Jamrach. After a time poor Little Jack was taken ill with a tremendous cough, so I let him out of the cage, and he used to sit almost under the fire, but he was too cute ever

to get singed. One day Little Jack was so bad that I thought
he could not last till the next day, so I sent John to my
friend Jamrach, to bring back another monkey of any
kind, as monkeys, like ourselves, cannot live alone. John
brought back a deal box, upon opening which appeared a
pinched wretched-looking face, with very bright eyes
attached to an apology for a body. After the new arrival
had been a short time in the house, he began to be tamed,
but the poor little fellow did not require much taming,
he was too ill. We made him a coat at once, and that he
was wise enough not to attempt to take off. I wanted a
healthy monkey, not a sick one, and at first was going to
send him back to Jamrach, but I doubted much whether
he would live to get there. I named this monkey Jamrach,
in honour of his former owner. I am strongly of opinion
that he is a retired organ monkey. I formed this idea
because, unlike most other monkeys, he no more minds
being picked up off the ground than does a human
baby. Again, when picked up, his great desire is
to crawl in underneath one's waistcoat or coat, and there
remain cuddled up as long as you will let him stay.
He and poor sick Little Jack struck up a great friendship, and they sit nestled together like babes in the
wood for hours without moving; still, occasionally, they
make mouths at each other and have rows when questions of dainty bits arise. My Jamrach is a comical-look-
ing monkey. When I examine him closely, I find his left
ear is torn as though a ring had at some time or other been
put in, and he had torn it out; his face and lower jaw are
quite bald, as though he were shaved every morning; on
the left cheek, just below the eye, he carries a tattoo mark.

How they managed to tattoo him I cannot conceive. His forehead is destitute of hair, and full of wrinkles, like a very old man. The back part of his head has more hair on it, but he has a bald place in the middle like the tonsure of the monks of old.

Jamrach is a very artful customer. Two baby children came to stay at the house : Jamrach at first could not tolerate their presence in the Monkey room ; he made terrible faces, and pouted his lips at them. The children nevertheless used to feed him with bits of sweetstuff, &c. This I suppose set Jamrach thinking, for he at once changed his tactics ; instead of swearing at them he suddenly became very civil and chattered Good morning, thanking them especially in his own way when he got the sweets. Ultimately it ended by his becoming the constant companion of the children, attending them everywhere, especially at meal-times. He likes to be looked at and talked to ; he takes everything with a serio-comic face which is very remarkable, but he does not like being laughed at.

MY SURICATE, JEMMY THE THIRD; JOE, THE TAME HARE; AND MY JACKASS.

As company for the monkeys and myself for many years past I have had a 'Jemmy.' All my suricates I call 'Jemmys.' The Latin name is *Suricata Zenick*. Jemmy is a very pretty little beast, somewhat like a small mongoose, or very large rat. His head is as like the head of a hedgehog as can be imagined. His colour is light brown with a darker stripe down the sides. He is an African animal, and lives in burrows on the plains, whence he is sometimes called the 'prairie dog,' or meercatze.

I should like now to say something of the habits of this pretty little fellow. Jemmy the Third (for I have previously had two Jemmys) was allowed the free range of the whole house. He was full of curiosity and restlessness, running continually from one room to another. He very seldom walked; his pace, on the contrary, was a short gallop, or rather canter. When on the move he always gave tongue like a hound on a scent. It was impossible to describe his melodious cry in words. When handled and petted he would utter a sharp bark, not unlike that of a dog, and if he was in a very good humour I could by

FIG. 1. JEMMY THE SURICATE.

imitating him make him bark alternately with myself.
His great peculiarity was his wonderfully intelligent and
observant look.   He had the habit also of sitting up on his
tail like a kangaroo ; his fore paws on this occasion were
like a dog's when begging.   He was very fond of warmth,
and would sit up inside the fender and warm himself,
occasionally leaning back against the fender and looking
round with the satisfied air of an old gentleman reposing
after dinner.

When the morning sun came into the room 'Jemmy'
would go and sit in the sunbeams and look out of the
window at the passing cabs and omnibuses.   While doing
this he had a way of turning round very sharply, and
looking with his little pig's eyes at me and back, as much
as to say, ' What do you think of that ? '   When breakfast
came up he would dance round me on his hind legs watching for something.   I often put him on the breakfast-
table, for if I did not put him up he would climb up un-
invited.   It was very amusing to see him go and smell
the egg, and, in his own language, swear at it for being
hot.   He could not understand its being hot enough to
burn his nose ; raw eggs were his special favourites.   His
great delight was to scratch about among the lumps of
sugar.   He was also very fond of cream, and it was most
amusing to see him try to get the little drops of cream I
had left for him out of the cream-can, as left by the milk-
woman.   I am obliged to have my cream in this little
can, otherwise the cats, Judy the marmoset, or somebody
else would be sure to have it before I come down. I placed
the cream-can on the floor, and it was fun to see Jemmy
try to force it open with his teeth to get the cream out ;

he used quite to lose his patience with this metal cream-can.

After breakfast Jemmy generally had a stand-up fight with the monkeys. He would inspect, from the outside, the bottom of the monkey-cage. If he discovered any portion of the monkeys' breakfast which he thought might suit him, he would immediately try to steal it by thrusting his arms through the bars. The monkeys invariably resented this indignity. The old, crippled monkey, Carroty Jane, could only make eyes and faces at him. The wicked, impudent Little Jack would jump up and down like an india-rubber ball, all the time well inside the cage, where Jemmy could not get at him. When Jemmy was fighting the monkeys he would stand on his hind legs and show his lovely white carnivorous teeth at them, turning up his sharp mole-like nose in a most contemptuous manner, all the time keeping up a continuous bark, into which fun the parrot generally entered, and barked like Jemmy also.

One morning, in the middle of the fight, Jemmy forgot himself for the moment in turning round, and gave the ever-vigilant Little Jack a chance. Little Jack seized Jemmy's tail with screams of delight, and pulled him straight up to the bars. Carroty Jane then joined in, and they were getting the best of it, when suddenly Jemmy turned sharp round and made his teeth meet in Little Jack's hand. Little Jack skirmished round the cage three or four times on three legs; then holding up his wounded hand, gazed mournfully and piteously at it, every now and then leaving off looking to make fiercer faces, and cock his ears at Jemmy. Never since has Little Jack ventured his hands outside the bars when a Jemmy fight comes on.

One of the funniest scenes that ever happened with Jemmy was as follows. Some seaside specimens had been sent me, and among the seaweed was a live shore crab about the size of a five-shilling piece. Little Judy, the marmoset, who will eat any quantity of meal worms, bluebottle flies, &c., came down at once off the mantel-piece and examined Mr. Crab, who was crawling about on the floor. None of my animals evidently had seen a live crab before. The monkeys were very frightened, and made the same cry of alarm as when I show them a snake or the house-broom. Judy plainly thought that the crab was a huge insect. The crab put out his two nippers at full length, and gave the marmoset such a pinch that she retreated back again to the mantelpiece, and from this safe height gazed down upon the still threatening crab, uttering loud cries of 'Chick, chick, chick,' alternated with her plaintive, shrill, bat-like note. Presently round the corner comes Mrs. Cat. The cat evidently thought that the crab, that was gently crawling about, was a mouse. She instantly crouched, head, eyes, and ears all intent, as if trying to make up her mind whether the crab was a mouse on which she ought to pounce or not. Hearing the row caused by the crab and marmoset fight, up comes Jemmy in full cry, with tail cocked well in the air. He also attacked the crab, but could not make head or tail of him. He did not like the smell, still less did he like the sundry nips in the nose that he received from the crab's claws.

A grand crab and Jemmy fight, which lasted nearly

half an hour, then took place, ending in the discomfiture of the crab, whose carcass when dead the marmoset and the cat, both coming forward, evidently desired to share. Although it was apparent that the taste of the crab was not agreeable to Jemmy's palate, yet he gradually ate him up, claws, shell, and all, simply that the other animals should not get a single bit.

Jemmy has teeth half carnivorous, half insectivorous. When he is at home in Africa he lives upon mice, beetles, &c. He probably digs these creatures out of the ground, for whenever he saw a crack in the floor, or a hole in a board, he would scratch away at it, as though much depended upon his exertions. When he was fed it was curious to observe how he always pretended to kill his food before eating it. He invariably retreated backwards while he was scratching and biting at his supposed lively food. The living food evidently was in the habit of escaping forwards. Mr. Jemmy took good care that it should not do so by scratching incessantly in a backward direction.

The cat's-meat man comes punctually every day at half-past one; when the cats hear the cry 'meat' they rush down into the area. When the cats ran down, Master Jemmy seeing them bolt, would run also, his object being to steal from one of them her ration of meat. By instinct or experience he had somehow found out that cats' claws are very sharp, and whereas his mode of attack upon the monkeys was face to face, the monkeys being clawless, he attacked the cats by ruffling his hair up and pushing himself backward. The cat, annoyed by being disturbed at dinner, would leave

off eating and strike sharply at Jemmy with her paw ;
that was his opportunity. In a moment he would
seize the cat's meat and bolt with it, but by a most
peculiar method, for when within striking distance of the
cat's paw he would turn round and back up to the cat's
face, and directly she struck at him, he caught the blow
on his back ; then he would put his nose down through
his fore-legs, and through the hinder ones, and have the
meat in a moment, leaving the cat wondering where it was
gone. Jemmy had by this time taken it into safety.
Under the table in my room there is just space for him
to crawl, where the angry cat could not follow him. In
this retreat he would finish up what he had stolen, and
then emerge, licking his lips, and probably laughing to
himself at the disappointed face of the cat.

Jemmy was always fond of getting under anything or
into any kind of hole ; his great delight was to get into a
boot, and when he got to the end he scratched as though
he wanted to get farther into the burrow. Frequently I
found my boot going round the room, propelled apparently by some internal machinery. This machinery
was Master Jemmy.

Jemmy was a greedy little fellow. John could not
bring up any kind of food into my room without Jemmy.
He would watch the cook broiling the chop down stairs,
and when John brought it up would follow close to his
heels; and what between Jemmy's pretty begging manner, the monkey's plaintive cries, and the parrot's demand,
it often happened that I myself got very little of the
chop.

I had hoped to have written a fuller biography of our

poor little Jemmy the Third, but, alas! Jemmy was taken with a fit. I did everything I could to relieve the poor little fellow, but the fits were too much for him, and I have since been busily occupied in making his skin into a mat and his bones into a skeleton. The last Jemmy died of eating cotton wool; this Jemmy died, I think, of eating too much, for he was as fat as a little bacon pig, and weighed 2 lbs., a great weight for such a little animal. It is curious how fond I become of dear little animals such as Jemmy, and how much I miss his pretty little ways as I sit in the Monkey room writing this memoir of my little pet.

When at Rye, in Sussex, on a sea fishery inquiry in 1879, I saw a collection of fancy rabbits, among which were some very beautiful specimens. In a hutch all by himself was a live hare, which when quite a little thing had been caught by a dog. My friend very kindly gave me this hare, in order that I might see what I could do in taming it.

When I turned the hare, which I called Joe, down on to the floor of my own room he exhibited great alarm, rushing about the room in all directions, eventually concealing himself behind some books. From his look, I think he must have some intelligence, for he watches me about the room with his beautiful dark brown eyes. He seems to know I am his friend.

It is quite evident that the hare depends for safety on keeping perfectly motionless. The colour of the fur is very much that of ploughed or fallowed ground, and his ears are always stuck back flat on his shoulders. When he gets up to run, he does not look at all like the same

animal. He will then cock his ears straight up in the air
as though there were wires in them, and it is surprising
how he can stand upright, as it were, upon his hinder legs.
These hind legs are somewhat analogous to the legs of the
kangaroo, and they enable the hare to propel himself along
at a most tremendous pace. I am told that a hare runs
better up hill than down. The hind feet are covered with
hair, hence the genus has been sometimes called *Dasypoda*,
or hairy-footed. I am not quite sure of the meaning of
the hairy foot, but I have an idea that it gives the
animal a firmer hold of the ground than if the sole was
naked. Hares' feet make good hat-brushes. Gunmakers
use them in their trade.

I tried the experiment of seeing whether Joe, the
hare, would live in the cage with the monkeys, my cham-
berlains, as they are sometimes called. I had some difficulty
in getting Joe out of the hutch. I had no idea that the
little fellow was so strong; he kicked tremendously with
his hind legs. It was very interesting to watch the monkeys' opinion of the hare, and what I have observed shows
me more than ever what amazing natural instinct these
animals have. They inspected the hare from the perch in
the cage, never attempting to come down till they had
ascertained the nature of their visitor. Little Jack was
the first to try experiments. Leaning over the bars of
the cage, he pulled the tips of the hare's ears; finding
the hare did not fly at him, he came down on to the floor
of the cage with an attitude of extreme caution and cir-
cumspection; then stretching out his hand and arm as far
as they would go, he gave the hare's fur a touch; finding
that nothing happened, he became bolder, and gave

the hare's fur a good pull. The hare would stand this
no longer; he jumped round with the quickness of a
' Jack in the box,' and gave battle to Little Jack, who,
like most bullies, showed himself an arrant coward. The
hare showed fight by holding up his fore-legs and scratching at Little Jack, and at last, using his fore-paws,
scratched Little Jack's face, implanting the blows in a
most workmanlike manner. It was curious to see Little
Jack's subsequent mode of attack. He would not face the
hare, but backed up towards him, using his tail as a sort
of shield. He then did what I never saw him do before,
put his head on the ground, and look at the hare from
between his hind legs. It was curious to see how very
soon the hare found out that Little Jack was a humbug, and
could not really hurt him, so he began to treat his attacks
with an air of off-handed indifference, and at last they
quite made friends together. The battle being finished,
the old crippled monkey, Carroty Jane, came down from
her perch very cautiously, and inspected the hare. Carroty
Jane is a good-hearted monkey, and of a very peaceable
disposition. The hare squatted quite still in the corner of
the cage. Jane went close up to his head, and the two remained there for some minutes simply gazing with wide-
open eyes steadfastly into each other's faces. This was a
curious scene, as the minds of these two animals, so very
distinct in their nature and habits, were evidently inter-
changing ideas. The result of this congress between
Jane and the hare was the conclusion of peace. Jane
began a chatter, a sure sign that she was in a good
temper and very well pleased. The hare showed that
he approved of the friendship by a quick movement of

D

the upper lip such as we see in ordinary rabbits, while
Jane showed her approbation by looking for fleas in the
hare's fur.

Joe lived in my room for several months. He chose
for his residence the interspace between my writing-
desk and the wall, and there he would sit all day. At
night, when everything was quiet, Joe used to hop out
cautiously, and, having looked me straight in the face for
a minute or two, would go to the fire, sit up on his hind
legs, and warm his white waistcoat. I am afraid I did
not succeed in taming Joe, though I tried my best; I
therefore sent him to the Zoological Gardens, to elucidate
if possible the question of leporines.

A great deal has been said and read about leporines,
which are said to be a breed between a hare and a rabbit.
Our friend Mr. Bartlett feels sure there is no such
breed; and one of his reasons is that hares are born with
their eyes open, and that they can run almost immediately after birth. Rabbits, on the contrary, are born
in holes, with their eyes shut for some days, and it is
many days before they can run. To Mr. Bartlett are
brought sometimes supposed hybrids between a cat and
a rabbit. Our friend says a cat with a short tail will not
prove the argument. He wants a rabbit with a long
tail. I have heard the following story of the great Duke
of Wellington being completely sold by a showman. A
man had advertised an exhibition of a hybrid creature
between a tench and a hare. When the Duke went to
examine it, the exhibitor told him he was very sorry he
could not show the specimen itself, as it had gone to Court
to be exhibited to the king; but, if it was any satisfaction,

he would show him both the father and the mother stuffed and in glass cases!

I have received a new addition to the menagerie in Albany Street. It is a jackass. My jackass is now sitting on the pole I use when out on salmon fishery inspections, and he has just eaten three mice which 'Bilzy,' the cat, has been kind enough to kill, when they came out at night to steal the seed from the parrot's cage. This cat lives upon cat's-meat, and she disdains to eat mice, though she will catch them for sport. The jackass does not bray, but he laughs most heartily, hence his name of Laughing Jackass. I cannot make him laugh when I like, and I do not know what is the cause of his cachinnations, but when he does laugh the ringing sound can be heard all over the house, and the other day much frightened a visitor waiting in the room below. My jackass is not a four-footed jackass—i.e. donkey proper—but an Australian kingfisher—the giant kingfisher, *Dacelo gigas*. The following is his history: It was seen flying over a park in the vicinity of Eltham by a game-watcher, who fired at and brought it down. The shot appeared to have only slightly grazed the wing, and the bird, when I first saw it, had been about a month in captivity, and seemed quite well and lively. Of course this stranger must have escaped from captivity ; most likely, I fancy, from a homeward-bound Australian ship, as the Thames is not more than four miles, as the crow flies, from where the bird was captured. The man who shot it was completely puzzled as to its species, and said gravely that he thought it must be a kind of sea-gull! Raw meat and fish seem to be equally acceptable to the palate of the aboriginal. I suppose he lives upon snakes and other reptiles

in his native country. My jackass would eat almost anything. He would eat any amount of sprats or little birds.
One day a gentleman brought a canary bird that was a
wonderful singer. The little bird's cage was left open for
a moment, but that moment gave Mr. Jackass an opportunity. He instantly seized the canary and swallowed
him right down, feathers and all. It has always been
a mystery in the house as to where that canary went ; in
this book now for the first time is the secret divulged.

When the jackass first arrived, the monkeys made
terrible faces and shook their cage at him. The parrot
ruffled up her feathers, and looked double her size. She
can tolerate any number of quadrupeds in her room, but
no birds. Little Jemmy, the suricate, immediately on
arrival, interviewed the jackass. It was the greatest fun.
Jemmy is rather a coward, though he pretends to be
brave ; he went as near to the jackass as he dared, ready
in a moment to take a spring back. The jackass, on the
contrary, stood his ground, and hoisted an enormous crest
like a cockatoo ; he then opened his bill like the bill of a
pantomime bird, and lunging well forward, took Jemmy's
head right into his mouth. This was quite enough for
Master Jemmy, who instantly went threes about, and
galloped away as fast as he could. Jemmy never tried
it on again, but he often went underneath the jackass's
perch and looked up at him, like the fox and the crow
in Æsop's fables.

The jackass sleeps in his cage, and he laughs every
morning when he sees the light coming through the
shutters. This is the London life of the jackass. Here
is the account of our friend when at home in Australia,

from the pen of that accomplished naturalist, Dr. G. Bennett, author of 'Gatherings of a Naturalist in Australia : '—

'This bird attracts attention more by the extraordinary notes which it utters than by anything conspicuous or elegant in its plumage. It is the great brown kingfisher of naturalists, called by the blacks "Gogera" or "Gogobera," probably from its note resembling the sound of the word. By the bush traveller it is regarded as an old friend and companion, because it enlivens the solitude of the bush with its peculiar sounds. It is the first bird heard in the dawn of the morning, when the woods resound with its peculiar noise ; and again at sunset its cry is to be recognised, as well as occasionally during the daytime ; hence its name "The settler's clock." In the stomach of specimens I dissected I have found the remains of lizards, snakes, and small Mammalia, together with caterpillars, gold beetles, and other coleopterous insects, which constitute its usual food. Unlike kingfishers, I never observed them procuring their food from the water.'

CARLISLE CATTLE MARKET

WHEN examining the train bills at Carlisle station in 1874, in making out my route for several days' official inspection of salmon rivers, I was lucky enough to meet my friend Mr. Bell, of Billholm, Langholm, Dumfries. He told me that (although it was not yet 9 A.M.) he had sold all his lambs at the market, and was going home. All of a sudden he said, 'If you like I will show you the Carlisle Cattle Market;' so finding the trains fitted in nicely, for a wonder, off we started.

No sight is more pleasant to me than a local market, for here we get a general idea of the people living in the neighbourhood near the county towns, and can inspect the local products. On going through the street by Carlisle Post Office, my first idea was that the principal products were old women, chickens and ducks, eggs, butter, and onions. The country carts were arranged in a row along the pavement; then came rows of old women, sacks, &c.; and then baskets containing live poultry, eggs, butter, and onions. The chickens seemed very happy; they were sitting in baskets, probably with the legs tied, and their heads and necks protruded through the netting, which kept them secure. The groups of living heads of ducks, chickens, &c., mixed in baskets looked very funny. I confess I could hardly understand the dialect of these good Cumberland folks; it is tremendously broad. My ears were, however, pretty well accustomed to it, because when in the 2nd Life Guards nearly all our troopers talked with a Cumberland accent; the reason being that so many of the men came from Cumberland that non-Cumberland recruits soon picked up the accent. For the same reason the soldiers of many marching line regiments talk with an Irish accent, because there are so many Irish in the ranks.

The Cumberland natives are a very strong, bony, tall, big people. I believe they feed the babies much upon oatmeal, and all oatmeal-eating babies grow up with big bones.

Such giants indeed are the Cumberland men that the chief constable told me a London tailor entered into a contract for clothes for the police, but when the tailor's foreman came from London to measure the men, he found they were such gigantic fellows that his calculated amount of cloth would run short, and he was obliged to break the contract. The Carlisle police are the finest body of constabulary I ever saw, and are the terror of the salmon-poachers on the Eden.

Leaving the poultry market, we visited the pig market; the pigs were mostly in carts, and kept down by nets. They seemed very clean and happy pigs; the price of a big ten-weeks-old pigling was thirty shillings. An old woman selling pigs told me she gave her pigs common coal to eat, and they were very fond of it. This fact is, I believe, well known to keepers of pigs; if it is not, let them give their pigs coal, it makes them fat. In the pig market is the weighing machine, and over it the arms of

Carlisle, viz. a heraldic lion, like nothing ever created, and apparently cut to fit the stone, two towers connected by a portcullis, and lines to represent, I suppose, water. The motto is ‘ Be just and fear not.’

To the west of the beautiful bridge across the Eden was the cattle market; I do not remember ever seeing so many cattle together before; the poor beasts were arranged in groups, generally with their heads in the centre and tails outside. Mr. Bell informed me that these were mostly Irish cattle, and that they were imported in very large numbers *viâ* the port of Silloth. They were mostly lean, poor-looking things, but doubtless would soon fatten on English pastures, turnips, and Thorley’s food. How is it that everything seems to breed so well in Ireland ; pigs, chickens, cattle, salmon, &c. ? Geese, also, breed freely in Ireland. At the far end of the market I espied an immense flock of geese. Just as I arrived, two men, Irishmen, were driving them to the river’s bank, and in they all plunged into the Eden for a wash and a drink. How these poor geese seemed to enjoy their bath ! and what a row they made in the water ! None of the poor birds tried to get away. As they came out on land I observed each goose flapped its wings and gave a kind of pleased note, which meant, I am sure, ‘ Well, that’s a grand bath, after that horrid steamboat voyage.’ The Irishmen did not seem to be up to the Southern plan of driving geese with a bit of red rag at the end of a long stick, nor did they use a crook to catch them by the leg. There were over 400 geese, the men said. The farmers bought them to turn out on the stubble. London printers generally have a ‘ wayzgoose ’ dinner in the autumn : a wayzgoose means, I believe, a stubble goose.

I should like to **know the origin of the** London printers' wayzgoose dinner.

In the middle of the river Eden stood a great white cow ; the water was **nearly** over her **back, her** ears were pricked forward, and her eyes stared out of her head as she bellowed incessantly to the Irish arrivals on the other side. I suppose **the** Irish cattle did not understand her Cumberland lingo, for they did not answer. This great white cow **in the Eden** reminded **me of a** picture **my** mother **used to show me when** a youngster, of Pharaoh's dream of the fat **and** lean kine coming out **of the Nile. If we had driven** an Irish cow into the river to bellow **in answer to the** Cumberland cow the old **picture would** have **been quite** realised.

On the west side of the bridge, beyond some hurdles, was the sheep market. These Cumberland hurdles, by the way, were quite new to me ; they have four bars, and the hurdles are joined to each other by a **most** ingenious and **simple contrivance of a bar** of wood. They **are** not called hurdles, **but ' flakes.' I believe the** great green racecourse-looking field, where the sheep market is held, is called the Scars. The whole place was a mass of sheep, each flock **was by** itself, and the sheep did not seem to get mixed **a** bit ; how this is managed I cannot possibly conceive. The river Caldew bounds the west end of the Scars, and **at its** junction with the Eden a grating was put to keep out the salmon **from the poachers above, but the winter's** floods carried **it away. In order to find the level of winter floods I** looked **out for the high-water mark, which was com**posed principally of **corks ; why so** many corks I cannot **imagine.** I also picked up several leaves of a very **ancient**

history of England. It seemed very well arranged and
written, and I learnt many dates from it which I had forgotten. I then stood on the raised bank of the Caldew to
examine the sheep, the shepherds, and the sheep boys.
The shepherds I have been accustomed to see in the South,
down Berkshire and Bedfordshire way, are quite different
from the shepherds I saw at Carlisle sheep fair. Our
southern shepherds wear smock frocks, leathern gaiters,
gigantic ironed boots, and always carry a crook, like the
bishops in the monuments and windows we see in cathedrals. The Carlisle shepherds had no crooks : how do they
get on without them ? and they were all dressed in ' go-to-
meeting ' costume, in fact, they were to my mind much
too great ' swells' in their dress to be shepherds. Dogs—
such a lot of sheep-dogs—mostly colleys, not the short-
tailed dogs of the Berkshire hills, but long-tailed dogs,
with most intelligent, thoughtful faces. A swell shepherd—
I was almost afraid to speak to him—kindly gave his
dog orders to move his flock where I indicated ; the orders
were given with voice and hand, the poor dog did his work
wonderfully well. He pretended to be very cross to the
sheep, but they did not seem to fear him, they only did
what he told them to do, and then they stared at him with
their laughless, but yet intelligent, faces. Why should
not sheep-dogs be employed as aides-de-camp to a general
in war? I believe they might be utilised. The general's
orders might be tied round their necks. If I were a
general I should certainly have a number of well-trained
colley messenger dogs attached to my staff. Here then is
a hint for ' The Duke ' and the War Office. One poor dog,
who I observed was doing his best to get his sheep into

position, and (as a dog-fancier at a dog show once told me) ''ad barked hisself 'oorse,' displeased his master—the master threw his stick at him. The dog gave a look of insulted dignity and disappointment, put his tail between his legs, and bolted then and there. I sympathised with that dog. I have often done my best, and then have been snubbed for my pains. I did not see at Carlisle sheep market the celebrated dumb sheep-dog, of which the shepherd said, 'I lets the dog run the sheep while I sit still and barks myself.' I am afraid there are many such shepherds among our noble selves.

From the bank top I espied a gigantic swell shepherd with a very small ash stick in his hand, running after some 200 sheep, both going as hard as they could. The sheep went faster than the man. Mr. Bell told me he was taking a cut; that is, he was driving some twenty or thirty sheep from the general flock as a sample to see if he would buy the lot. After looking for a minute or two at ' the cut,' the swell shepherd began hunting the sheep again all by himself. The sheep dodged him and he the sheep, and that poor man kept running after the sheep as hard as he could, with a thick coat on, and a great comforter round his neck on a very warm morning, for at least twenty minutes. I believe there was one sheep in the lot he wanted particularly, but never got him, and perhaps he and the sheep are still dancing quadrilles on Carlisle Scars at this moment ; but I suppose he knew his own business.

There were between 30,000 and 40,000 sheep in the fair that day. Every owner has his mark, mostly made with ' reddle,' a kind of rouge, sold in large quantities

to Madame-Rachelise the sheep's pale faces. The total
value of the lot of sheep on the Scars was very great.
The money transactions take place seldom by cheque,
generally by notes and gold. Mr. Bell showed me the
money he had received for his lambs. I not only saw,
but smelt the money from afar. It consisted of a roll
of Scotch bank one-pound notes, nasty, dirty, ragged
pieces of paper, looking only fit for the fire. These
notes, I understand, are sometimes quite intolerable; the
notes from Wick are the worst, there is a charming odour
of fish about them. Mr. Bell's notes smelt of sheep.
However, my friend did not seem to despise them at all.

As we were leaving the Scars, lo and behold! an old
woman tending a gigantic black pot hung over a fire by
three sticks; she was stirring it, and inside was about two
bucketsful of delicious-looking soup. The old woman gave
me a great bowl of her soup, and a bit of bread and salt
for three-halfpence. I enjoyed it amazingly, and had
another pennyworth. It was magnificent soup, made, I
think, principally of sheep's heads, peas, onions and other
excellent things.

When the market was over I accepted Mr. Bell's kind
invitation to his house up among the hills, as he offered
to show me his museum and to tell me more about sheep,
&c. He is an enthusiastic naturalist, and until lately had
a considerable number of living animals about his house;
he has been obliged to part with most of his collection,
but he still has remaining a kangaroo and a pair of storks.
His storks live in a field with the cows, and form a great
addition to the natural beauties of the domain; they
pick up worms and grubs in the fields and hedges, but

he cannot obtain any frogs for them. I had no frogs in
my pocket to give the storks, but I had a lucifer-match
box full of little toads, about the size of beans. I
had found these toads hopping in great numbers about
the garden of Corby Castle, on the Eden, when I called
to ask permission to inspect the salmon loops. When
I opened my toad-box, I found the poor little things
all dead and in a jelly. I had been sitting on them
when in the 'machine,' as they call a fly in Scotland.
In the pleasure-grounds of Corby Castle I was almost
frightened by coming upon a huge giant, looking out
of the wood. The giant was twelve feet high, carried
an immense club, and had only one eye. His name
was Polyphemus. He was cut out in stone some fifty
years ago; Goliath of Gath must have been about his
size.

Mr. Bell has built a very nice little museum, in
which there are some good specimens of natural history of
all kinds, especially some human bones brought from the
Crimea to Glasgow to be ground up for bone manure.
On our road from Carlisle, just as we were going into the
town of Langholm, we observed an appearance on the top
of the trees in the wood opposite, on the other side of the
Esk. This phenomenon was like a cloud or evening fog
rising; it was not, however, near the ground, but was of
a pyramidal shape, about twenty or thirty feet in height
and about twelve feet wide. This cloud was probably
composed of gnats; these great clouds of gnats are not
uncommon about the woods in this part of Scotland in the
autumn: perhaps some of our readers may have observed
similar great clouds of insects hovering over the woods. At

the junction of the Black and White Esk he showed us an old archway where water-ousels breed every year. I am glad to find that he considers water-ousels do not injure the salmon eggs.

I was much interested in watching through my field-glass from the road, sixteen blackcock and two grey hens basking in the sun by a hayrick; they seemed very happy and comfortable. There are a great number of these birds about strictly preserved by the Duke of Buccleuch. It was a pretty sight to see them fly over the hill-top. I could never bring myself to shoot or injure such beautiful birds. Mr. Bell has recorded a curious instance of affection of a blackcock to his wife. He remained about her after she was dead and had even become a skeleton. Close to this bridge, near Castle Orr, a locality was pointed out to me called the 'Hand fasting place;' the tradition was that people could come there and get married for a year and a day, the marriage contract lasted no longer; the country people here think that there is a 'bushel of wedding rings' buried near this place, but they have never yet been dug up. Near Castle Orr there are some curious-looking enclosures made with stones on the hill-side. These are called 'Kepe or Kebe houses;' the sheep are driven into them to be fed when the snow is on the ground. There are also smaller houses for ewes with lambs. It is a common practice among the shepherds if a lamb dies to take the skin of the dead lamb, tie it on another live lamb, and the mother will then suckle it. If the skin of the dead lamb was not put on, the mother would drive it away. Lambs so brought up are called 'Kebe lambs.'

We saw some fine colley dogs about. Mr. Bartlett, who was with us, pointed out a curious fact, that the peculiar brown and chocolate-coloured streaked dogs generally, if not always, have one brown eye and one white eye.

The shepherds up in these Scotch hills are a curious class. They used formerly to take their dogs to church every Sunday. The dogs would sneak quietly underneath the seats, and remain as quiet as mice during the service; but when the congregation came to the psalm which concluded the service, the dogs without any sign or signal from their masters would suddenly get upon their legs and howl loudly in concert with the psalm. They never howled at any psalm but the last. The shepherds do not now take their dogs to church—for this reason, that the parson does not want the assistance of the dog choir—but somehow the dogs always know when it is Sunday. The shepherds know their sheep by their faces. Mr. Bell had a lad of fifteen on his sheep run who was very clever at this. He knew every sheep in the run, and it is said that if he had once seen a sheep he never forgot its face.

The shepherds on these hills are very fond of bracksey mutton. This is simply the flesh of the sheep which die on the hills. I was told that this bracksey mutton forms a chief part of their food throughout the year, and that they will eat it when it is in a horrible state. I believe they put it up the chimney, and make a sort of ham of it. From what I hear of it I don't think it very likely to be patronised by Fortnum and Mason. The dead sheep are the perquisites of the shepherd.

Sheep-washing does not do much injury to the river, but anglers complain of bits of wool getting into their flies

when fishing. I find, however, that all about this part of
the world the rivers are very much injured by tanners.
They put lime on the flesh side of the skin, and leave it
there for a certain time; the lime loosens the wool, which
then easily comes off. The tanners then take these lime-
saturated skins and wash them in the river, thereby doing
great injury to the fisheries. In summer-time the maggots do much injury to the sheep; carbolic acid is a good
thing to destroy them. The shepherds do not keep a
sufficient look-out for flies; they do not seem to know
that maggots are deposited by flies.

In former times the hill shepherds used to spear the
salmon kelts in very large numbers when they came into
the burns among the hills to spawn, but since the Esk
Association has been started there is but little poaching
going on. This lack of poaching I am sorry to say is not
universal in Cumberland. At another place, which shall
be nameless, there used to be people who carried on kelt
killing as a business, and just as a tradesman may be
called a tallow-chandler, cheesemonger, &c., so these men
were called 'Kipperers.' One of these kipperers was a
dwarf, a very little fellow with a very big head. Upon
one occasion he tied a leister fast round his wrist and
stuck it into a big salmon. The salmon struck off quickly
down stream, pulled the little dwarf (whose name was
Joey) off his legs, dragged him through the bridge, and
very nearly over a mill weir below. They put caricatures
all over the town of little Joey riding triumphantly on the
top of a salmon with a leister in his hand, like Neptune
riding the waves. Not long ago Joe the kipperer died,
and when about to depart, he told his friends to look into

the small of his back and they would find a charge of shot. He said, ' When I was out a-kippering a long time ago, when I was a lad, old Tipple of —— Farm warned us off. We wouldn't go, so the old gentleman ups with the gun, and the consequence has been that I have carried about under my skin a charge of old Tipple's shot for the last forty years.'

An old shepherd who lived upon the hill-side had been accustomed, as man and boy, to spear salmon on his sheep run. When the Salmon Act came in he was obliged to leave off, as he called it, his legitimate sport. A great number of salmon were subsequently seen spawning on the very shallow where the old man used to leister them. One of the conservators asked him to come down to look at the salmon. The old man groaned a heavy groan, and said, ' I canna gang; I will no go; I could no keep my hands off of them; I could no resist the temptation.'

AN ELEPHANT IN ALBANY STREET.

EARLY one Sunday morning, in October **1874, there came** a tremendous ' rat-tat ' at **the door.** I never will receive visitors on a Sunday, and could not therefore imagine who could be calling at such an early hour. ' John,' the Buttons, announced **Mr.** Jamrach's foreman, who came with a very **long face,** and looking **very miserable.** ' **What's up ?** ' I said ; ' nothing the matter with the **governor, I hope ?** ' My **friend** Jamrach is daily and hourly in such **close communication** with wild animals, that I thought possibly **the big bear,** the tiger, the hyena, or one of the numerous **wolves** which a **day** or two before I had inspected in the back **yard close to 180 St.** George's **Street East, had collared Jamrach, and injured,** if not eaten him up.

' **The old man's all** right,' said the foreman, ' but the **elephant is dead, and** the **governor thinks he has** been **poisoned, or that there has been foul play of some** kind ; and as **Jerrard and a lot of 'em refused** to open him, the governor says **he would** be **very much** obliged if you would make the *post-mortem* examination.'

' But where **is the elephant ?** ' said I.

' Oh, he is laying **stiff** on the **straw in our** stable-yard, but I'll fetch him here in **two hours if you will** open him.'

'Right you are,' said I ; 'cut away and fetch him.'

On my return from church I observed a great litter of straw in the street in front of the house, which indicated to me that the elephant had really arrived.

'Where's the elephant, John?' I said.

'He's laying at the bottom of the stairs, close to the kitchen door, sir ; and I can't move him, and the men is gone.'

So I rushed down to the kitchen, nearly stumbling over the beast, who was lying, stomach uppermost, at the bottom, blocking up the kitchen door, with his four legs in the air. John informed me that they had brought the elephant in a cart. They tipped him on to the pavement into a large piece of canvas, and, with the assistance of some men who were standing by, got him to the top of the kitchen stairs. They then gave him a shove, and rolled him down stairs, and he came down head over heels like the tumbling nigger we see as a child's toy. I have often told the servant-girls, who for some unknown reason will never report arrivals, that if 'even an elephant were to come downstairs they would not tell me,' and when an elephant did really come downstairs they never said a word.

With the assistance of some friends who came to see the animal, we got the elephant into the casting-room. We put him in a kneeling position, as though he were going to have a howdah put on. When properly posed I searched for external wounds, and quickly discovered that the elephant had an awful 'black eye.' His right eye and eyelid were much swollen and inflamed, and there was a soft place above the eye, which showed there was fluid under the skin. I have forgotten to state the measurements of my new friend. From the tip of trunk to end of tail, nine feet; body, four feet seven inches long; height, about four feet; weight, as much as six men could move.

The case being so important—it was thought to be elephant murder—I sent to my friend Mr. Bartlett, who kindly came down at once. As there seemed to be some doubt about the cause of the black eye and swelling on the forehead, I determined, as I had to go to Lydney to the meeting of the Severn Board by the nine o'clock express train that evening, although it was Sunday, and quite contrary to the rules, to begin the *post-mortem* then and there.

I therefore dissected off the right side of the skin of the elephant's face, and was pleased to find that there was no blood diffused below the surface of the skin, and that the fluid under the skin was not blood, nor was the skin stained, nor were the bones fractured or bruised.

The cause of death, therefore, it was satisfactory to find, was not a blow. Thinking that I should never perhaps have so good an opportunity of making a cast of an elephant, I directed my secretary Mr. Searle to begin early the next morning to make a mould of him, and see that he was taken to the Zoological Gardens, with the request that the Prosector would be kind enough to finish the *post-mortem*. He subsequently reported that the cause of death was 'inflammation of the lungs in the first stage.' Although Jamrach by this sad event lost his beast, whose price was 350*l.*, yet it was very satisfactory to know that the animal died from natural causes, and not from a malicious wound, as was originally suspected.

Being away on Monday and Tuesday, I was not able to be present at the *post-mortem*, but on taking off the skin of the elephant's face I discovered a very rare specimen, for from underneath the skin slipped out a small slimy substance, the colour of new-melted lead, about a quarter of an inch long, and like a tear as cut on French tombstones. This I recollected from Professor Owen's lectures was a gland peculiar to the head of the elephant. I at once turned out the most valuable book in my library, viz. the 'Catalogue of the College of Surgeons,' and found the following passage:—'Preparation 2103.— The scent-gland from the side of the head of the elephant, the duct of which opens at a short distance behind the eye. The gland is of a flattened and lobulated form; a section has been removed from one side to show its thickness and compact structure. It is stated to be in activity, and to secrete an unctuous fluid having a strong musky odour at the period of sexual excitement.' Mr. Bartlett says the presence of this gland is a mercy, as it enables those in attendance on the elephant to ascertain when he is beginning to lose his temper.

About a month afterwards I managed to finish the cast of Jamrach's baby elephant. The mould, when filled with plaster, was a terrific weight, but by means of lever, chains, and other dodges, I managed to turn it over, so that the outside plaster could be chipped off. I found that the front and back entrances to my little kitchen, where I made the cast, quite barred its exit. Up the stairs, therefore, he must go. 'Round the corner' was the difficulty, as plaster will not bend; so I took a sharp thin saw and cut the elephant right in half. By the assistance of the two dustmen, we then managed to carry Mr. Elephant in bits, cut up like a traitor of old, up the kitchen stairs. At one moment the cast of the head part was in danger. Mr. Edon, who was alongside of me, was crushed out of the work by the narrowness of the passage, and the whole weight came on me. Luckily I thought of my shoulder, and, by supporting the weight, saved an accident. The careless dustmen kindly knocked off an ear and one of the legs, and the tip of the tail. We, however, put on these dismembered limbs again all right. I made an ornamental saddle and girths and crupper, and put them on the elephant, and he now looks beautiful in the ante-room of my fish museum. The 'Artist's Elephant' at the south-east corner of the Albert Memorial looks quite a 'guy' by the side of my little beauty.

SALMON EGG COLLECTING FOR AUSTRALIA.

EVERY one who knows what is going on in the salmon world is aware that near the mouth of that beautiful river, the Dart, is a mill-weir—a very great obstruction to fish. They must also be aware that Christmas week and the week after is the time when salmon are most ' at hill,' turning up the gravel and making their nests. The Dart rises in Dartmoor, where there are some splendid spawning grounds, and were it not for the Totnes weir and the pollutions of mines at the top, and wool-works in the middle, the Dart would indeed be '*fluvius piscocissimus.*'

It was from the Dart that in Christmas week, 1875, I undertook to collect salmon eggs to be sent direct to Melbourne in January by the s.s. ' Durham.'

After many letters and telegrams as to the state of the water, the nesting of the fish, &c., the right moment at last arrived, and I started for Exeter, and thence to Totnes.

Early the next morning, on looking over Totnes Bridge, I found that the tide was up. I adjourned, nevertheless, to the weir, and waited till the water had fallen low enough for us to begin. Mr. Garland (lessee of the fishery), his men, and two water-bailiffs were present. When the water had dropped to a certain point, 'All right now, sir,' said Garland. 'Slip her round then,' said I, and away went the boat from the shore, the oars making that peculiar rattle and rubbing noise so melodious to the ears of salmon fishers. As the boat advanced the net was quietly dropped into the water, she made a great circle in the weir pool, and we then pulled swiftly to land. 'Steady, men, steady; keep the lead line well drawn,' I cried; then as the net was dragged nearer and nearer to the shore I felt the line, and from a particular shake in it felt certain that we had some salmon, and that the net had ' fished well.'

When she came into shoal water the shouts of those assembled were great; we had indeed a splendid haul. The men wanted to pull the fish out on land, but I would not allow it, as I am most careful never to injure fish. The splutter the poor frightened fish made when they found themselves in danger was wonderful. ' Leave them alone; they will soon be quiet,' I said. I then went into the water and examined the captives. The poor fish were regularly 'blown' by their exertions to escape, but in about five minutes they began to leave off spluttering, and, strange to say, ranged themselves in a row side by side, with all their heads directed towards the deep water, like cavalry horses tied to a picket-rope.

I then put my hands deep into the water and examined them one by one. They never flinched when I touched them—I suppose they knew I was their friend. Mr. Garland wished me to put the fish that had not spawned over the weir, and for this purpose had provided long and shallow wicker baskets containing rushes and soft moss. As I

touched each fish I cried out what he or she was. Thus,
'Female, not ripe; bring the basket;' the basket was
then brought as near me as possible. I then gently
caught hold of her ladyship's wrist (the thick part above
her tail) with the right hand, while the left hand slewed
her round till she lay broadside on. Then kneeling down
in the water, I quickly slipped my arms under her and
popped her with a jerk into the basket, the lid was put
down instantly, and she 'danced Jim Crow' in the basket.
I examined her again, after which two men carried her
away, and slipped her into the mill leat above the weir;
she doubtless then made the best of her way, as fast as
her tail would propel her, up towards Dartmoor, wondering
doubtless, in her scared mind, what had happened to her,
and what it was all about.

In this manner I examined all the fish in the net,
putting the unripe ones into the baskets, and sending
them to be turned down on the upper side of the
weir.

At last I had only the ripe fish left in the net. It
was then my assistants' turn to help me. When I had
got a fish to suit me I put him into the basket, and let
him get a little faint. The iridescent colours of the salmon
when he is getting faint are very beautiful; coruscations
of lovely emerald and gold shoot all over his scales as he
quivers like a man with the ague. I fancied also that his
face changed, and an expression of 'What a fool I am to
have been netted!' came over it. When he had got a
little quiet I slipped a sheet of house-flannel under him,
one assistant held his head, and one his tail, and thus his
struggles were reduced to a minimum. It is necessary to

be more careful with the females than the males. The fish must never be kept too long out of water; all fish must be nursed when returned to the water. If they go on their side and lie still, they are in danger. I therefore make it a rule to go into deep water with every fish that has been spawned, and hold his or her head against the stream. As the fish recovers I relax my hold, and in a few minutes he will give a great gulp with his gills and swim away uninjured.

I now give the score of the salmon caught in three hauls below Totnes Weir: first haul, females eight, males eight; second haul, females two, males five; third haul, male one; total, twenty-four. Many of these were large fish, two were not less than three feet eight inches in length, and were, I should guess, nearly thirty pounds in weight.

This shows how preserving sea-kelts will increase the general size of salmon in a river. These big fish made Garland stare. 'We never gets them big ones in the summer-time; they never comes up till late, when they knows we must not catch them.'

'No, Garland,' I said, 'they know the law as well as you or I do. Salmon get more and more clever every year, and I really believe they know every amendment in the Act of 1873. What they pray for most now is an Anti-Pollution Bill, and I trust they will get it this next session.'

I calculated I had obtained about twelve or fourteen thousand eggs from these Dart salmon. They were very fine, healthy-looking eggs. Some of them I packed in moss by the side of the river, in the boxes in which they were eventually to go their long journey to the Antipodes.

On January 4, 1876, I went to Lancaster to continue collecting salmon eggs for Australia. On my arrival I was met by Mr. Thompson, lessee of the Skerton and corporation fisheries on the Lune ; who prophesied that if there was no flood in the night, we should catch some fish the next day, either at Skerton or Halton Weirs just above Lancaster.

We began early the next morning by fishing Skerton Weir. The net at Skerton is taken round the pool at the base of the weir not by a boat, but by a horse and cart. The old mare—'Grey Fanny '[1]—knows her work as well as or possibly better than her master, and she seldom or never makes a mistake. The net being piled up in the cart, Mr. Thompson drove the mare across to the other side along the shallows at the foot of the pool. When they got to the other side a long rope was passed to Mr. Thompson's assistants, who walked along the base of the top of the weir, over which a strong current, dangerous to those not accustomed to walk on weirs, was running.

All being ready, the old mare walked leisurely back again along the way by which she had come. Mr. Thompson all the while was paying out the net from the

---

[1] Grey Fanny is a wonderful animal, and seems to enjoy fishing ; they say she suffers much from rheumatism, except when she is in the water, and then she is all right. This fishing mare, old ' Grey Fanny,' has been working the nets at Skerton Weir for nearly seventeen years. She is a very old-fashioned customer ; sometimes a flood takes her cart off its wheels and swings it with the stream. Old Fanny, however, knows what to do. She has never been toit (Lancashire for ' upset ') yet. It is very funny to see her look at the struggling salmon with her great eyes and stiff ears. I am sure she enjoys the sport.

back of the cart. It was not necessary to guide the mare, as she knew the road in the river quite well; nevertheless, she nearly got out of her depth every now and then, and it was amusing to see her manœuvre herself out of trouble.

The result of two hauls at Skerton Weir was one male salmon, five jack, and a roach. I was very pleased at this failure of fish, because a new fish pass had lately been put up under the superintendence of Mr. Walpole and myself, and certified at Skerton Weir, and if it had not been efficacious we should of course have caught many salmon *below* this weir, for it is the first weir at which the fish arrive after leaving the sea. I was very pleased also to hear such good reports of the diagonal board which I put up at Skerton some five years ago. They say the fish like it even better than the pass.

Mr. Thompson then determined to try the 'Ladies' walk' draft. This is a pool situated some half-mile down the river, not far above the bridge which connects Skerton with Lancaster. There are several islands between Skerton Weir and the bridge, and we walked the shallows between them, in order to drive off any fish that might by chance be making their nests there. I disturbed one pair of very fine fish which had just begun making their nests in the gravel, and I found one nest not quite finished. I tried to get some eggs out of this nest with my hands, but the current was so rapid and the water so deep, that although I saw a few eggs dancing about in the stream I could not catch them.

Having beaten down the shallows between the islands, I found there was no other way of getting to the drafting place than by walking across a very broad piece of the river. I can tell pretty well, looking from the bank, where it is safe to walk in a river. This time I miscalculated, for close under the bank, at the further side, the water deepened most suddenly and unexpectedly. The bottom of the river was formed by huge round slippery stones, the current was excessively strong, and I was as nearly as possible carried off my legs. Mr. Edon, who was behind me, was, as well as myself, in a very awkward difficulty, if not in danger. Mr. Thompson, however, who knew the ground, shouted out to us to take another path, and we ultimately landed safely.

In the meantime Grey Fanny had somehow or other managed to drag across the river not only the draft-net, but also two of the Local Board of Conservators. We then took a shot round the 'Ladies' walk' pool, and caught two hen salmon, one quite done, the other not ready. Time was getting on, so we hastened back to Mr. Thompson's mill at Skerton, and trotted away to Halton Weir, about two miles off, sending the nets up the river by boat. Below the mill-tail at Halton we discerned two fish on their nests, but although the shot was made with the net as quickly as possible, we missed them and caught only a little grilse containing a few eggs. This draft was provokingly spoilt by an old tin kettle getting in the way of the net, and rolling her up beautifully. Looking over the iron bridge at Halton we saw to our great delight a lot of salmon on their beds. There is a little island just below the weir, and the northernmost side of this island had been chosen by the salmon to deposit their eggs, the poor brutes not having sense enough to know that this spot where they were putting their eggs would be dry in the summer, and that the eggs and fry would probably perish.

The splashing the fish made as they turned up the gravel and hunted each other about was grand to behold; we could plainly see the fish hunting and driving each other, and fighting as only salmon can fight. The old males have terrible teeth, and inflict bad wounds when fighting. When the salmon were quiet I could only see the tips of their tails waving just above water, and also their back fins like a forest of masts. I confess I do not understand the meaning of this, as salmon do not burrow with their heads, but, on the contrary, thrash up the gravel with a whirl by means of their tails, the lower edges of which are in consequence very often scarred and wounded.

Mr. Thompson and the water-bailiff undertook to catch these fish off the spawning-beds, a difficult operation, on account of the swiftness of the current, which runs very fast from over the weir just above, and the artfulness of the salmon. Next to a fox there is no more artful creature than a salmon. His sense of sight is very great, and he can hear *in the water* as far as, or even farther than, we can on land.

By a very cleverly arranged sweep of the net they managed to enclose some of these fish, the remainder scuttling away into the deep below. I was rejoiced beyond measure to find in the nets three hens and one male, all three hens being quite ripe. The water-bailiff assured me that those fish which escaped the nets would seek refuge in the pool below, so we sent back to Skerton for Mr. Thompson's big one hundred and forty yard net. When this arrived we fished the pools below the weir.

taking altogether four draughts, with the following results: —1st, two cocks and two hens ; 2nd, two cocks ; 3rd, two cocks and one hen ; 4th, four cocks ; the total number of fish at Halton Weir being ten cocks and three hens. One of the males was a magnificent fish, four feet three inches long, and weighing over forty pounds. This fine fellow knocked me right over with his big tail when he was spluttering about on the bank. I took the greatest care of him, and he swam off all right.

To me it is the greatest puzzle why the male fish always preponderate over the females. Among both trout and salmon there are often seven cocks to one hen, but in the spring a considerable mortality takes place among the *male* salmon, while a few females alone die a natural death.

In the case of trout, the cocks invariably bolt *up* stream, the hens bolt *down* stream. Female trout also hide themselves, thrusting their noses into rat-holes and any places they can find under the bank. In birds, by a wonderful provision of nature, the hen generally has a coat the colour of the ground upon which she sits on her nest ; thus the female pheasant has feathers to suit the foliage and vegetation on the ground : the male bird, on the contrary, has most resplendent feathers. I observe that by the same rule the cock salmon, when at the height of spawning, wears a Joseph's coat of many colours, and the purple ground, variegated with sealing-wax-red coloured spots on the sides and cheeks, is very beautiful. Hence in the Severn district they call them ' old soldiers.' The hen salmon, on the contrary, wears a plain russet suit, and does not often adorn herself with red spots, although I have sometimes seen them on her cheeks.

As each shot of the net was drawn in, I waded deeply into the water, and examined the fish swimming about inside the net, in sufficient depth of water for them not to get stranded, because if they touch the ground, immediately they begin to knock themselves about. I caused the basket to be floated on the top of the water near to the spot where I had got the salmon by the wrist with my right hand. Feeling where his head was with my left hand, I got his head and shoulders into the bend of my elbow, just as a nurse carries a baby in her arms. When I found the fish had put his weight into my arms, I jerked him up into the basket, and took him ashore.

It was quite dark before we finished our work, and then, in order to get out of the field where we were fishing, we had to go up a steep bank, through a hedge or two, and over some high palings, not a pleasant job to accomplish in the dark, dressed in wet waterproofs, and carrying tins heavy with eggs, water, and moss.

The next morning I proceeded with Mr. Thompson some twelve miles further up the river to Burrow Hall, a little way beyond Hornby, my friend Mr. Fenwick, chairman of the Board, having kindly invited me to try my luck at his fishery. Immediately on arriving at the water-side, we discovered eight or ten fish spawning on the shallow. I had anticipated catching all this lot at one haul in Mr. Thompson's trammel, but as my back was turned only for a moment, the local water-bailiff marched straight into the river, and drove all the fish off the spawning beds in a moment. This was dreadfully aggravating, as we lost all the fish off the beds, and also lost half an hour in sending for another net. When it at last arrived

Mr. Fenwick's keeper managed a clever long shot of several hundred yards, and we got a good haul of salmon. I passed them out of the net, with the following result :— Females twelve, not ripe three, nine spawned out. Males five. Seventeen fish at one haul and not a single egg ; this was again provoking, but it could not be helped. Hearing that there were fish on the spawning beds about a quarter of a mile lower down, we made a long shot for them, and were just congratulating ourselves on the prospect of good sport, when, to my deep regret, the net suddenly got on to a 'fast.' The net was swimming down beautifully, but all of a sudden the root of a tree caught her about the middle, and there she hung in two great bags.

Three men pulled the boat up to where she was fast and hauled on the net, while all present pulled on the line hauling up stream, but our efforts were in vain. At last, by means of main force, the men in the boat pulled up the net from the stump, tearing a hole big enough to let a sheep through without touching. Mr. Thompson, having a needle with him, quickly mended the hole, and we made another long shot without touching a single fish.

It was then getting on for five o'clock, and we were a long way from the carriage, but we determined to try one more shot in the pool just below. In order to get to this pool Mr. Thompson had to shoot the boat down a very nasty rapid, but managed it admirably, and in a few minutes laid the net round the pool. I could see from the corks, and the feel of the ropes, that she fished well. They landed her on a beautiful sloping gravel bank. The score of fish was as follows : Males eleven, females nine—no less than twenty fine fish. Of these two females were not ready,

F

the others had done spawning; one only gave us eggs. It was past dark when we got to the village, glad enough to get rest and some bread and cheese.

During the day's fishing at Skerton the cold was something terrific. The wind carried freezing sleet with it. They said it was called in Lancashire a 'Robin Hood's wind,' i.e. the only wind that Robin Hood could not stand. I found it to be much warmer in the water than out of it.

Having got a fair quantity of eggs I brought them to London; and Mr. Thompson kindly went out the following Monday to collect more for us. The result of our fishing in the Lune was altogether about 16,000 eggs. The icehouse on board the s.s. 'Durham' was built under the superintendence of Mr. James Youl. Altogether there were collected about 175,000 eggs. I tell the number of eggs by counting them into a measure glass. There are 1,000 eggs in a nine-ounce glass. The 'Durham' sailed for Melbourne punctually to her time on January 20, 1876.

SALMON EGG COLLECTING FOR NEW ZEALAND.

SALMON egg collecting is one of the most difficult, and I
may say dangerous, tasks that fall to my lot. Salmon
eggs are by no means to be picked up as easily as fowls'
eggs. Those only who have gone through the difficulties
of collecting these treasures can know the anxiety connected with the task. The first thing is correspondence
to get proper official leave, about which I am most particular; then follow other correspondence, telegrams, &c.,
to fix times and places; nevertheless, in the second week
of January 1878, I went at it once more. The Government
authorities of New Zealand, having expressed by telegram
to Sir Julius Vogel, agent-general in London, their desire
to have a further consignment of salmon ova sent them
this spawning season, I told Sir Julius that I would do my
best for them, though it was late, very late, this year to
hope for much success.

The ship chosen to take the eggs was the 'Chimborazo,'
a big steamer, sailing from London on January 21, direct
to Melbourne, the eggs to be there transhipped to New
Zealand. I now proceed to relate my adventures in collecting salmon eggs on the North Tyne.

In the collection of salmon eggs, as in every other
matter, the great rule is to take for granted that you will
find nothing anywhere; I therefore go fully prepared for all

F 2

eventualities. Here then is a list of my 'spawning kit.'
First, the waterproof dress; this very useful garment is in
fact a diver's dress, and when properly put on, admits not
a drop of water. It has however one fault; it is apt to
freeze when I am out of the water, and then one feels en-
cased as it were in a suit of inflexible tin armour. Second,
the spawning tins: long experience has shown me that
the best form of vessel in which to spawn fish is no paltry
little tin, but a bath large enough to bathe a good-sized
baby in. Third, a long shallow basket, to hold the
salmon immediately they are caught, such as ladies use to
carry their clothes when travelling; such a basket makes
a capital salmon cage. It is easily sunk to the proper
depth with stones, and the salmon live well and do not
fret in it. The fish can remain alive in the water in this
till they are wanted. I find a big 'crinoline net' does not
answer, for the fish are apt to turn on their sides, and get
faint; besides, there is a difficulty in getting them in and
out. Fourth, house flannel cut into lengths of one yard;
this is absolutely necessary to hold the struggling salmon.
Those who are unaccustomed to spawn salmon, have an
awkward habit of putting their fingers into the gills of the
fish, and if the fish's gills are injured and bleed he suffers
much from it. I never to my knowledge killed a fish in
my life while spawning it. Fifth, dry towels; these are
most necessary, as the slime from the salmon makes one's
hands very slippery, and it is a very bad thing to have
slippery hands, for you may lose a valuable fish in a moment;
besides which, wiping the hands warms them, and when
working in the water at this time of the year the cold to
the hands and arms is fearful, or, to use the expression of

the cabmen, 'all my fingers is thumbs.' Sixth, bottles for experiments with milt and ova. Seventh, 'Sphagnum' moss to pack the eggs in the tins and cans. Eighth, wooden boxes tied up in threes or fours to pack the eggs at the river side. Ninth, a huge landing-net. This is very useful for catching fugitive fish, which may happen to escape round the side of the net. Tenth, nets ; one long heavy trammel and two smaller trammels are best. Eleventh, ordinary luggage, and especially a bottle of scented hair oil with which to well anoint the chest and arms and tips of the ears when working in the water, a most excellent and serviceable plan. I took this hint from the Es-quimaux.

Thus equipped, I started for Newcastle, writing all the way in the train, of course. Arrived at Newcastle, I took the train to Chollerford, where the Chairman of the North Tyne Committee had kindly made all the arrangements for me. The next morning a drive of eleven miles to Bellingham, and thence by train to Reedsmouth. We dressed ourselves in the station, and proceeded to find Sergeant Harbottle, the head of the Tyne salmon watchers, the water-bailiffs, and my man, Mr. Edon, who had gone on before us.

The main river of the North Tyne was too heavy for us, no net could possibly stand ; so Harbottle had judi-ciously made his first shot in the river Reed, just above her junction with North Tyne. He had marked down several pairs of spawners on this bed, and hoped to get the lot for me. We came up just in time to see our assistants with very long faces. It appeared that they had, though the water was then running rapidly, got the net across, and some fish in her. Just as they were bringing her round she caught on a rock, and immediately rolled 'leads over corks.' Just at that moment there came a heavy spate from above. The men on the bank could not hold the net, and she straightened herself out beautifully, letting every fish in the net, of course, escape. We managed, however, to secure three half-spawned fish, from which we got a few eggs.

We then packed up the wet nets and the kit on a cart, and marched off to a shallow in the North Tyne, about a mile above, where we thought we might have luck. During our walk thither a regular winter's storm came on; the telegraph wires sung out their music as if laughing at us, and far away in the north was a great jet-black angry-looking cloud, showing that a heavy storm was gathering upon the moors and great hills that separate England from Scotland. We had no time to lose, as we knew the rain from this cloud would soon send North Tyne down in a heavy spate. Turning off the highway we passed down a hill to the river bank, and then the cart with the nets went across the river, while I waded over, not very pleasant work in a rapid rising river, with great rolling slippery boulders under one's feet. However, we got to the island, and determined to fish the stream on the other side of it. There was great difficulty in getting the net across, the stream was so strong and rapid. At last Harbottle and six men got her over, and then beginning some sixty yards above, the trammel was run down stream to her. Great was the excitement when we quickly perceived from the bobbing of the corks that the fish on the spawning bed were 'masked' in the trammel. She's a beautiful

net is my trammel, though some find fault with her.   She's
like birdlime to a fish ; let her once touch a fish's fin,
and she has the rest of him pretty quickly.   Down came
the trammel right on to the net below in true orthodox style.   Look alive, lads, round with them both on to
the bank.   Three fish !   Instantly I was on to them as
they kicked about in the water.   First, male ; second,
female ; third, male.   The males fine big fish, with red
coats on them, as though they were going to a Horse
Guards parade, and beaks on the lower jaw enough to
frighten one.   The female, alas ! had not an egg in her ;
had done spawning long ago.   As I told Sir Julius Vogel, it
was very late for eggs this year, and I was right.

While I was examining these fish the river spared us
not, and I quickly observed that a bank of pebbles on which
I had just been packing eggs was covered with water.   We
were all therefore only too anxious to be off, as a long stay
on a desolate island for a winter's night, in the middle of
the North Tyne, was not a pleasant prospect.   Several of
the party got into the cart ; the more the safer, as the
cart would be heavier in the stream, and less likely to
tip over.   As I was waterproofed up to my neck, I walked
behind in the water, holding the cart-tail with one hand,
the precious egg can with the other.   The man whipped
up the horse, and he managed to drag his heavy load across
the river, the old cart (already over the axles in water)
rolling about like a ship at sea as the wheels tipped up
over the boulders below.

At last we got ashore all right ; the cart then went
back for the nets and the other men, some of whom
waded, others rode across.   My friend the chairman had

brought with him a curious-looking basket, made by the peasants in Germany, very handsomely worked in wicker. This basket he carried on his back, like a **Parisian** *chiffonnier*. We had laughed at his basket, but we did not laugh now, as he produced therefrom a capital luncheon, beer, &c.

As we sat on the bank we saw the North Tyne gradually rising. Lap, lap, came the little side waves at our feet; the island on which we had been standing became smaller and smaller, and at last down came North Tyne with a mighty rush; the stones which a few minutes before had caused the ripples and the 'hovers' so dear to salmon fishers, quickly ducked their heads under water, and where there had been a loud resounding rapid before, there was now a swift black deep stream, running like oil. This sudden spate was caused, of course, by our friend the black storm on the hills. In this part of Northumberland spates come on very quickly, owing to the mountains being so steep, and the moors drained so much more than they were in former years.

With the spate in the river came the storm upon us, a regular spiteful gentleman, fresh from the caves of Æolus, iced rain, sleet, and snow. I was cold, very cold, but I would not let it be seen. I felt my wet suit of waterproof gradually freezing, and becoming like a suit of armour, especially about the arms and throat; so we packed up and walked away as fast as we could, and got a sort of shelter under a railway arch, where I managed, with the help of a water-bailiff, to get off the frozen dress; and then for a walk—I hate walking—into Bellingham. As we went along a blacker cloud came over and it began to snow, not in nice heavy flakes, but little sharp cutting spikes, the size of peppercorns. The howling wind drove these along like a volley from an infantry regiment.

At last we arrived at Bellingham, and on our way home in the dog-cart, a heavy winter snowstorm was on, and kept on all night. The next morning everything, from the distant hills down to the window-sills, had put on a white nightcap. We could see with a telescope the river tumbling over Chollerford dam in the distance. We at once concluded that it would not be of the least use to try for eggs, certainly not to-day, may be many days, as all that snow had to melt and come down off the hills into the river in the form of water. 'Besides, Buckland,' said my host, 'you're a fortnight or three weeks too late to get the run of spawning salmon off the ridds.' 'Yes,' I said, ' I know that ; but when Sir Julius and the New Zealanders say "Go and try," of course I must go and try.'

So I packed up, waited half a day at a country railway station, and got that night to Carlisle, to try what my old friends the salmon in the river Caldew had to say.

At Carlisle station Sergeant Nicholson, head water-bailiff of the Eden salmon watchers, was awaiting me. Nicholson assured me that there were plenty of salmon in the Caldew, and that the water was nice and low. The Caldew is a little river that runs into the Eden just below Carlisle. The Eden Board of Conservators had allowed me to fish here. As in fox-hunting a knowledge of Mr. Fox's ' little game ' is necessary, so in salmon matters a special knowledge of the times and seasons of those silent but artful rascals, the salmon, is indispensable. It is a known fact that salmon, if left alone, will attempt to stock a river, more or less, from top to bottom. The largest salmon are always the last to spawn, and they spawn much lower down the river than their juniors, who go to the higher waters.

Knowing this fact, I concluded it was most probable that the heavy fish of the Eden would run up the Caldew to spawn. The Caldew is a pretty little river with fine spawning tributaries, but it is completely blocked about a mile and a half from the Eden by a weir, over which, I trust, a pass will one day be made. I told Nicholson to be waiting for me at the hotel with nets, and to be ready to start with me as soon as it was light the next morning.

After a time we arrived at the weir, where I was met by the occupier of the mill. Near the mill is a suspension bridge over the river; under the bridge is a very deep hole. Looking downwards from the bridge we could see some huge salmon gently balancing themselves in mid-water. I at once held a consultation as to how to catch these gentlemen. Flinging a rope across the river, we got the big trammel into the edge of the pool where the water began to shallow. Nicholson and I then ran the small trammel through the pool. We touched one heavy fish, for I felt the cork line go tug, but the meshes of the trammel were, I suppose, too small to hold him or her.

By that time a considerable number of idlers had assembled. I do not like idlers of any sort, and at once began to make use of them, setting them to work to stone the pool. We did this for about five minutes, and sent into the pool a continuous volley of stones to drive out the salmon on to the shallow below; but these 'water-foxes' knew what we were after, quite as well as we knew ourselves. 'Come out of the pool.' 'No, thank you, not so long as that net is at the hall door,' said they to themselves. It was no go. So I determined to send my trammel through the hole. She behaved very well, sailing steadily down. Not a fish; the rascals had all disappeared, like frightened rats in a barn, under the great shelves of rock in the pool. We then determined to try the pool underneath the weir, just above the bridge. With great difficulty Nicholson and I managed to get the net across the apron of the weir, over which the water was running pretty swiftly. The stones at the sides of the weir, being varnished with ice, were very slippery, the board of the apron of the weir being like glass itself. We managed, however, to get the net across with only the loss of my big landing-net, which is now somewhere at the bottom of the pool. This was a pretty narrow escape for me; either I or the landing-net must have gone. I gave the landing-net the preference. About two minutes after the net had been in, the corks and the splash showed that there was a fish in her. I halted the men at once, and went in directly up to my armpits. In the middle of the trammel was a lovely female; she had got the outside string of the trammel into her gills, and this held her nicely for me. Alas! she was done, not a single egg in her. I let her go, and she left a tremendous wake behind her, as the poor frightened fish scuttled back into her pool. She weighed about 18 or 19 lbs.

We then decided to try the Factory shallows, some half-mile below.

The success of salmon egg collecting depends upon very small circumstances.

Looking over the river bank towards the Factory pool, what should I see but an old woman standing on the bank just in the very middle of this happy spawning-ground. The old woman was picking stones out of the river bed with a sort of curved pitchfork ; she had a huge petticoat, under which probably pockets existed, so that without doubt she often picked out other things from the river besides stones. I am sure that old woman was a salmon poacher with a stick in her pocket, and tapes round her waist on which to hang under her petticoats the salmon she gaffed.   Stone picking of course had driven away any fish that might have been on these beds.   A curious-looking party was this old woman, and when I came home I found her portrait in my little marmoset, only the little monkey is much prettier than this horrible old Cumberland native.

In spite of the old woman's kind operations, we took a shot with the net at the shallows, below where she had been picking stones.   We got two fish, a splendid male, as strong as an ox, difficult to handle, and a lady fish, who had evidently sent out her cards, with 'thanks for kind enquiries.'   And here I found the great use of my big wicker basket for carrying ladies' ball dresses.   Thrown into the river from above, it floated down nicely. Nicholson, opening the lid, shook Mr. Salmo Salar out of the net into it without once touching him.   This basket makes, in fact, a splendid salmon-cage, where the 'beasts,' as the Tay fishermen call them, can be kept all right in mid-stream without a possibility of escape, and in which they can be handled with much greater facility than with a 'crinoline net' or a landing-net.   After a consultation we agreed it was of no use going on any more, as the fish we had caught showed us the spawning season in the Caldew was already over; so we 'up nets,' and made for the station just in time to catch the last fast train to London.

As the Avon, Devon, is one of the latest of English rivers, as a last chance I sent Edon there, and a day or two later I received a telegram saying that he had achieved great success at Kingsbridge, near Plymouth, and would be home by the night mail. Very early the next morning Mr. Edon appeared at Albany Street with a can, and with a face radiant with joy. With triumph he opened the can, and showed me such a lovely lot of salmon eggs, with an iridescent rich bloom on them like a ripe Hamburgh grape.

The first shot of the net had produced sixteen salmon; among these were three males and two females, from which he procured the splendid lot of eggs he had in the can. The eggs ran out of the fish like shot out of a shot belt; in fact, they were very ripe, and could not possibly have been in better condition. What luck!

On his arrival at Albany Street, all hands immediately set to work to pack eggs. Captain Smith kindly came up from the New Zealand Office from Sir Julius Vogel. He told me he had room in the ship for eighteen boxes of eggs. By one o'clock we had packed the eighteen boxes, got them into a van, and were just starting for the West India Docks, where the 'Chimborazo' lies, when Mr. Capel, of the Cray Fishery, Foots Cray, arrived with a box containing fifteen hundred trout eggs, which he had taken from a fish of about one pound and a half weight, some four hours previously. These eggs were presented by Mr. Capel, in answer to a request made by a New Zealand correspondent some few weeks before.

Just before it got dark we arrived, all of us riding in triumph in a one-horse van through Whitechapel, at the 'Chimborazo,' in the West India Docks. On the deck was Captain Hall, who received us with great cordiality. The 'Chimborazo' is an enormous vessel, 388 feet long, 42 feet wide, and 2,500 tons, 500 nominal horse-power, working up to 3,000. Sailing on Monday, January 21, she hopes to get to Melbourne on Tuesday, March 5, or in about forty-three days, it may be less. At the building of the Tower of Babel of old, there could not have been, I am sure, a more busy scene than the loading of the 'Chimborazo' in the West India Dock, but yet there was no noise and no confusion. The men would work all night. Huge barges of coals were lying on each side loading; and I am told that her furnaces will eat a thousand tons of coals between here and Melbourne.

Everybody carrying a box or two of eggs, we arrived at the icehouse on board ship. Captain Smith opened it, and when I looked in I perceived that a portion of the bottom was covered with boxes of eggs and ice. These were Mr. Youl's boxes, that he had packed some three or four days previously. Searle and myself bundled through the 'man-hole' of the icehouse. Captain Smith handed us the boxes of eggs, and Searle and I shifted with the ice-axes and ice-forks the great slippery blocks of ice on to the top of our own boxes, filling up the interstices with broken bits. When we first got into the icehouse it was jolly cold, but we were so busy shifting the blocks of ice that we soon had no time to be cold. The dimensions of the icehouse were 10 ft. by 7 ft. and 6 ft. It will hold ten tons of ice, which will be packed on the top of the boxes. I am glad Sir Julius has taken my advice and has utilised the icehouse of the ship. At my very first interview with him I told him I had for many years thought that the cost and labour of building a huge icehouse to carry salmon eggs might be saved if arrangements could be made to utilise the ordinary icehouses of Australian ships. I am now convinced that my plan of packing the eggs in the ship's icehouse, when it can be properly done, is a good one. Expense is thereby saved, and should the experiment prove successful there will be little difficulty in sending salmon eggs every winter to Australia and New Zealand—a consummation of our labour in which my friend Mr. James Youl and myself have been deeply interested for so many years past.

We trust these English salmon eggs may be the parents of many salmon which in future years may become established at the Antipodes, to the great increase of the wealth and prosperity of our good friends in New Zealand.

I calculate the number of salmon eggs packed in the eighteen boxes to be over twenty thousand.

John Hunter was, in my opinion, one of the greatest men, if not the very greatest, England ever produced. For this cause any reminiscence or relic that belonged to or was connected with him becomes to me an object of reverence and extraordinary value. Some years ago my respected master, Professor Owen, promised me, to my delight, that he would give me the bedstead which once belonged to John Hunter.

The kind-hearted Professor has now been so generous as to confide this relic to my hands. It arrived as a present to me on my last birthday. The bedstead consisted of two fluted front posts and two square back posts, besides the wooden skeleton which formed this regular old-fashioned four-poster.

The limbs of this bedstead lay for a long time in my room until the *quasi*-Hunterian presence should indicate to me what to do with it. One morning the inspiration came all of a moment, and I cried out, 'Eureka! I know what to do with it—I'll make it into a chair.' So then and there I measured out the bedstead, calculated the depth, height, weight, size of its limbs and ribs, and at once left off all other work, got a good saw, and cut it up so as to make a chair.

Wishing to complete the job, I tried to finish off the chair, but was beaten, as I had not the proper cabinet-maker's tools; so I sent for a working dealer in old furniture. I thoroughly impressed upon him the importance and value of the charge entrusted to his care, and seeing my anxiety about it, he has made really a most excellent job of it. The chair was completed September 22, 1879.

Thinking that the chair, now ready for use, ought to have a proper official inauguration, I asked my old friend Dr. Wadham, of Park Lane, physician to St. George's Hospital (who had been selected by the staff to preside at the annual dinner, which always takes place on the 1st of October at Willis's Rooms), to occupy it as the presidential chair on that occasion. To this he most kindly and readily assented, and delivered from this Hunterian throne one of his usual eloquent addresses to his colleagues and the old students there assembled. As we all know, John Hunter was surgeon to St. George's Hospital; and in the board-room of that institution he died, October 16, 1793.

Previously to the chair being sent for Dr. Wadham's use, I recollected the solemn admonition of John Hunter himself to his assistant, Mr. Clift, handed down from Clift to Professor Owen, from Professor Owen to Professor Quekett, and enforced upon me by my father, namely, ' Label everything.' I therefore had a brass plate fixed in an artistic style to the chair, in such a position that no one can sit down without seeing the inscription, which is as follows :—

G

THIS CHAIR

IS MADE FROM THE BEDSTEAD OF

JOHN HUNTER,

BORN FEBRUARY 14, 1728. DIED OCTOBER 16, 1793.
BURIED AT ST. MARTIN-IN-THE-FIELDS, CHARING CROSS.

RE-INTERRED

WESTMINSTER ABBEY, 1859.

It was first used by Doctor Wadham, president at the annual dinner, St. George's Hospital, October 1, 1879. The bedstead was given to me by Professor Owen, F.R.S., &c., who writes,—

'This is a genuine relic of John Hunter. Mr. W. Clift bought it at the sale of the furniture in Leicester Square. It is the frame of the bedstead on which John Hunter lay when brought from St. George's Hospital.

Frank Buckland, M.A., M.R.C.S.,
Inspector of Fisheries ; House Surgeon, A.D. 1851.

Besides the inscription I have affixed to the chair a photograph of the bust of John Hunter which is now at the north-east corner of Leicester Square, near the house where he lived, and a photograph of the statue which stands in the centre of the Museum of the College of Surgeons. This statue was erected by subscription on the occasion when John Hunter's remains were transferred to Westminster Abbey. It is by the late Mr. Weeks, and is a copy in marble of the celebrated picture of John Hunter in the council-room of the college, by Sir Joshua Reynolds. If my readers have not seen this statue, they certainly should ; it must be a living likeness of this great man, of whom I now give a description from the 'Life of Hunter,' by Jesse Foot, published in 1794.

'John Hunter was about the middle stature ; he was

rather robust, but not corpulent. His shoulders were broad and high, and his neck remarkably short. His features were hard, cheeks high, eyes small and light, eyelashes yellow, and the bony arch protruded ; his mouth was somewhat underhung. He wore his hair curled behind. His dress was plain and none of the neatest. He was frequently seen to smile in conversation, but it was generally provoked from a ridiculous or satirical motive.'

It is recorded that when Hunter's portrait was placed before Lavater the physiognomist, after deep study he exclaimed, 'That man thinks for himself.'

I now give short extracts from various Hunterian Orations. The Hunterian Oration is annually delivered in the theatre of the Royal College of Surgeons on John Hunter's birthday, namely, February 14.

Abernethy says of him, ' Profoundly contemplative, his mind had not been taught to act in imitation of others, he disliked to read as much as he liked to think.'

Cline records, ' Much as he did, he thought still more. He often told Mrs. Cline that his delight was to think.'

Travers writes, ' He was capable of large and comprehensive views of natural phenomena, and endowed with a microscopic faculty of seizing and analysing constituent parts and bearings.'

In the life of Hunter, by Sir William Jardine, ' Nat. Library,' vol. iv., we read : ' He was in no small degree indebted to the friendship of Sir Joseph Banks, who not only allowed him to take any of his own specimens, but procured him every curious animal production in his power, and afterwards divided betwixt him and the British Museum all the specimens of the animals he had collected in his voyage round the world.'

The Museum of the Royal College of Surgeons in Lincoln's Inn Fields is, I fear, for the most part regarded by the general public as consisting of a collection of all the horrors of nature, of deformities, monstrosities, and malformations, both human and animal, so collected and arranged as to form an enlarged 'Chamber of Horrors,' rivalling that in Madame Tussaud's exhibition. Some fifty years ago, before science had dissipated the clouds of vulgar ignorance which then obscured the public mind, I believe the museum was more or less calculated to inspire feelings of dread and sensations of discomfort. In the present day however we are all better educated; the days of the gold-caned and white-wigged physician have passed away; no longer does the pseudo-learned doctor open the top of his gold-headed cane to smell in a graceful manner the aromatic powder therein contained, for the purpose of keeping off infection. Nay, rather has the learned professor of the present day exchanged his smelling-cane for the microscope, his gold snuff-box for his stethoscope, and his wig of learning for the considering cap of severe study and acute observation.

Hunter—the great and immortal John Hunter, whose remains, through my humble exertions, I feel proud to say, now rest in honour in Westminster Abbey, instead of being consigned to an ignominious and obscure corner in a crowded London vault—was indeed, as a physiologist and surgeon, one of the greatest men this country ever produced. I say this advisedly. The great men of the world are for the most part generals, statesmen, lawyers, &c., and we all admire them for the benefits they have conferred upon human civilisation; but to the sick man writhing in agony from the fierce sting of a cruel and remorseless disease, who is the great man? To whom does he look for human assistance but to the man of science; the student of Nature who has deeply investigated the laws of health and disease, and has arranged and practically applied them to the alleviation of human misery and suffering? John Hunter therefore as the founder of the system of modern surgery, and the discoverer of many of Nature's sanitary laws, may be justly regarded as one of the greatest benefactors to the human race. The discoveries of Hunter were not made in a moment: the conclusions he came to were not arrived at without vast labour of both mind and body. Nature is jealous of her secrets—nay, very jealous; always a witness to the truth, she gives her evidence only under very severe cross-questioning and cross-examination. In his investigation of disease therefore John Hunter was not unfrequently foiled, and could obtain no answer from the subject before him; it was then his custom to call another witness, and if he could not get at his fact directly, he would indirectly. The human stomach, the great cook-shop of the human system, refused in many instances to inform the enquirer how she prepared the flesh of animals, the leaves of vegetables, and the products of the mineral kingdom, and formed therefrom dishes and *entrées* which should be palatable to the absorbent and form good blood, invigorating the mental powers and building up anew the body of man, whose construction is, as the Psalmist says, so fearful and wonderful. Hunter therefore was in the habit of getting at the secrets of the *chef de cuisine* by calling at the minor cooking restaurants, asking a question here and a question there. He enquired of the cow why she had a double stomach—a front kitchen and a back kitchen; of the camel, why he carried a system of water-works whose supply was at command at any moment within his gigantic thistle digester. He asked the horse why he had such a small stomach and such large intestines; the sheep, why such a large stomach and such small intestines. He saw in the gizzard and crop of the bird a machine which performed not only the duties of digestion, but also of a crusher and mincemeat maker. The entrails of fish (to others an abomination) became to him samples of another mode of Nature's operations; and thus he went down and down in the links of created beings till at last the lowest link of all was before him. And of what did that consist? A stomach, a simple stomach—a stomach unprovided with eyes, arms, legs, or brain, but yet—oh! strange to say—having the power which other stomachs higher in the system have not—namely, the power of knowing and choosing what is good or bad for their digestion.

In his investigations into the functions of digestion and other functions of the animal kingdom, Hunter collected a vast museum, an assemblage of bottled facts, which no human philosophy can deny, no ideal metaphysicians dispute or question.

By his will, John Hunter directed this museum to be offered in the first instance to the British Government, and in the year 1799 Parliament voted the sum of 15,000*l.*

for the purchase, and an offer being made of the museum to the Corporation of Surgeons, it was accepted on the terms proposed by the Government. An admirable synopsis of the contents can be obtained of the porter at the college, price sixpence; we learn from this that there were in 1875 40,701 specimens. Great facilities are given by the council of the college to visitors who wish to study.

Since Hunter's death, to the great credit of the nation and its rulers, this magnificent collection has been kept up, added to, and fostered under the care of Mr. Clift, my friend Professor Owen, the late lamented Professor Quekett, and the present able and industrious curator, Professor Flower. From the utmost parts of the world, habited and uninhabited, come monthly and yearly, as if by intuitive instinct, all that is rare, curious and instructive in the animal kingdom, each to add its quota of information towards the elucidation of what Nature does in her private laboratories.

Passing into this glorious museum, we ask ourselves upon what order and plan are all these miscellaneous objects arranged. On entering, we find immediately upon our left specimens of the tissues and skeletons of plants, upon our right specimens of dried humanity—mummies from the catacombs of Egypt, from London churchyards, and from the museums of ancient quack doctors. Between these two limits are galleries full to plenitude of, all intermediate forms of animal life, some miles of glass preparation bottles, and some acres of dried specimens. Examining these as we walk along, the idea strikes us to ask ourselves what general law governed all these various creatures when in life?—why were they created, and why did they live? The answer is simple and easy. The great law of nature, to which all living things must submit, is, 'Eat and be eaten;' and in conformity with this law are all animal machines contrived and made to work. The plant eats decayed vegetable and animal substances; the herbivorous animals eat the plants; the carnivorous eat the herbivorous; man, as lord of all, lays his claim of power upon all and over all.

We therefore find that all animals may be well called eating machines. Looking at them as simple machines, we find the ultimate object of their structure is to procure food, and so admirable is this structure that every part of the body is in harmony with its neighbour, so much so that one single bone will tell the comparative anatomist what the rest of the body must have been like; what its food must have therefore been, and thence what the external conditions necessary for its well-being in life; and these rules become of the greatest importance to the researches of the geologist, who by the application of these laws is frequently enabled from a single fossil bone to draw a picture of animal life as it *must* have existed in the times long past when this earth was yet in its infancy.

We place the skull of a deer and of a tiger side by side, and compare them. The teeth are the objects that first strike us as presenting the most marked differences. In the deer we have the front teeth made for nipping grass, boughs of trees, &c., and the hind teeth beautifully constructed for the comminution of the same. Not so in the tiger; here the teeth are mightily different. The great canines grin savagely at us; they are bayonets, daggers, and flesh-hooks combined; sharp are their points, cutting their edges. We open the gaping jaws, we find the back teeth set like scissors, so as to bite up crude masses of blood-stained flesh. The deer is an herbivorous animal, the tiger a carnivorous. The teeth of the deer would be useless to the queen of the jungle. The fangs of the tiger placed in the mouth of the deer would cause its death by starvation. We now walk to the cabinet where the skeletons are arranged. We see here the skeleton of the deer made with the utmost lightness consistent with strength; we find that it is constructed for swiftness in flight and bird-like speed. The bones of the tiger are, on the contrary, like bars of iron, solid, massive, firm in their structure. The horn-covered toes are no longer suited for flight, but in the form of claws are elongated into curved, sharp-pointed hooks, not fitted for continuous running, but rather for seizing and holding a living prey. Yet observe the pad at the sole of the foot—how noiselessly, how quietly do these cushions of natural velvet carry the destroyer within reach of the destroyed! How marvellous is the elasticity of this mighty framework of gigantic osseous strength!

We next go to the gallery where various forms of eyes are displayed. What a difference do we behold! The beautiful dark-coloured open eye of the timid deer enables it to see its enemy from afar, and to ramble in midday in search of luxuriant pastures. The eye of the tiger is that of a nocturnal animal. It has a most wonderful mechanism for making the best use of the scanty rays of light from the moon or from the rising or setting sun. It is fierce, cruel in its aspect. Pity it knows not; once

fixed on its prey it is deadly and glaring till its appetite
is satisfied with fresh blood. Let us now examine the
stomachs of these two animals. That of the deer is
formed in a complex manner for the digestion of vegetables.
It is a natural hayloft, so formed that there shall be a
receptacle, a meal-bag, for containing the collected food
when the animal is at pasture. Besides the bag, we find
a true digesting stomach, which shall be called into
operation when the owner is in safety and able to eat its
dinner in peace and quiet. The stomach of the tiger, on
the contrary, is a simple bag, a mere receptacle and
digester of the flesh it devours. The cook who presides
over it is a 'plain cook,' serving up 'simple joints.' The
deer's stomach has a complicated larder and a grand array
of stew-pans, over which a 'professed cook' presides,
sending up the crude food, not sufficiently comminuted
by the teeth, back again into the mouth to receive an
extra mincing by the process which is called 'chewing
the cud.'

Thus then we see that these two animals are broad
examples of structure being always in conformity with the
food of the animal. The business of the deer is to eat
herbs ; his whole anatomy is constructed in conformity
to this end; his limbs enable him to seek his food, his
teeth to procure it, his stomach to digest it. So with
the tiger, his teeth are carnivorous, his claws carnivorous,
his stomach carnivorous.

Throughout the whole series of the animal kingdom
we find this law prevailing. Watch a dog, a cat, an
elephant, a flea; what seems to be *the* one idea in these
creatures' heads? To eat, to sleep, and to eat again.

The dog is most friendly to his master, and shows him the greatest attention, when dinner is on the table; the cat is most lively and most complacent when she hears the well-known tread of the cat's-meat man in the street, and at the words 'Mēēt, mēēt,' carries her tail erect and in a true cat-like manner. The elephant is a terrible mendicant, always supplicating alms with outstretched trunk. The flea takes his supper of human blood when the sleeper retires for the night, and rouses him again at early morn when his insect stomach craves for breakfast. All these creatures are constructed with the object they have principally in view. The trunk of the elephant tears down the luxuriant vegetation of the jungle; the trunk (or piercer) of the flea sips its food from the skin of the most savoury mortal it can discover in a day's hopping, be he lord or serf.

Over John Hunter's grave in the north aisle of Westminster Abbey, close to the stone bearing the inscription 'O Rare Ben Jonson,' is the following inscription deeply cut in brass:—'The Royal College of Surgeons of England have placed this tablet over the grave of John Hunter to record their admiration of his genius as the gifted interpreter of the Divine Power and Wisdom at work in the laws of organic life, and their grateful veneration for his services to mankind as the founder of scientific surgery.'

TALKING-FISH, EYES OF MUMMY, ANTIQUITIES FROM PERU.

When staying at the Elephant Hotel, at Newtown in Wales, in May 1875, Mr. Charles Thomas, of Newtown, was good enough to call upon me in order to show me what he called his 'talking-fish.' I candidly confess that his curiosity was entirely new to me. On opening the box which contained this treasure, Mr. Thomas produced a double jug. Each jug is somewhat of the shape of an ordinary toilet water-bottle; the two jugs are united at the base by a junction very like that which united the Siamese Twins, and the bottles are again united by a kind of handle that passes between them at the top. The top of one of the bottles is plain, the top of the other is rudely fashioned to represent the head of a seal. Mr. Thomas poured water into the bottle which has the open mouth, and gently turned the water in the bottles from side to side; he then stood them on the table, and from the seal's mouth immediately proceeded a cry amazingly like that of a seal. It sounded something like this: 'Ma-maar-mamaar-mam-a-ma-a-a-r.' The same effect was produced by emptying the water out and simply blowing into the bottle. I have no idea how this sound is produced, neither has Mr. Thomas. Of course there must be some kind of whistle in one of the bottles, but where it is and how it works we cannot tell, nothing being visible from the outside.

Seeing I was interested by his talking-fish, Mr. Thomas said he thought he could puzzle me again with another curiosity in the 'Powis Land Museum,' at Welshpool. Mr. Thomas was quite right, for he did puzzle me again. He showed me there some very remarkable thimble-shaped bodies, which would be well represented if the top of one's little finger were cut off at the root of the nail, and stood on the table. These remarkable objects were, he said, *the eyes of mummies*, and were found in the shrunken skin of the eyes of dried mummies of the ancient Peruvians at Areca; when the mummies were handled, these objects were found loose in the cavity of the eye. They are conical in shape, with a flattened base; they are of a dark amber colour, and, in fact, very like amber. On holding them up to the sun the light is concentrated as by a lens, so that a brilliant spot, like a speck of flame, appears just where the centre of the eye would come in a human being. When inserted in the mummy these eyes must have a ghastly effect. The section shown naturally at the base presented a laminated appearance, like an onion; and a small portion when burnt showed that they were decidedly formed of some animal matter. The structure was very like that of the crystalline lens of the human eye, which when hardened in alcohol splits into three segments, each of which is again separated into layers, leaving a central nucleus.

Notwithstanding the structure of these dried substances

found in the eyes of Peruvian mummies so much resembled that of the lens of the human eye, I was inclined
to think that they were really the bisected lenses of some
fish.

By subsequent investigation I ascertained beyond doubt
that these curious objects are the *lenses from the eyes
of cuttle-fish*. Collectors of Peruvian antiquities, please
examine your collections.

Mr. Thomas has resided for upwards of the last twenty-
five years in Peru, both in the interior and on the coast.
He has travelled and explored a great deal, and has
brought home with him a large collection of prehistoric
pottery, which is now in the Powis Land Museum at Welshpool. I know nothing about pottery, but I should think
there are some rare treasures in this collection. The
shapes of the vases and jugs are most artistic and elegant ;
they are made of clay or earthenware, and are very light.
Nearly all are in some way connected with animals ; some
are in the actual shape of animals ; others have figures of
animals worked into their substance, such as parrots, monkeys, lizards, toads, fish, pelicans, &c.

Mr. Thomas also showed me a leather-cutting knife
(modern, of course). The handle of it is hollow and inlaid
with beautiful filigree work. In the hollow are placed
little portions of metal, which tinkle as the knife is moved.
The object of this is, I am told, that the master may know
whether the workman is going on using his knife, or
whether he has laid it down in idleness. In Mr. Thomas's
collection are also some very remarkable wooden staves,
carved with grotesque figures. They look like staves of
office used by some of the South Sea Islanders. They

were found buried very deep in the guano at Morro de Guanape, islands to the south of Truxillo, on the coast of Peru. Altogether, Mr. Thomas's collection is most interesting.

The Powis Land Museum also contains a fine collection of local antiquities and works of art.

MY TAME OTTERS.

Mr. Matthias Dunn, of Mevagissey, Cornwall, informed me, in February 1873, that there were two young otters for sale, which had been caught by fishermen on the Cornish coast, while rowing along the sea-shore in a small boat, going to their crab-grounds. When off a high cliff the men saw two young otters taking their morning bath in a quiet inlet; the otters instantly made for the shore, and quickly hid themselves under a jutting rock. One of the men landed, got hold of them and brought them into the boat, and tied them fast with a strong cord. When these youngsters found their liberty gone, they set up a very shrill noise, whistling would hardly express the name of the sound. The men were about to resume their work, when, more than 150 yards away along the coast, they saw the dam making directly for them, and lay on their oars to notice the effects of the screams of the young on the parent otter, expecting the mother to show the white feather. She swam, however, boldly up to the boat, and tried to climb into it, but its height out of the water prevented her from doing so. Three times the otter made the attempt to mount the sides of the boat, and each time failed.

The affectionate and plucky mother was eventually killed, and her two young ones brought ashore. As soon as I heard of their capture, I determined to secure the pretty creatures for the Brighton Aquarium.

The two poor motherless baby-otters arrived at Albany Street about twelve o'clock on a very cold day, the parcels delivery man having kindly carried them about London for nearly three hours. They were in a large hamper, with some straw. I found the little things curled up like the 'babes in the wood,' and their pretty little bright eyes looked up at me imploringly, as much as to say, ' Please do not hurt us; we are dreadfully frightened, hungry and sleepy, and we have lost our mother.' Knowing that otters cannot do long without water, I put into their basket a basin of water, and they drank greedily of it. I then sent for some sprats, and was delighted to find that they would take them out of my hand. Altogether they ate nearly half a pound of sprats between them. Not willing to trust anybody to take my prizes to Brighton, I determined to see them safely thither myself. A four-wheel cab not being available at the moment, I put them in their basket between the doors of a hansom. On arriving at Victoria station, after taking my ticket, I looked at the otters to see how they were getting on. I was horrified to find one lying on his back, apparently dead, while the other looked by no means so fresh as I could have wished. I had a bit of a shindy with the porter, who wanted to put my basket in the guard's van. If this had been done both the otters would probably have perished between London and Brighton. I therefore appealed to his humanity, showed him the poor little otters, and asked him where I could find a fire. He then kindly showed me into the waiting-room, and lighted the burners of the gas stove. I put the

H

basket with the otters on the top of the stove, and
turned up the gas as high as I dared without burning the
animals: still the poor sick otter did not move, but the
other one got better. I then sent the man to explain
the circumstances to the superintendent, and get his leave
to take the basket with me into a first-class carriage.

Just as the train was starting, a man came by with
foot-warmers. I procured one, and placed the otters in
their basket upon it. Seeing that the man had another
warmer to spare, I took that also into the carriage, and
opening the lid of the basket, carefully slid it down between
the two little animals. I then left them alone. When
we got to Croydon I examined them again, and was much
pleased to find that the healthier of the two was lying full
length half asleep on the foot-warmer, while the other one
opened his eyes, of which I was glad, for I really had thought
he was dead. One ate some sprats, which I carried in my
pocket, but the sickly one would not look at them. Feeling sure he wanted more warmth still, I considered what I
should do for a wrap for him. Having no rug or great-
coat, I was for the moment puzzled what to do. After
thinking for a minute I recollected I had got on my sealskin waistcoat, so at once took it off, and covered him over
with it. Both the poor little animals then went fast
asleep, and I determined not to disturb them any more till
I arrived at the Aquarium.

Mr. Lawler met me at the station at Brighton, and we
jumped into the cab without looking at the otters.

A few minutes after we left the station I felt something nip my leg, and looking down into the basket, I
found that it was empty. Both otters were loose in the
cab. My foot-warmers had, in fact, been so effectual that

I had made them *too* lively. I told Lawler to keep perfectly quiet and do nothing, and even if he was bitten not to move his legs. The otters soon came out from under the seat and looked impudently at us. I did not care what they did, I was so pleased to find they were alive. When we arrived at the back entrance of the Aquarium I asked for a small landing net, and then passed the cushions of the cab out of the window to the man, who seemed somewhat astonished at my proceedings. I intended to catch them with the landing net; so I shut up the windows, and prepared for an otter-fight in the cab. I had not long to wait before I saw the tail of one of the otters projecting from under the seat. Recollecting that pictures of otter-hunting sometimes represented the huntsman as 'tailing the otter,' I thought I would try if I could accomplish the feat. So, watching my opportunity, I caught the otter by the tail, gave him a twist, and dropped him into the basket like a shot. He snapped and snarled dreadfully, and tried to turn round to bite me, but I was too quick for him, and the lid of the basket was down in a moment. The other otter then climbed up on to the seat of the cab, and seemed to be looking for his comrade. I opened the lid of the basket, and he seemed inclined to go in. While he was making up his mind, I opened the lid with one hand, and gave him a push with the other and in he tumbled; so I had got the two all right. When inside the Aquarium I gave them some more sprats and another drink of water. We then shut them up in their basket, and put them by the engine furnace, where I left them as jolly as otters could be, though I regret to say the poor little fellows did not live very long after this.

MY OTTER TOMMY.

ON Friday, April 2, 1875, when returning from a salmon inspection at Cardigan, I halted for a minute to take the temperature of the water of the Teify, as it passes under the bridge at Llechrhyd. A coracle fisherman came running up to me to ask if I would like to buy an otter. We were much pressed for time, so I had only just a minute to run into the cottage garden and examine him. He was loose in a pigsty, and as handsome a little beast as ever I saw. The fisherman, when lying in ambush for wild ducks, between Llechrhyd and Cenarth Falls, in January, saw something just at the dawn of day swimming past him in the water; he caught it by the tail, and it turned out to be a little baby-otter. Though a baby, the otter fought and bit tremendously; but the fisherman firmly secured him by putting him inside the sleeve of his jacket. Hearing the proposed destiny of the otter was to be hunted, I at once bought him, and directed him to be packed up quite warm and sent to Albany Street. During the next day, when all was quiet, I had a grand opportunity of watching him. At first he was very savage, and bit fiercely at everything. I gave him as many fish as he could eat, and he then began to get tame, so tame in fact that he would allow me to stroke his head with a pencil. I then took the otter down to my Fish Museum at South Kensington, and, for want of a better place, was obliged to put him into an aquarium, and I am afraid it did him no good, as the next morning he was found to have suffered much from the cold. Being in want of a cage, I searched for something that would do, and was fortunate enough to discover an old wooden pedestal which had been used at the exhibition of 1872 as a stand for a statue : turning it over right on its side, I found it to be hollow, and by nailing wire and boards across the bottom I made a capital big cage.

When in the aquarium, as it was getting dark, the otter began to whistle in a most beautiful way. At first I thought it was the note of some bird—something like the robin. The whistle was repeated several times sharply, and then followed by a musical kind of rattle. I have no idea of the mechanism of the whistle of the otter; prairie-dogs and marmots also whistle. I believe it is not under-stood how they manage to do it. Lieutenant Juel, commanding officer of a Norwegian man-of-war, who had come to consult me about the fisheries of his country, told me that otter-shooting was a favourite sport in Norway. They either tracked them in the snow, or else called them by imitating the otter's own whistle.

Tommy, as the otter was christened, lived in his cage a long time, and became a great attraction to visitors. He soon learnt to answer to his name, and if a stone were thrown into his tub of water he would dive for and gambol with it in a kitten-like manner. During the summer of 1878 the attendant Edon informed me that Tommy used to come out of his house, especially on moonlight nights, and play about on the roof of his cage; but, as far as we know, he never then went far away. We should never have known this had not a policeman seen him on the top of his cage. We could not conceive how he got out; but it was afterwards discovered that Master Tommy had scratched a hole underneath the straw of his bed, through which he used to squeeze his india-rubber-like body and crawl up the interspace between the cage and the wall; but at daylight he used to go back again by the same road into his cage.

One morning in the following winter a mysterious circumstance took place. The padlock which fastened the wirework of the cage was missing, and Tommy was gone. The question was, whither? As my badger got loose and was seen in the drains in Kensington Gardens (where for aught I know he is still alive and well, and I hope he is so), I expected to hear of a wonderful discovery of a live otter in the Serpentine. In order to induce Tommy not to go to the Serpentine, I ordered the lad Joe, the assistant, to put Tommy's food as usual in his house, so that he might not suffer from hunger.

For several days we knew he was not far away, because he ate his food, and we could see his tracks in the snow. One night, as Joe was hunting the bushes about with a lantern, Tommy followed the light, and Joe and the policeman on duty managed to circumvent the foolish little rascal, and drive him into his cage. He was dreadfully thin and scared, and seemed only too glad to get back to his comfortable home. I had previously borrowed a cat-trap from Mr. Bartlett, but Tommy was much too artful to go into it.

With care and plenty of food the otter soon recovered. Mr. Edon found he could imitate his whistle exactly by sharply twisting the glass stopper of a bottle in its socket.

I suppose that my Museum must be a ghostly-looking place in the middle of the night. An Irishman who was put on as policeman, was terribly frightened one night. When going his rounds, as he was flashing his bull's-eye about, suddenly from the side of the stove there appeared two eyes of fire, glaring with demoniacal fierceness at the Bobby. Poor Bobby trembled, groaned, and quickly retreated backwards from the supposed ghost; in doing so, he fell down three steps on to his back, which added much to his previous alarm. It turned out that the demoniacal eyes were simply the glass eyes of my big Scotch fox, which Edon had stuffed in a curled-up attitude. The light from the bull's-eye lantern happened to hit the glass eyes just at the right angle. The stuffed fox was afterwards placed upon the straw on which the cast of the elephant rests. Edon put a chain round his neck, and it is often amusing to hear visitors argue whether the animal is really dead or alive.

In April 1879 my friend Mr. Charles Hambro wrote to say that his keeper had captured an otter near his residence, Milford Abbey, Blandford, Dorset, and that the animal was so little injured that he thought it would do well in captivity. It had been taken by a steel trap, but so lightly caught that only the extreme end of the toe was held, so that no bones were broken, and no internal parts injured.

At my request Mr. Hambro presented this otter to the authorities of the Westminster Aquarium, where it was placed in the tank previously occupied by the manatee, and which was built originally for otters. The manatee had died in March, and the otter was installed in its place. The tank was most admirably suited for the purpose, and being constructed with immense sheets of glass, was really a palace for the animal.

This otter did not live very long, so at the request of the Directors I sent up Master Tommy from the Museum, and I am glad I did, as the sight of the otter swimming about in his transparent house is an exhibition quite unique. I have often suggested this exhibition of otters to gentlemen connected with aquaria, but the Westminster Aquarium was the first to carry it out.

Not only is this a very pretty sight to ordinary visitors, but the naturalist had, for the first time, an opportunity of learning the habits of this Kee Door, or water-dog,[1] in hunting for his prey under water. Otter hunters, fishermen, and gamekeepers know doubtless the habits of the otter when on land, but their mode of swimming under water, and their manner of catching fish[2] in the

[1] The Welsh for otter is ' Ci dwr,' which signifies water-dog—not at all a bad name.

[2] Besides the cannibal fish of the waters, the fish have to run the gauntlet of many animals living a great part of their time, not in the water, but in the air, or breathing air. Thus, for instance, the sea fish have to encounter the attacks of whales, porpoises, dolphins, a great many species of seals, besides gannets, divers, and a great number of other fish-eating sea-birds ; and here let it be remarked that the walrus does not eat fish : he uses his tusks and wire-like whiskers for routing

water are probably as unknown to them as they were to myself until lately.

I will now venture to make a few remarks upon the structure and mode of fishing of this interesting British animal, which in elegance of form and perfect structure is one of the most graceful animals that has been placed by the Creator on this earth.

When living fish are placed in the aquarium, the otter ascertains the fact in a moment, and his beautiful intelligent face gleams as it were with satisfaction as he goes into the water. The first thing to be observed is the wonderful way in which he glides off his board. He does not go in with a run and a jump, but dives head foremost, almost without disturbing the particles of water, certainly without the slightest splash or noise.

This he is enabled to do mainly because his head is formed in a beautiful wedge-like shape, a structure admirably adapted for the work he has to do. On each side of the head, near the nostrils, are situated a great array of whiskers. These whiskers are found also in the lion, cat, seal, rat, hare and other creatures which get their living in darkness or else under water. Each whisker springs from a great root. This root is composed of a bunch of nerve-substance, and is connected by means of another nerve with the brain. In the skull of the otter, as in the skull of the lion, we find therefore that the hole through which this great nerve going to the whiskers passes is very large, showing that the nerve is also very

in the sand, and turning up therefrom shrimps and small edible arctic molluscs. In tropical climates the fresh-water fish have the crocodile for an enemy.

large. The instant the otter is under the surface of the water we see these whiskers come into play ; the otter expands them to their full extent, and they form as it were a circle of sentries, so that when under water these highly sensitive whiskers guide him in all his movements. This is obvious by the way the otter, although not in pursuit of fish, is enabled to turn the corners of the aquarium and avoid obstacles as they occur.

The next thing we observe is that, when hunting under water, the otter is guided more by sight than by sense of smell. He keeps his eyes wide open all the time, and turns his head right and left with a quick motion, as though looking for his prey. I am however puzzled to know why it is that the otter's eyes should be so exceedingly small. They are prominent and rat-like, and altogether not very unlike small black boot-buttons. Why the otter should have such small eyes, and the seal such large ones, I am not as yet certain, but there is doubtless good reason for it.

When the otter is pursuing a fish, it is most interesting to observe his manner of swimming. He does not use his fore and hind legs as does a horse or dog, but folds his front paws alongside his body while he strikes out vehemently with his two hind legs. This causes his movement to be apparently by jerks, but the jerks are so exceedingly rapid that the creature progresses in the water with extreme velocity, almost as quick as a pike when he darts at his prey.

I have elsewhere explained that the use of the tail of the rat is to balance himself when passing along places difficult to walk on, and **that the use** of the beaver's tail is **not** to build his house, as is stated **in** old natural history books, but to **act as a** support when the animal is sitting up, tripod fashion, at his **work.** When swimming the beaver uses **his tail** to enable him to rise **or sink in** the water, whereas I find that the otter carries his **tail** extended straight **behind** him, **so** that he guides **himself, and turns very quickly** in and out among the sunken **roots of** waterside trees. This graceful **act** of turning is **well seen** in the Westminster otter when he seizes the fish. **At that moment he** instantly turns, and forms himself as it were into a ball, so that the fish has not the slightest chance of escaping.

I have **described, when** writing **of** the anatomy of the guillemot, the wonderful bubbles **of air** that invariably follow that **bird** when under water, and I have explained how the **air is stored** underneath the feathers, **and given out when the bird is** diving. **In the otter a somewhat similar phenomenon can be observed. As** he swims along under water **he is followed by a train** of the most **lovely** air-bubbles, which appear exactly like beads **of quicksilver.** The origin of **this air** I cannot quite make out. A large proportion **of it comes** directly **from** the lungs. **This is** important; **the otter** evidently **has** some difficulty in **sinking in the** water, he therefore **lets out the air to enable him to go down; but at the same time a** good **deal of air comes from underneath the fur.** When the **seal dives no air appears to come from underneath his coat.**

The **otter, it has been remarked, always** takes **the** largest fish **in** the tank first, leaving **the smallest fish till** the last. He never attempts to eat them under water, but always comes to the bank-side to have his meal. The otter invariably begins to eat the fish by crunching up the head, never the tail; holding his prey by his fore paws, so that it has not the least chance of escape, and munching it into very small bits. I have prepared the skull of an otter, and find that the canine teeth are very trenchant, and almost scissor-like in their action; they are conical in shape, much sharper than the canines of a dog or cat. When a fish is caught the otter immediately transfixes it through the head with his sharp canines, the action of which is such that the fish is held by them as in a rabbit-trap, and cannot escape. The otter holds the fish for some little time between his canines before he begins to eat, waiting till it is quite dead and quiet. In eating he never uses his canines at all, but bites at the fish with the side of the mouth only. The molars and the præ-molars are also very sharp, but capable of crushing any substance into very small bits.

In January 1871 my friend Dr. Norman of Yarmouth sent me a huge otter. It was packed in a baby's cradle in which the various members of the doctor's family had been successively reared. This grand otter measured four feet three inches from tip of nose to end of tail, the tail being one foot three inches long, and weighed thirty-two and a half pounds immediately after it was captured near the North Pier, Yarmouth.

When dissecting the body of the beast, I discovered what I believed to be a new fact as regards the œsophagus or gullet of this animal. Holding up the pharynx, I poured down thin plaster into the stomach, which, of course, hardened, showing its full capacity ; it was nine and a half inches long, and fifteen inches round, and would hold rather over three pints of fluid. The œsophagus was nineteen inches long, and, strange to say, was a very small tube, the size of a half-inch gas pipe, hardly big enough to admit one's little finger, and only one inch and three-quarters round. I expected to find it a large dilatable tube, as in other fish-eating creatures : why the gullet should be so small I do not know, but the description given above of the teeth, and of the manner in which the otter eats, shows that the structure of the teeth is adapted to this peculiarity in the gullet. If the otter did not cut up his food very small he would be choked. In the seal, on the contrary, the gullet is a large capacious bag, down which the fish is slipped in a moment. The reader should observe the seals when fed at the Zoological Gardens ; the fish are bolted, and not masticated.

In my Museum at South Kensington there is a preparation showing this very curious construction of the gullet of the otter. I have remarked that every time the otter swallows his food he gives a gape, something like yawning. This must have something to do with the large size of the stomach and the small size of the œsophagus.

I have also in my Museum the cast of an otter when skinned, showing the muscular structure of the beast. I observe that all four feet are webbed ; that is to say, a membrane connects the toes as in the foot of a duck ; the hind feet are very much larger than the fore feet, a fact accounted for when we have learned that the otter uses his hind legs and webbed paws much more than his fore paws when going rapidly through the water.

The following account of the otter is given in ' La Petite Vénerie,' written by a most observant French sportsman, M. D'Houdetot :—' This wolf of the river resembles the fox in size, but the badger in conformation. The skin as long as the otter is alive does not become wetted. The paws are very short and webbed; he swims better than he runs. His "spoor" resembles that of the fox, but is larger ; and the heel is never marked in the spoor. The otter has yearly two to four young ones, which she lays up in a burrow excavated under the roots in a bank at the water's edge. The otter eats beetles, cray-fish, insects, frogs and water-rats, but his chief food[1] is fish, which he often kills for the pleasure of killing, as do the marten, weasel and polecat. Otters are taken by traps, or are shot ; but are no longer hunted in France with dogs, as formerly.' The following account of the old French mode of training otter-hounds is given by M. De la Conterie :—' The puppy hounds are allowed to go to an extreme point of hunger : then the whipper-in, who is accustomed to feed them, takes a caldron of soup, and calls them to him. He walks straight into a river or horse-pond and places his soup-dish at such a distance and depth of water that the

---

[1] As regards the food of otters, my friend Captain Salvin writes me :—' Otters will kill and eat rabbits. I keep mine almost always on meat, and often give him rabbit. In the wild state, when frozen out, otters will catch rabbits in their holes. They often kill water-rats, water-hens, &c. My otter is very fond of a fat frog. When it eats eels it puts them constantly into its water dish to help them down. The otter should be called the " water mart," it is so like the tribe in all its manners and customs.'

puppies can get at it without losing foothold of the bottom. Urged by hunger, and by fear of the water, the puppies make many ceremonies before they will go in; but "hunger dares everything." When the puppies have been in the water once it is all right; the second time they hesitate an instant; the third time they run to the soup caldron in the water just as though it was on land. All hounds when excited will run precipitately into a river or pond after a hunted stag or fox; but it is another thing to train hounds to take water at daybreak on a cold morning on the chance of finding an otter.'

All dogs will follow an otter's track with eagerness; but his track is not often continuous, as he will constantly pass over from one side of the river to the other.

'The otter swimming noiselessly in the water frequently leaves his retreat without the huntsman seeing him, but rarely escapes the hound's perception. When the otter comes up to breathe, he shows very little of his body, seldom more than the tip of his nose for a second, which is time enough for him to breathe. Fishermen are great enemies of the otter; they catch him in trammel nets, which are set under water. The number of otters destroyed annually in France is about seven to eight hundred, most of them taken with traps and nets. The Chinese have taught otters to hunt and catch fish; they are said to keep otters as we do packs of hounds. In former times the otter was much trained in Sweden for catching fish.'

Our author then tells a capital story how, when on a sporting expedition, he called upon his uncle, a canon of

the cathedral town through which he was passing. He
told his uncle he would not stop to dine, because he knew
it was a fast day, and his uncle would have no dinner. The
worthy old clergyman persuaded him to stay. Dinner-time
arrived, and upon the table was placed smoking hot what
appeared to be a roast hare. 'Not hare,' said the canon,
'it's an otter.' By official authority the otter has been
declared *maigre*, i.e. food fit for a fast day.

THE COSTERMONGERS' AND POOR MAN'S MARKET.

THE Londoner who is perchance at a loss to discover something he has never seen before in this great metropolis should pay a visit to the cattle market at Islington. On Mondays and Thursdays, on those days only, we may observe cattle and sheep being driven through the streets of London. These are the market days at Islington. The market begins very early, and at ten o'clock the gates are closed, and no cattle are allowed to be driven through the London streets again that day until after six in the evening.

Every Friday in the year a very different market is held among the pens at the Islington Cattle Market. This begins at one and lasts up till six exactly, when the great bell announces the time for a general clearance. I feel certain that few of my readers are aware that this most curious phase of civilisation exists amongst us. It is the market for the poor, the moderately poor, the out-of-work people, the very poor, and especially for the London costermongers—quite a class among themselves. At this market almost every conceivable article used by civilised man can be purchased, at prices ranging from one penny to twenty pounds. The articles sold in this

I

market are rarely new; they are second-hand—we may almost say third or fourth hand. To this place, in fact, gravitate the shreds and the refuse of Great London and its vicinity—the 'jetsam and flotsam' of this huge city.

On entering the northern gate (my visit was paid in September) we find the pen which on cattle market days is occupied by the calves devoted to the sale of old, very old clothes. These garments are mostly, if not altogether feminine, and the customers belong to the gentler sex. The sellers are women. There are four of them in the same calves' pen, one at each corner, each with a bundle of clothes before her. One picks up an article of dress, and sells it by Dutch auction. She starts with two shillings: 'Child's jacket for two shillings, fur and all.' After a great deal of chaff and wrangling as to the worth and condition of the article, she tosses it over the heads of the bystanders to some customer for the large sum of fourpence. In the other corners are selling babies' half-worn shoes, old caps and bonnets, gowns, jackets, shawls —in fact, the contents of an ordinary rag-shop. If these garments could only speak, what tales of misery and starvation they could tell! It is a curious thing, that if one of these saleswomen, after putting an article once up for sale, puts it down on the ground unsold, she will never pick it up or take money for it that day.

In the interspace between the rest of the calves' pens are allotments of ground for which the holders pay six-pence a day. Laid out on the bare paving-stones may be seen a most curious conglomerate of household goods, all in a broken and dilapidated state. I attempt a catalogue

—a bunch of rusty horse-bits, broken birdcages, chairs without legs, old clocks, chairs without bottoms, rusty nails of all sizes and shapes, lids of saucepans, birds' eyes, clock weights, bell pulls, glass stoppers for bottles, broken fishing-rods, piles of old boots and shoes one would have thought long past service, buckles, old straps, stirrups, old saddles, empty physic bottles, bits of broken looking-glasses, oil bottles, odd volumes of books, bits of stair carpet, oil-cloth, &c. &c., besides cough drops, medicines for rheumatism, and patent nostrums of all sorts and descriptions.

In order to provide for the commissariat of the thousands of people who attend this market are here to be met vendors of baked potatoes hot from the can, huge deep-sea oysters fresh from the sea, whelks, mussels, cockles, stale buns, sherbet, ginger beer, sheep's trotters, ham sandwiches, cold fried fish and bread for a penny, hot sausage and bread for three halfpence. The articles of food for sale are really fresh and in excellent condition, as these dealers know quite well that neither the poor man nor his wife will buy any food that is not really of excellent quality.

At the end of the avenue we come to the poultry market. Here, on a fine day, can be seen for sale immense quantities of live fowls, ducks, geese, turkeys, pigeons, &c. Some of these birds are of the very best possible kind—some of the very worst.

Irish ducklings can be bought at fourteen or fifteen pence each. They are of course very thin, but yet are bought up by the poor with the idea of fattening them for home consumption. Irish goslings are sold in large numbers, and fetch from half a crown to three shillings. 'Widows,' *alias* old hens, are to be bought at a shilling each. Most of these widows are sold by the hawker from the hand, as it would be a dangerous experiment to let them try to stand on their feet. They might betray their age and infirmities. In the spring of the year these bird dealers have an ingenious device of dressing up the combs of old hens so as to give them the appearance of birds in full lay.

Adjoining the poultry market are offered for sale a number of German hen canaries. At this time of the year large crates containing small cages of German canaries come to this country. These birds are all hens. In the market they are, of course, warranted all cock birds. They fetch, cage and all, from one to two shillings each. The German dealers do not send over the cock canaries until they are clean-moulted and in song. These birds are not sold in the streets, but in shops, where they fetch from 4s. 6d. to 6s. each. They begin to appear in London in the month of November.

Alongside the poultry are also cages containing other birds and a few 'monk' parrots. 'Monk' parrots are sickly parrots, which have caught cold on their passage from abroad to the wholesale dealers in Liverpool, London, &c. Grey monk parrots were being sold at five to six shillings. Had they been healthy birds, each would have been worth a pound.

Near the canary stalls the market is occupied by rows of costermongers' barrows, new and second-hand, all for sale. There are also carriage and truck wheels and springs in abundance; in some cases there are only portions of wheels. The spokes of wheels are much used for the rounds of ladders, and are well fitted for the purpose.

There are also numbers of carts containing live pigs; these are sold by higglers or pig jobbers, who go round the country collecting them. The pig market can always be found by the noise the pigs incessantly make.

The eastern side of the market is devoted to old carriages and harness. Here may be seen old hansoms, broken-down four-wheelers, carts and vans of every age, shape and description. I was much struck with the collection of the metal portions of what once had been first-class harness, especially the coronets, intricate monograms, coats of arms, and other heraldic devices, which had been taken off old harness that had seen better days. These metal armorial bearings were polished up equal to new, and really looked beautiful.

Near this carriage department we came upon a lively scene, namely, the horse market. In this were to be found goats young and old, but the poor things were in very bad condition. Some Nannies are sold as milkers, and a most ingenious device is used by the dealers to give old goats the appearance of being in full milk. A very young, innocent-looking kid of another goat plays a prominent but not willing part in this transaction. Almost every description of goat is to be found here. The large male goats are bought for stables where many horses are kept. I believe the reason of this is that goats will run from fire, and the horses will follow them out of the stable should it catch fire. Goats are sometimes used as food, and in some cases sold for venison.

Jerusalems, *alias* living donkeys, are plentiful in the market.   In September mokes, as they are called, are at a discount owing to many circumstances; to wit, the winter is coming on, the lively time of the year is nearly over, and there is no more demand for mokes to assist at the sea-side, children riding, school treats, excursions, bean feasts, &c.   In the spring of the year, on the contrary, good donkeys, also small ponies, fetch high prices from the gipsies.   The gipsies frequent places such as Epping Forest, Hampton Court and the suburbs of London resorted to by school treats, &c., and make a great deal of money by providing donkey rides.   Good working donkeys are in the spring worth 3*l.* to 4*l.* each.   In the autumn a good donkey can be got for from 1*l.* to 50*s.*   Donkeys are largely used during the busy fruit season by the costermongers.   But many of them cannot afford to keep a donkey during the winter, so that in October donkeys are very cheap.

In horses a large business is done.   Those principally sold are screws, such as kickers, jibbers, roarers, broken-winded, bolters, and vicious tempers.   Every infirmity to which horseflesh is liable may be here found represented.   Among the horses are some fine specimens of 'racks,' that is fleshless horses, simply skin and bone. They are principally bought up by the knackers, not for the flesh, but for what they really are, for the skin and bone.   Every portion of a rack not sold for cat's-meat is of some value to the knacker.   The ultimate destination of the horses for sale, not racks, is for the carts of costermongers and little tradesmen.   The operations in horse dealing are principally done by horse copers before sending the animals into the market, and, *caveat emptor!* Old horses are apparently turned into young ones by judicious trimming, grooming, and feeding up according to their ailments and infirmities. When tied up for sale the horses are certainly not kindly used, being kept awake and lively by sticks or whips.

Adjoining the market there are sales which take place weekly of Russian and other foreign ponies. They are sold by auction in large numbers. These ponies are strong serviceable animals, and are received here without shoes on their hind feet. This is to prevent them from kicking and injuring each other when in the hold of the steamer that brings them over. These horses and ponies are bought up by speculators in numbers varying from forty to fifty, and are taken round to country fairs. They fetch from seven to twelve guineas each. Altogether the Islington market on a Friday is a most curious and interesting sight. Take a tram from the top of Tottenham Court Road to the ' Brecknock Arms; ' you will be within two minutes' walk of the market. The best time to go is on a Friday when the weather is fine; the height of the market is about four o'clock.

RELICS IN THE ASHMOLEAN MUSEUM, OXFORD.

I HAVE taken an opportunity lately of inspecting the Ashmolean Museum at Oxford. This museum was one of the first, if not the very first, ever instituted in England.

The Ashmolean Museum was founded by Elias Ashmole, in 1679. Ashmole's monument is at Lambeth, with the following inscription :—'Hic jacet inclytus ille et eruditissimus Elias Ashmole, ob : 18 Maii, 1692 Anno : ætat. 76. Sed durante Museo Ashmoliano Oxon : nunquam moriturus.'[1] The collection was, however, commenced by John Tradescant, who visited England first in 1600 ; it was then called 'Tradescant's Ark.' For many years it was under the curatorship of my father's old friends, Philip Bury Duncan, D.C.L., Fellow of New College, Oxford, and John Shute Duncan, D.C.L.

The following are some of the more remarkable relics in this interesting collection :—

Model of ancient British village, discovered at Standlake, near Oxford. It appears that our ancestors lived in circular holes in the ground, five feet across by three or four feet deep. Huts or tents were probably erected over these holes ; they must have been very warm and comfortable. I shall try a house of this kind myself. Soldiers on a campaign should take the hint.

The Alfred jewel found in Newton Park, Somersetshire

[1] L sons' *Environs of London*, p. 330.

with the inscription in **Saxon**, 'Alfred commanded me to be made.' **Alfred** died in 901. The jewel is therefore nearly 1,000 years old. I have described this elsewhere.[1]

A lock of hair of King Edward the Fourth, taken from his head when his remains were examined in the chapel of Windsor Castle, March, 1789. This is a very small lock, and the colour of the hair is quite faded. This specimen shows what a long time human hair will resist decay. Edward the Fourth died 1483, nearly 400 years ago.

A portrait of the head of King Charles the First (who died 1649), taken immediately after the coffin was opened in the vaults of Windsor Chapel, 1813 : near it is the printed description of what occurred on this occasion, written by Sir H. Halford.

The hat worn by President Bradshaw when he condemned King Charles the First. It is made of thick leather, and has a brim three inches wide. The cavity for the head is thirty-five inches round, and inside the leather is an iron cage, a round iron plate protecting the top of the head ; slips of iron protect the sides.

Helmet and cuirass worn by the Pikemen in the days of King Charles the First.

A shoe of the Hermit of Dynton ; who was clerk to Simon Mayne, one of King Charles the First's judges. The hermit died at Dynton, 1660. This shoe is made entirely of patches of leather nailed together. A picture shows that his dress was made of the same material, and in the same way.

A pair of bellows which belonged to King Charles the Second, beautifully inlaid.

Boots of Prince Henry, Duke of Gloucester.

Candle snuffers used in the sixteenth century.

A pewter plate from off which King Charles the Second dined the day before the battle of Worcester.

King Henry the Eighth's hawking glove, a thick glove of the same sort of leather as is used now by hedgecutters. It

---

[1] *Logbook of a Fisherman and Zoologist*, p. 372.

must have been made to fit a man with a large hand ; the wrist part is highly ornamented.

A sword presented by Pope Leo X. to King Henry the Eighth, when he first assumed the title of *Fidei Defensor*, or Defender of the Faith.   The hilt in crystal is set in silver.

A portion of an old stump, apparently uninteresting, but to all Oxonians *the* most interesting object in the collection.   It is a portion of the stake used when Cranmer, Latimer, and Ridley were burnt outside the Bocardo Gate at Oxford, at the place now marked by a stone cross let into the street opposite Balliol College.   The lower end of the stake is pointed, the upper end charred and burnt.   This curiosity deserves a special case to itself.   These poor martyrs, who were called the ' Noble Three,' were burnt A.D. 1555.

A marvellous picture of the battle of Pavia, 1525.   The soldiers are all in very heavy armour.   The artillery of the period is most interesting.

Queen Elizabeth's watch and chain.   The watch case is highly ornamented with turquoise stones ;   externally it appears to be made entirely of turquoise.

Queen Elizabeth's riding-boots.   These are made of a soft flexible leather resembling thick chamois leather.   The sole is thick and strongly made ;   it is nine inches long.   The Queen wore high heels, they are two inches high.   The boots measure fifteen inches from the heel to the top ;   Queen Elizabeth must have had a very pretty foot.   These boots lace up on the outside. The ladies' high-heeled walking-boots which extend high up over the ankle, must have been ' developed by the process of selection ' from Queen Elizabeth's boots.   Inside the Queen's boots I discovered a small portion of satin, once white and forming the lining ;   it is now coffee-coloured with age.   These boots must be about 300 years old.

Lady's shoe, time of Queen Anne.   It is the very model of ladies' shoes now to be seen in the ladies' boot-shops in London. It is high-heeled, and measures eight inches long, by two and a quarter wide at the sole.

A still smaller sandal shoe of black satin. This belonged to the late Duchess of York. The sole of this lovely little shoe is eight inches and a quarter long, and one inch and a half wide, a regular Cinderella's shoe. Where is the lady now whom it would fit?

Small picture of the 'Via Dolorosa,' or road to Calvary, formerly supposed to have been made of humming-birds' feathers, now pronounced by the best authorities to be made of transparent enamel. This is said to be the finest specimen of the kind known, and the art is supposed to have been lost. This most valuable specimen belonged to the queen of James II.

Very fine old painting (1651) of the now extinct bird the dodo. The head and foot of the dodo are in the university museum. A big frog, beautifully painted, is by the side of the dodo.

A collection of native arms from Fiji and the South Seas. Amongst these, without doubt, are those collected by Captain Cook in his second voyage, many of which are figured in his 'Voyages.'

Three specimens of man-traps—most formidable-looking things. I have a man-trap in my own Museum at South Kensington.

A spring gun on pivot, used formerly for poachers. It is so contrived that it will only fire direct at the poacher. The lock is admirably protected from wet, by wood. Spring guns were made illegal about 1826.

An ancient basket-hilted sword, a large portion of which is completely enveloped and grown over by the root of an old tree. How I should like to know the history this sword might tell!

CURFEW AND CHARTER HORNS.

AMONG the many curiosities of natural history of which I am always in pursuit, nothing gives me more pleasure than the discovery of an ancient Charter Horn.

When at Ripon in October 1863, I took the opportunity of inspecting the celebrated relic of antiquity, the Ripon horn. I went to call on the Horn-blower, and found him living in a little house down a court, not far from the Unicorn Hotel. He had been horn-blower for thirty-three years, and his father was horn-blower before him for thirty years. He always walks bearing his horn in front of the mayor when the mayor and corporation attend church. The horn is a common cow's horn (with a metal mouthpiece), curved in shape, measuring three feet six inches long. It is carried by means of a leathern strap across the bend of it.

At nine o'clock every night the Ripon horn-blower goes with his horn to the door of the mayor and blows three long blasts—rather a dismal but yet musical sound. He also gives one blast at the Market Cross. In former times the mayor was called 'the Wakeman,' and the blowing of the horn, I believe, indicates two things : first of all it answers the purpose of a 'curfew' bell, and at its sounding in former times people were obliged to put out their fires, a wise precaution, considering the carpets were rushes, and the houses were built of wood. It also indicates the watch-setting, and the law in Saxon times was something to this effect :—If anybody after horn-blowing or watch-setting was robbed ' on the gate-syd within the towne,' the wakeman was bound to compensate the person robbed if it was proved that he ' and his servants did not their duties at y^t time.'

The horn in the blower's possession is not the original horn. This is kept at the house of the mayor. I called upon the mayor and asked him to allow me to examine it. This ancient horn is handsomely mounted, and fastened on to a black velvet scarf made to be worn on the shoulders. At the junction of the scarf with the horn are miniature silver models of a spur and crossbow. On the horn is this inscription :—' Antiquis et honorem et premia possi—(I cannot quite construe this)—Vetustate lapsum restituit.— J. Aiselbie, ARM., 1703.' On the lower part—' This horn was again restored, 1854.—H. Morton, Mayor.' Attached to the velvet scarf are several silver plates. Every mayor on resigning office adds, or is supposed to add, a silver plate. I made a note of some of the dates as follow—1570, 1593, 1595, 1602, 1658.

Some of the plates, bearing coats of arms and bosses, are shaped like a sailor's hat. Several also are of curious antique shapes. I was informed that the oldest badges are those of a ' wakeman ' who lived in the time of Henry VIII., the name of one Gayscar, wakeman in 1520, being marked especially. The title of Wakeman was exchanged for that of Mayor in 1604. Hugh Ripley was the last wakeman, and the first mayor.

I was told that the horn itself is certainly of a date not later than the Conquest; that its form is true Saxon, and that there was another horn of similar shape made of ivory preserved in the **vestry** of York Cathedral.

In former **times Ripon** was famous for the manufacture of spurs. Ben Jonson says, ' As true as Ripon rowels.' ' There is an angel if my spurs be not right Ripon.' ' Whip me with wire beaded with rowels of sharp Ripon spurs.'

I was fortunately able to examine a specimen of a real Ripon spur. The rowel was so ingeniously placed that the sharp points of the star of which it was composed would not show themselves unless pressed against something. This effect was produced by a most ingenious guard. I recommend our London spurmakers to look into the matter, as the revival of Ripon spurs would probably be acceptable to equestrians.

Ripon was also celebrated for some centuries for making saddletrees and crossbows.

When passing through York I took the opportunity of examining the horn there. Not having time to go the regular rounds of the cathedral, one of the vergers conducted me at once into the ancient vestry, and unlocking an old oak chest, displayed this valuable relic to my admiring eyes. It is made of the lower end of a very large tusk of an elephant, and is of the same peculiar semi-curved shape as the Ripon horn, which, however, is not of ivory, but of simple cow-horn.

I am not quite sure whether the hollow of the horn is the natural cavity of the tusk, or has been scooped out by artificial means. It is of a dark mahogany colour, reminding me forcibly of the tusks of the mammoth found frozen in the ice in Siberia, and its surface is polished like a marble monument ; this is caused, I imagine, by the touch of human hands for many generations past.

The most authentic history of this remarkable horn is given by Sir William Dugdale as follows :—' Ulphus the son of Thorald, who ruled in the west of Deira, by reason of the difference which was likely to rise between his sons about the sharing of his lands and lordships after his death, resolved to make them all alike ; and thereupon coming to York with that horn wherewith he used to drink, filled it with wine, and by the ceremony enfeoffed this church with all his lands and revenues.' By this relic, I understood the Chapter still retains possessions of great value. In former times the horn was adorned with gold mountings, and slung with a gold chain ; but it was stolen from the church in a general seizure of ecclesiastical property. Afterwards Thomas Lord Fairfax became its possessor, the golden ornaments having been stripped from it. He bequeathed it to his son Henry Lord Fairfax, who restored it to the church. In 1675 the Dean and Chapter re-adorned it with silver-gilt, and engraved upon it an inscription commemorative of the circumstances. The horn is adorned with four rings, or straps of silver, and on that which protects the rim are representations of various animals, all being emblematical : thus, the griffin signifies honour ; the unicorn, chastity ; the lion, courage ; the doe, affection ; the dog, faithfulness. I find that ' Deira ' was one of the two kingdoms—the name of the other was Bernicia—out of which Northumbria was formed in the early part of the Saxon government. The capital of the kingdom of Deira was York. The horn, therefore, will date somewhere between A.D. 560 and 600. There is, I believe, no reason to doubt the authenticity of this ancient Saxon horn, though from whence, and by what means, the Saxons obtained so fine a bit of ivory I cannot conceive. After some research I have obtained further particulars relative to ancient horns. In the 'Archæological Journal,' vol. ii., there is an interesting article upon the usages of domestic life in the Middle Ages, in which I find the following :—'The warriors of the North drank from horns, as did the Homeric heroes, ages before them, and as the people of most countries have done where horn-bearing animals were known. In the ninth century the Saxon King of Mercia gave the monks of Croyland his "table horn, that the elders of the monastery might drink out of it on feast days, and sometimes remember in their prayer the soul of Wiglof, the donor." The same Wiglof gave to the refectory of Croyland his gilt cup, embossed on the exterior with barbarous victors fighting dragons, which he was wont to call his crucible, because a cross was impressed on the bottom and on the four angles of it.' This was doubtless a specimen of that skill in working precious metals for which the Anglo-Saxons were famous, and for the exercise of which Eadrid, in 949, rewarded his gold-smith Alssige with a grant of land. Horns continued to be appendages of the table until after the Conquest, although other drinking vessels were in use also. We see them represented in the Bayeux tapestry, and find from wills and other notices that they lingered on the board or in the hall for centuries after the date of that historic needlework. The mouth of the horn was not unfrequently fitted with a cover like the old-fashioned Scotch mull. In the collection of antiquities in the British Museum is preserved a very large drinking-horn of the sixteenth century; so great, indeed, that it was evidently intended to try a man's capacity for wine. It is formed of the small tusk of an elephant, carved with rude figures of elephants, unicorns, lions, and crocodiles, and mounted with silver; a small tube, ending in a silver cup, issues from the jaws of a pike, whose head and shoulders enclose the mouth of the vessel. The following legend is engraved upon it :—

> Drinke you this, and think no scorne,
> Although the cup be much like a horne.

The remains of an iron chain are attached to this horn, which was probably suspended in the hall of some convivial squire of the olden time, whose guests were at times summoned to drain it, or to pay a shilling fine. This custom of drinking from horns is by no means yet obsolete, for when a student at the German University of Giessen, I myself frequently became a victim to the fashion of drinking, or rather trying to drink off an immense curved cow-horn which had been filled with Bavarian beer, a most difficult task, for if the horn is not held in a peculiar manner, and gradually elevated by an experienced hand, the beer invariably rushes down the incline of the horn with considerable violence into the face of ' the fox,' as the new student is called.

In the Museum at Canterbury there is an excellent specimen of an ancient curfew, and also of a curfew bell. The curfew, or ' cover fire,' which was used long ago to

K

put out the hearth-fires when the curfew bell rang, is a large curved piece of metal something like the front half of a Life Guardsman's cuirass enlarged.

'And what may this be?' I inquired, as I kicked my foot against a piece of metal under one of the cases. 'Oh, that's a curfew bell,' was the answer. Lucky curfew bell to have escaped the marine store dealers these many hundred years, even though you have lost your clapper; yet unhappy curfew bell to be so little prized by the present inhabitants of Canterbury! Surely such precious local antiquities as the curfew and curfew bell are worthy of tender care, and a good place in the cases. A new clapper, too, should be fixed to the poor old bell, and thus he might once again lift up his voice in the streets of Canterbury, to be heard by the subjects of Queen Victoria, after being silent for centuries, and possibly having given out his last-sung notes (quære, what are they?) to the subjects of King Henry I.

When at Carlisle, after the Salmon Disease Inquiry, I had just half an hour to spare. I had previously read in the guide-book that in the Chapter-house at Carlisle there was a very ancient Charter Horn. Canon Prescott on my application kindly showed it to me, telling me that the object in question was called the *Horns of the Altar*. What was my astonishment, on examining this specimen, to find it to be a walrus skull without a lower jaw, with tusks about eighteen inches long! The skull itself was marked out with faded colours, so as somewhat to resemble a human skull.

I afterwards obtained the following information about this curious Charter Horn.

In the year 1290 (as appears by the Pleas of Parliament) a claim was made by the King, Edward I., and by others, to the tithes on certain lands lately brought under cultivation in the Forest of Inglewood. The Prior of Carlisle appeared on behalf of his convent, and urged their right to the property on the ground that the tithes had been granted to them by a former king, who had then enfeoffed them by a certain ivory horn (*quoddam cornu eburneum*), which he gave to the Church of Carlisle, and which they possessed at that time.

In 1530 Thomas Tonge, Norroy King of Arms, made an heraldic visitation of the north of England, in which he recorded as follows: 'Be it noted that the Monastery of Carlisle was first founded by King Henry I., the second year of his reign. And the said King Henry gave unto the said monastery a great horn of venery, having certain bonds of silver and gold, and the verses following engraven upon it: *Henricus primus noster fundator opimus, dedit in teste cartam pro jure foreste.* And by the said horn he gave liberty within the Forest of Inglewood.'

The Cathedral of Carlisle has had these two fine walrus tusks, with a portion of the skull, in its possession for a great number of years. They appear in ancient inventories of goods of the cathedral (1674), together with other articles of the altar furniture, as, 'one horn of the altar in two parts,' or 'two horns of the altar.' So antiquaries came to the conclusion that these were identical with the 'ivory horn' referred to above. Communications were made to the Society of Antiquaries (see 'Archæologia,' vol. iii.), and they were called the 'Carlisle Charter Horns.' Bishop Lyttleton, in a paper read before the society in 1768, said the 'horns' were so called improperly, being 'certainly the teeth of some very large *sea fish*.' He quoted this passage from Ray's ' Itinerary : ' ' They have preserved [at Carlisle] two *elephant's* teeth fastened in a bone like a scalp, which they call the Horns of the altar.'

The late Professor Harkness, F.R.S., in a paper communicated to the Cumberland and Westmoreland Antiquarian and Archæological Society in 1875, thus described the tusks and disputed their title to be called Charter Horns :

' The so-called horns consist of two walrus tusks clamped by an iron bolt to the maxillary bones of a walrus; the inter-maxillary bone and the nostril-bones are gone *in toto*; the tusks are misplaced--that is, the right tusk is in the left socket, and *vice versâ*, so that the grooves characteristic of walrus tusks are to the outside, instead of inside as in the living animal. The tusks are broken at the upper end, one very much so, and these fractures are more modern, judging from their colour, than the fractures which have taken place at the tips. Holes exist in the upper parts of the tusks in which have been copper nails, as shown by the green tinge. Iron nails and nail-holes exist in the bone, and iron rust shows that it has had an iron rim round its back which is sawn off smooth, and in such a plane that the horns hang against the surface of a wall, tusks down, as in the living animal. In the front part of the bone there seems to have been a metal plate, probably of silver, which may have held the donor's name. The iron bolt which now holds the horns together is much later in date than the iron nails in the bone.'

'I have no doubt the tusks and bones have been subjected to very rough usage after they came into the Cathedral. When first presented there is every reason for inferring that the sockets of the tusks would be perfect, or very nearly so. An accident could never have broken and destroyed them in the manner they now appear. The sockets, when perfect, would retain their tusks, or if they came out, a small portion of glue would have fixed them permanently. The mode in which they have been both broken suggests the idea that the tusks were held near the points and wrenched violently outwards. This would destroy the outer sides of the sockets.'

'We may safely conclude that these "horns" are not Charter Horns at all, but that they were given to the Cathedral at Carlisle by some traveller, at a time when such things were considered valuable curiosities, probably *tempore* Henry VIII., and that they were used for the decoration of the altar, being hung from a nail in the wall behind. Further, we may conclude that they have been violently pulled to bits, probably by the Puritans, and rudely patched up again by the iron bolt which now holds them together, and which may have been concealed by embroidery tacked on by the irregularly placed copper nails.'

I cannot quite understand how a walrus's skull and teeth came to be considered so valuable as to be promoted to the dignity of a Charter Horn of a great cathedral like Carlisle. I am afraid Bishop Lyttleton was not a naturalist, or he would never have called the tusks of a walrus the teeth of some very large fish.

It seems not improbable that they were presented to

the Church as an offering by some traveller, and used as an ornament to the altar. Such offerings were frequent, both at the smaller altars of cathedrals and in churches.

Another Charter Horn, the Pusey Horn, is preserved at Pusey House, near Faringdon. This horn is an ox horn, two feet and half an inch in length, and a foot in circumference at the larger end, and dark brown in colour. It is mounted round the middle with a ring of silver-gilt, and supported on two hound's feet. At the small end is a hound's head of silver-gilt, made to screw in as a stopper. Thus without the stopper it served as a hunting-horn, and with it as a drinking-horn.

On the silver ring is the following inscription :—

𝕴 𝕽𝖞𝖓𝖌 𝕶𝖓𝖔𝖙𝖚𝖉𝖊 𝖌𝖊𝖇𝖊 𝖂𝖞𝖑𝖑𝖆𝖒 𝖕𝖊𝖈𝖔𝖙𝖊
𝖇𝖞𝖘 𝖍𝖔𝖗𝖓𝖊 𝖙𝖔 𝖍𝖔𝖑𝖉𝖊 𝖇𝖞 𝖇𝖞 𝖑𝖔𝖓𝖉.

The traditional history of the Pusey Horn is that Canute being encamped in the neighbourhood of Pusey, and the Saxons at a few miles' distance, an officer of his army, the ancestor of the Pusey family, discovered an ambuscade formed by the Saxons to intercept the King. He gave information to Canute, who, in consequence, escaped the danger, and for this service gave to the officer and his heirs the manor of Pusey, to hold by the tenure of this horn.

Another Charter Horn, the Borstal Horn, was granted by Edward the Confessor to Nigel, his huntsman, by whose descendants it is still preserved. Nigel having slain a wild boar which infested the forest of Bernwood, near the King's palace at Brill, Bucks, received a grant of land with the custody of the forest of Bernwood, to hold to him and his heirs 'per unum cornu quod est charta prædictæ forestæ.' Upon this land Nigel built a lodge called Borestall, in memory of the slain boar.

The Borstal Horn, or Nigel's Horn, as it is also called, is the horn of some kind of ox or buffalo, and is of a dark brown colour. It is two feet four inches long on the convex bend, and twenty-three inches on the concave, and three inches in diameter at the large end. It is tipped at each end with silver-gilt, and fitted with wreaths of leather to hang about the neck, ornamented with an old brass seal-ring, a brass plate sculptured with a horn, and several lesser plates of silver-gilt with fleur-de-lys.

Figures of the Carlisle, Pusey, and Borstal Horns are given in the 'Archæologia,' vol. iii.

PRE-ADAMITE LITTLE MEN, BEASTS, BIRDS, AND FISHES.

A NEW THEORY OF CREATION.

SOLOMON has said there is nothing new under the sun. Until March 11, 1876, I had always believed Solomon was right, but I have now really something new to relate. It is a new theory of creation—very startling, I admit, at the same time very amusing.

An elderly man called upon me and stated he had a box of fossils he wished to show me. He is the coachman of a clergyman at whose house I once stayed when out on inspection duty. He said he was 'no scholar, but he was an observer of nature.' The coachman's theory is this:— According to his idea, there were three periods of time in the earth's history—viz., 1st, thousands of years before Adam; 2nd, thousands of years before Noah; and 3rd, our own time. In the thousands of years before Adam the world was peopled with 'giants and little men;' and he had in his box a great many of these little men turned into fossils, showing their customs and habits. He had brought specimens of the little men for me to examine. He did not know what had become of the giants. He then took out of his box a fossil little man, a little woman, and a baby. The little man is about four inches

high, like 'Hoddy Toddy, all head and no body;' the
little woman is shorter, but much fatter; the baby is
about as big as a large bean. The coachman is sure his
theory is right, because he has picked up a leg (rather
gouty) and a pair of feet, about as big as beans, in the
same field; so that they *must* have belonged to this tribe
of pre-Adamite little people. He does not know exactly
what the habits of this small people were, but he thinks
'they buried themselves in the earth; they lived like
wild animals, and came out of their holes and caves and
fed in the fields like rabbits; they hadn't much intellect;
nobody had intellect before Adam, who had the breath of
life blowed into him.'

'Types of these little pre-Adamite people now remain
in our own time. They are existent in every village,
in the form of silly people who runs about and knows
nothing.' The little people 'lived upon the fruits of the
earth before they knew how to till the ground.' To prove
his theory, he brought some of the pre-Adamite fruits
upon which the little people lived. Thus there was a
tomato. On one side the tomato had been exposed to
the sun, on another it had been covered from the sun with
leaves. Then there were some fossil walnuts. One had
been cracked and showed the contents inside. Then there
was a 'dough-fig,' showing the stem quite plainly; an
orange which had been peeled; a 'sturshum' (nasturtium)
seed; a fruit that had tumbled into the mud, and there
were marks where the little people had been trying to
scratch it out. There were also a mushroom and half an
egg, showing the shell, the white, and the yolk.

Along with the little men there lived a number of

very curious animals; thus there were a fossil bat, a fossil
mole, and other animals he could not make out.   Besides
the animals, all very little, there were a great number
of birds and fishes of different kinds.   The best specimen of a bird was a fossil partridge, about an inch and
a half long, and the size of a large filbert; he called my
attention to the frightened look of the bird.   A fossil
pheasant did not look so frightened.   There is a fossil
goose that looks particularly alarmed; in fact, so frightened
that he has dislocated his neck.   There are no bones in
these fossil birds, 'they are all pressed together.'   These
birds still preserve the frightened look caused by 'the
sudden destruction of period that come on 'em.   They
lived on the hills with the little men, and when they saw
the waters of the deluge a-coming up they couldn't get
away in time, and they looked with surprise at the water.'
The frightened appearance of these birds still remaining
on them is a certain proof of the deluge.   Somehow or
other, most of the birds are very much crushed, but he
'don't know what crushed 'em.   Their feathers 'as all
gone away through the lapse of hages.'   He had also a
collection of fossil fish that lived at the time of the little
men; thus there is a sprat, a minnow, an eel, a gurnet, a
smelt and a mackerel, all diminutive, the same as the
people.   The eel is particularly remarkable; 'he was
going quietly along through the water, when he was took
with a sudden change of period, and became solid all of an
instant.'   The great triumph of the theory is 'a fossil
bird's nest,' there is even 'a mark where the bird leaned
his head over,' and he has found a bird, he thinks, that
built the nest.   There are not many insects, only one

fossil black-beetle. 'As the black-beetle lived in the period
so many hundreds of thousands of years before Adam, he
has now turned into a beetle, white with age.'

My readers will doubtless wonder what all this means.
The coachman has been over twenty years in the employ
of his master, with whom he goes out shooting a great
deal. At these times he has made his collection of pre-
Adamite little men, fruits, birds, beasts, and insects that
were living thousands of years before Adam.

These wonderful curiosities are really *nothing but
common flints.* His little men, legs, birds and fishes are
simply fossil sponges, or portions of flint, which, by an
imaginative mind, may be said somewhat to resemble the
various forms attributed to them. His 'fruits of the
earth' are fossil echini; his fossil bird's nest is simply a
flint waterworn sponge, somewhat resembling a small
bird's nest.

He was, however, right in two cases, as he produced
some fossil 'sherk's' (shark's) teeth, and the fossil ear-bone
of a whale. I thought it would be too cruel to tell the
coachman that his curiosities were only flints, and he went
away quite satisfied with the converts he had made. Of
course I purchased this unique collection for my museum.

The thought suddenly struck me that after all the
coachman's theory is not wholly new. I remembered the
story of Deucalion and Pyrrha, and turned to my 'Ovid,'
where we have the stony origin of mankind set forth long
ago. The following is the history of Deucalion:—The
son of Prometheus, King of Thessaly, and husband of
Pyrrha, daughter of Epimetheus. In his reign came the
deluge, or universal flood, which drowned all the world.

Only he and his wife got into a small ship, which was carried to Mount Parnassus, and there stayed; and there dry land first appeared, after the waters were abated. He, consulting with the oracle of Themis how mankind might be repaired, was answered, if he cast his great mother's bones behind his back; whereupon he and his wife cast stones over their shoulders, and they became men and women.

Here are the very lines of Ovid. The oracle says to Deucalion and Pyrrha,—

> Discedite templo;
> Et velate caput; cinctasque resolvite vestes :
> Ossaque post tergum magnæ jactate parentis.

Pyrrha, with a woman's instinct, guesses who the great parent is.

> Magna parens terra est; lapides in corpore terræ
> Ossa reor dici; jacere hos post terga jubemur.

Then they go and throw the stones, and the stones thrown by Deucalion turn into men, and those by Pyrrha turn into women. The gradual metamorphosis of the stones into men and women is too long to quote, but is one of Ovid's very best bits. He winds up by saying that the origin of the human race from stone accounts for the hardihood of mankind.

> Inde genus durum sumus, experiensque laborum;
> Et documenta damus, quâ simus origine nati.

May not, again, the idea of the origin of mankind from stones be in some mysterious way connected with the real fact so well put in the following words, ' *Pulvis et umbra sumus*'? or to go further back, may it not be an instinctive hazy idea of what we read and believe in Genesis, 'And the Lord God formed man of the dust of the ground'?

When going over Melrose Abbey I found the same idea embodied in the following beautiful epitaph :—

The Earth goeth
  On the Earth
    Glistring like gold.
The Earth goes to the Earth
    Sooner than it wold ;

The Earth builds
  On the Earth
    Castles and Towers,
The Earth says to the Earth
    All shall be ours.

THE CRUISE OF THE 'JACKAL.'

THE Herring Commission of Inquiry being duly appointed by the Home Office in August 1877, it became the duty of my colleagues, Messrs. Walpole and Young, and myself to arrange our plans, in order that our official duties of inquiry might be performed as efficiently as lay in our power. After due consideration we determined to hold our courts of inquiry on the east coast of Scotland previously to visiting the west coast and the outlying islands, inasmuch as during the month of August the herring fishery on the east coast is at its full height, whereas on the west coast the fishings do not begin till the spring of the year, and we had been informed that we should meet on the east coast with many of the fishing crews of the west coast, fish curers, as well as the fishery officers of the Scotch White Herring Fishery Board.

Those who followed the published reports in the papers of our various inquiries might like to know the exact order in which the courts were held on the east coast. I therefore give them in their proper order :— Edinburgh, Eyemouth, Anstruther, Montrose, Aberdeen, Peterhead, Fraserburgh, Banff, Buckie, Lossiemouth, Burghead, Inverness, Bora, Helmsdale and Wick.

It then became necessary to continue our inquiry into
the fisheries of the Orkneys and Shetlands, and also many
of the outlying places on the west. For this purpose
the Lords Commissioners of the Admiralty placed at our
disposal H.M. gunboat 'Jackal.' The 'Jackal' first met
the Commission at Aberdeen on September 4, 1877, and
there the plan of our future expeditions was arranged
with Captain Digby.

H.M.S. 'Jackal' is a gun-boat of 340 tons; her length
is 160 feet; her breadth 25 feet; her horse-power 150;
officers and men, 60. I find that if the roof were taken
off the church I attend, St. Mary Magdalene, Munster
Square, Regent's Park, and the 'Jackal' let bodily down
into it, she would exactly fit the main aisle. Her bowsprit, however, would project considerably beyond the
east window of the church.

She is a paddle-wheel steamer, built in 1845, and
lately repaired at Devonport. One of her first duties
was to act as an escort to Her Majesty Queen Adelaide
when visiting Madeira. She has also been to the West
Coast of Africa, and, as far as I could judge, had escaped
fever.

The 'Jackal' is a splendid sea-boat. Her officers know
her little peculiarities; she is a good, smart, obedient creature, and does her best to perform her various duties in
looking after the herring fisheries. She has a nose as keen
as her African four-footed namesake (*Canis aureus*) for
anything going wrong with British herring interests on
the coasts of Scotland, and she helps much to provide the
British Lion with food, in the shape of thousands of crans
of herrings.

We held our court at Wick early on the morning of
September 4, and the same afternoon started to board the
'Jackal,' then lying with her steam up.

When walking down to the pier, through Pulteney
Town, I was perfectly amazed at the wonderful fleet of
herring-boats in the harbour; they were so close and
thick together that it would not have been difficult to
walk from one side of the harbour to the other across the
boats without seeing the water. The quays were also
covered with herring barrels, all disposed orderly and in
due form, forming a vast army of herring barrels, each
set bearing its own peculiar brand as affixed thereon by
the Government officers.

The captain's boat, called the 'whale boat,' was waiting
at the pier-head, manned by four sailors and a coxswain
to steer. They were true British man-o'-war's-men, fine
strong active brave tars. We were assisted down the
very slippery stairs, the luggage neatly piled away, the
boat shoved off, and we were away. I had never in my
life before been on board either a man-o'-war or a boat
belonging to a man-o'-war. I was, therefore, entering
into a new phase of existence, of which, you may be sure,
I was not unwilling to take advantage. The extraordinary
ease with which the captain's boat went through the
water was surprising to me. The men were such thorough
oarsmen that the boat slipped through the water with an
easy velocity which I only once before experienced, and
that was when riding in Sir Benjamin Brodie's London
visiting carriage, the most comfortable carriage that ever
was or ever will be invented.

The whale-boat was soon alongside the 'Jackal,' and

when we got near, the man pulling the bow oar laid in his oar and cleverly caught his ship's side with a boat-hook. Captain Digby was on deck to receive us. Of course, the moment I set foot on the deck of the 'Jackal,' I raised my hat in salute to the commanding officer. Her Majesty, too, is supposed to be always present on board the British ships of war. Captain Digby introduced us to the officers of the ship, who at once, by their kindly welcome, made us feel quite at home.

Preparations were at once made for starting, and for the first time I heard the merry boatswain's pipe. In obedience to the pipe the sailors came running from the forecastle to hoist in the boat. The run of the man-o'-war's man is peculiar; it is a short, quick, heavy tramp; the men get over the ground very quickly, and seem to concentrate their strength in a manner that only efficient training could bring about.

At a given word the men caught hold of a rope, pulling all together; up came the boat and hung on the davits, where she was properly secured. Then came another pipe from the bow of the ship, and a hoarse kind of order, which I afterwards found out to signify 'All hands up anchor.' It sounded thus, 'A-l-l h-a-n-d s-u-p a-n-k-e-r-r-r-r!'

Everything seemed to be regulated in the most perfect clock-like manner by means of the boatswain's far re-sounding whistle, piping merrily to the musical click of the capstan, the iron tongue of which gave out a sound like the hammer on a blacksmith's anvil. The anchor being up, I heard sundry sharp tings of musical bells, the meaning of which the engineer officer explained to me

L

as signals to the engine-room; the paddles then began to
turn slowly, and we were off.

The first thing the 'Jackal' had to do was to pass
through a fleet of herring-vessels coming in with their
fish and nets. There was not much wind, and the steering
of the 'Jackal' was, I need hardly say, simply perfect.
Having got clear of the herring-boats, the captain gave a
signal for full speed, and the paddles began their pit-pat,
pit-pat. Captain Digby having arranged all the affairs
connected with the ship, then invited us down to luncheon,
the first of many acts of courtesy for which we were
indebted to him. Luncheon over, we went on deck, and
for the first time entered the chart-house, a comfortable
little deck-house in which the ship's charts and all other
necessary paraphernalia of navigation are kept. We were
by this time off Duncansby Head, the extreme N.E.
promontory in Scotland, and the principal outpost of
that terrible place, the Pentland Firth. In the distance
we could see the Great and Lesser Skerries, and the Isle
of Stroma.

As we passed the Pentland Firth, between Duncansby
Head and South Ronaldsha, the ship rolled considerably;
it was not a disagreeable motion. The officers told me
it might have been on account of a gale somewhere
away in the Atlantic to the westward, or else that it was
due to the rapid currents of the Firth. The waves were
ugly, dark-looking fellows, and could have been very
nasty had they chosen to put on their white night-caps,
and give a ball in honour of the 'Jackal' and her pas-
sengers. Not liking these big waves, I consulted friend
Young's barometer, and recollecting the old Horatian

sailor (Horace, Ode III.) who went on the perfidious sea
for the first time in a brazen cuirass lined with oak, I
vowed a testimonial to Young's barometer if it gave good
weather during the cruise of the 'Jackal.' This votive
offering had the desired effect, for we escaped really bad
weather throughout our wanderings in Scotland.

Through the Pentland Firth rushes the great eastern
Gulf Stream of the vast Atlantic, flowing with the
tremendous force of united tides through the narrow
opening between the mainland and the Orkneys—an
awful place, where King Neptune lives, and where his
racehorses frequently get loose and have a stampede.
When we were about three parts across the Firth we
saw the headland on the extreme south of South
Ronaldsha. Gradually nearing it, a big steamer was reported by the look-out man. This was the 'Pharos,' the
Government steamer of the Northern Lighthouse Board,
which carries oil supplies to the lighthouses on the northern
coasts of Scotland.

When we got to the eastward of South Ronaldsha
the ocean swell began to abate, and the 'Jackal' seemed
to shake herself for a fresh start, having successfully
crossed over the eight miles of turbulent and angry waters
which form such a barrier between the Orkneys and the
mainland. When we got to a certain point on the ocean,
which the captain had marked out by a pencil dot on the
chart, a wave of his hand to the steersman caused the
'Jackal' to point her nose to the west: we then went on
a westerly course till we arrived at a small island called
Thieves Holm, near the west end of Shapensha Bay, and
then we saw the lights of Kirkwall town; the red light

at the head of the pier showed the authorities of the ship
where the anchorage lay. Again once more the cheery
boatswain's pipe, and orders were given to stand by for
letting go the anchor. The ship began to go slow, slow,
slower, slower, stop. At last Captain Digby's orders came
to let go the anchor ; instantly, the boatswain's pipe, the
musical rattle of the chain cable as the anchor plunged
with a foam and a rush into the dark waters, and we were
at Kirkwall. We then had to go ashore in the boat, a
proceeding I did not like at all, for it was pitch dark, and
we had to thread our way through a lot of craft at anchor ;
but the officer commanding the boat brought us to the
pier all right.

Having arrived late the night before at Kirkwall, and
having to hold an inquiry at ten the next morning, and
leave at three in the afternoon, I had not much time to
look about. By getting up early, and by sacrificing
luncheon, I was able to get a general view of the place.

The following facts I have picked up from various
sources. In Orkney there are sixty-seven islands, out of
which twenty-seven are inhabited. The population in
1871 was 31,241. The largest island is Pomona, on which
Kirkwall is built. The town consists of one long, narrow
street, of foreign aspect, swarming with children. I went
into the office of the *Orcadian* newspaper, and was surprised at being recognised by the editor, who at once
thanked me on behalf of the pigs of Newcastle for what I
had done for them. I could not recollect much about it
till he told me that I had written an article in *Land and
Water* in June 1871 urging the necessity of placing
drinking-troughs for the poor pigs that were brought to

the Newcastle market, sick and seedy after their long voyage from Ireland. The result of this article, this gentleman in Kirkwall told me, was that the pigs now have proper drinking-troughs placed for their accommodation in the market at Newcastle.

It is impossible to fix the exact date at which Orkney was discovered, but a Danish historian states it to be about three hundred and eighty-five years before Christ. Dunnet Head, in Caithness, was designated Cape Orcas before the birth of Christ. (Query, is *Delphinus Orca*, the ca'ing whale, so named from this promontory?) The Roman Emperor Claudius invaded and conquered these islands. Those brave and clever soldiers, the Romans, seem to have been everywhere in Scotland. I wonder whether Claudius issued rations of herrings and finnon haddies to his soldiers? The name Kirkwall, as Anglicised, is the Danish word Kirkjuvagr (Kirkevaag), signifying Churchbay, a capital name, as the church stands quite at the end of the bay.

Looking out of the hotel window in the early morning I could see St. Magnus Cathedral, a venerable pile seven hundred years old; built in the reign of Henry II., A.D. 1177. It is built of red sandstone, and is not at all unlike Yarmouth Church on a small scale. I had not time to go into the cathedral, but observed that the sandstone at the great gate was very weather-worn in consequence of the stone slabs not having been placed flat, as they lay in the quarry, but turned upon end. The same weather-worn appearance I have noted on the stonework of the door of Durham Cathedral.

I was told I ought to go to visit the 'Maeshow,' about nine miles from Kirkwall, to see some wonderful Druidical remains. The meaning of the word Maeshow is not known. It was a great chambered barrow built on the surface of the ground, and afterwards covered with layers of small stones and earth.

The stones of Stennis, near Kirkwall, are also remarkable Druidical remains; there are thirteen stones upright and ten in number have fallen down. I wanted to see if I could find any confirmation of the idea that the Druids used to get these heavy stones placed one on the other by utilising earth or snow; but unfortunately I had not time to go and see them.

On Salisbury Plain the Druids first made firm the two uprights; they then made an inclined plane of snow, and levered the third stone on the two uprights; when the snow melted, of course the stone remained *in situ*, and the means by which it had got there were not apparent. Common earth would have served the same purpose. This at least is my theory.

In a shop immediately opposite the hotel, I observed some curious soft shawls, such as I had never seen before, and also some remarkable thick woollen fishermen's socks, made in bright Spanish-looking colours. These shawls are hand-knitted by the fisher-wives of Shetland. They are most industrious women, and knit all day long when the husbands are out fishing. The socks are made in Fair Island, of which more presently.

Speaking of woollen goods, Mr. Bartlett informs me that recently he had some wool sent him to know from what animal it had been taken. He proved that it was wool pulled from the large mastiff of Thibet—another instance of my friend's great sagacity.

When the official meeting was over at Kirkwall, the crew in the captain's whale-boat came up to the landing-place to get our luggage. We got into the boat, and were quickly once again on board the 'Jackal.'

Immediately on our arrival on board, the boatswain began to pipe up, and the sailors to trot merrily about the beautifully clean decks. We went below at once to luncheon, and soon perceived, from the noise above, that the 'Jackal' was getting under way. This time her nose was pointed due east, and away she went, pit-pat, pit-pat with her paddles through the beautifully clear water. We shortly passed the island of Shapensha.

Before we started from Kirkwall the captain gave the order, 'Leadsman in the chains!' Immediately in the centre of the paddle-box stands the leadsman. The lead consists of a long, heavy weight, like an enormous clock-weight. This the man swings well forward in such a manner that the weight shall be at the bottom by the time the ship has made her way up to the lead. The plunge made by the lead into the sea sounds to a landsman like a heavy thud, and is a good imitation, on a small scale, of Zazel taking her dive into the net from the top of Westminster Aquarium. The lead takes down with it a lot of air, and as the big bubbles ascend from the bottom of the sea, gives the appearance of a rocket with a long tail of diamonds. The navigating lieutenant was with the captain on the stage between the paddle-boxes directing the steering of the vessel, and this without the least noise, so perfectly are all duties carried out on board this admirably managed ship. Captain Digby allowed me to examine the navigation charts. To a landsman like myself the numerous figures on these maps are not usually very interesting, but when out on the ocean among a lot of islands, the figures assume a personal interest. In these maps the lighthouses are marked with a tiny red spot surrounded by yellow. The course of the ship is laid down on the chart by the officers in a pencil line, according to the lights and headlands.

The first land we saw after leaving North Ronaldsha was Fair Island, a very interesting place. From the deck it appeared like a huge solitary rock, without trees, herbage, or habitations:

Dorsum immane mari summo.

Of course we did not land on this island, it being a very dangerous place; and, in fact, there are only two points where access can be obtained by boats. It is here that in 1588 one of the ships composing the Spanish Armada was wrecked; some of the survivors are said to have remained on the island; it is believed that the present inhabitants have a mixture of Iberian blood in their veins. The women are famous for their skill in knitting curiously bright coloured stockings, the patterns of which are said to have been taught them by the shipwrecked Spanish seamen. No grain is grown on this island, consequently supplies must be sent from Orkney or Shetland. I learnt that the honest fishermen of Fair Island, having such few opportunities of communication with the mainland, are most greedy after newspapers, and that they will come out in their boats to beg for newspapers, which are thrown to them from the passing steamers.

Wishing to know more about this curious place, I sent a copy of *Land and Water*, directing it to the Principal Inhabitant, Fair Island. In due course of time I received from Mr. W. Lawrence, of Fair Island, a long and interesting letter, of which I now give an abstract.

Fair Island lies in mid-channel between the Orkney and Shetland Islands, twenty-five miles distant from each group; it forms part of the parish of Dunrossness, which is the southernmost part of the mainland of Shetland. It is about three miles long by about one and a half broad. In clear weather the Orkney and Shetland Islands can be seen from it; but when the weather is in the least hazy or overcast, nothing can be seen but the rolling waves of the Atlantic and German Oceans, whose action on its coast-line has hollowed out many deep caverns, while pyramidal stacks and cliffs rise perpendicularly from one to seven hundred feet above the level of the sea, forming rock scenery grand beyond description, and a safe retreat for the countless number of sea-fowl of all kinds which repair to it during the breeding season.

The name Fair Isle is evidently a corruption of Faraoc, which signifies in Icelandic Isle of Sheep. Torfacus calls it Fava in his historical account of Orkney and Shetland, and tells how the leader of Earl Ronald's expedition against Earl Paul crossed from Orkney to Shetland, landed in the Isle of Westray, and wrenched the islands from the grasp of his rival. This is an historical fact of the middle of the twelfth century, and the present inhabitants of Fair Isle have the same legend by tradition, without any historical record of it. The same tumuli, sepulchral steatite urns, and rude stone implements, which are so numerous in the Orkney and Shetland Islands, are also found here.

The present population of the island is about 200, nearly equally divided between males and females. Fishing and farming form their principal occupations. The fishing is prosecuted in their small fragile skiffs, which are only the first step above the Greenlander's canoe, yet in them the fishermen feel safe in all weathers, and as there is generally an inexhaustible supply of fish around the shores of the island, they seldom fail to earn sufficient for a competent livelihood. The fish are sold to the proprietor of the island, who salts and cures them and sends them to market. The principal fish caught are cod, ling, and saith.

Each fisherman holds a croft or small farm of from five to ten acres on the pastoral part of the island, which is about two-thirds of the whole. On this they keep from one to three cows, two to three ponies for bringing peats from the hill, and a few sheep and poultry. The islanders are thus supplied with milk, butter, eggs, potatoes, fish, and mutton or beef for winter use.

The proprietor of the island also has a store, where all sorts of groceries, fishing material, &c., are kept, and he makes an annual visit for the purpose of settling with the fishermen and doing any other work required. The gross rental is about 150*l*. There is no poverty under any ordinary circumstances. There is an excellent library, the gift of Lady John Scott, of Spottiswoode. In point of intelligence the active Fair Islander will make a favourable comparison with any of his own rank or class in either the Orkney or Shetland Islands. The establishment of regular postal communication has proved a great boon to the people.

Fair Island has been the scene of many disastrous shipwrecks. From its position in the centre of a gateway between the Atlantic and German Oceans, where great and yearly increasing numbers of vessels are continually passing and repassing, in clear weather it proves an excellent beacon to guide the approaching mariner; but in dark nights or foggy weather, surrounded by rapid tides and dangerous eddies, and without a lighthouse, it has too often proved itself a dangerous rock, on which many a goodly ship has been dashed to pieces. In 1868 the German ship 'Lessing,' with 465 emigrants on board, ran into the island during a dense fog. This, fortunately, happened during fine weather, and the emigrants were saved; but the vessel, which was valued at nearly 30,000*l.*, became a total wreck. In 1877 no fewer than five known wrecks took place on the island, the estimated value of which was above 30,000*l.* Happily only two lives were lost in these; but during December 1876 the wreckage showed that two vessels at least had run into the island in dark nights, and not a soul was left to tell the tale.

The island seems to be a general rendezvous for all sorts of seafowl common to the Northern Ocean.

The common and black-backed gull and the kittiwake are here the whole year, but are much more numerous during the breeding season than at any other time. The eider-duck, the guillemot, the puffin and sheldrake come about the middle of April and remain till October. The puffin and guillemot seem by general consent to have fixed

on the 12th of August as the day of their departure.
Thousands may be seen a day or two before that date,
but only a few solitary birds after it. The little black
guillemot remains here the whole year.

The Solan goose and fulmar come after the breeding
season. The stormy petrels breed here, but, though their
young are frequently seen, the nests are rarely if ever
found. Swans and many different kinds of geese visit
the island yearly for a few days in spring and the beginning of winter. Nearly all the different kinds of
cormorants are found here the whole year round; they
often drift ashore in considerable numbers, dead or
very much weather-beaten, during long-continued storms.
Although many different kinds of duck may be seen, the
eider-duck appears to be the only one that breeds here.
Herons come in great numbers during autumn; as many
as twenty may be seen at a time, but more generally they
arrive in pairs. Some time ago a pair of white-tailed
eagles had their nest on the island, but they have now
deserted it. The white falcon is often seen during winter.
Goshawks, sparrow-hawks, and merlins are very numerous.
There are only five pairs of ravens, but a great number
of hooded crows. Owls and rooks come in considerable
numbers during autumn, especially after strong gales of
south-east winds, and generally remain all winter; probably
they are blown across from Norway.

Wild pigeons are very numerous, and so are starlings.
Plover, snipe, lapwings, curlew, sandlarks, and dunlins are
also pretty plentiful. Larks, linnets, sparrows, wrens,
redbreasts, wagtails (both the common and pied), are
plentiful also. The swallow visits the island in his season.

The birds are allowed the full freedom of the island without molestation, with the exception of the gulls and eider-ducks, on whose nests terrible raids are made. Every nest that can be reached by any means is pillaged either for the eggs or for the young birds when they are ready to fly. Many a good meal is made both on the eggs and the birds. Frequently as many as twenty-four dozen young birds are taken at a time. Great numbers are also caught in gins for the sake of the feathers; but with all the slaughter they never seem to be missed out of the common stock.

Fish abound, cod, saith, and ling being the principal kinds caught. The saith is the chief fishing of the island, but great numbers of cod are annually taken within half a mile of the shores of the island by smacks from Orkney and Shetland.

The Dutch carry off great quantities of herrings during the months of June and July. A few barrels of herrings are sometimes taken by the fishermen here when they 'pan,' which means when they are forced above the surface of the water by the saith; the fishermen then scoop them into their boats with hand-nets: this generally occurs in the month of August.

Numbers of large whales are always seen for a few weeks during the autumn while the herrings are on the coast; they often come within rifle-shot of the shore day after day for a week at a time. The ca'ing whale is never driven ashore here. There are a good number of seals, the large white seal (*Phoca barbata*) and the common little black seal: they are frequently caught by the fishermen; they lie up in the caves, and the fishermen go in with clubs and kill them; sometimes as many as five being killed at a time. The large ones are about twelve feet long; and the small ones about half that size.

There is a large fish that comes along and commits great havoc among the seals about the month of November. It is said to be from twenty-five to thirty feet long, but not thick in proportion to its length. There are no otters on the island, and the only wild animals are the rabbit and the mouse.

Captain Digby told us that the people on the island of St. Kilda, another desolate island on the extreme west coast of Scotland, complained of a very peculiar disease, called the 'boat fever.' It appears that for years past, after a boat has landed on the island, the people have been subject to a kind of feverish attack. This they call the 'boat fever.' This boat fever is no new thing; it has been recorded as being in existence a hundred years ago. I think I am close on the solution of this phenomenon. The fever only occurs on St. Kilda when a stranger boat lands, and only when the wind is blowing from the east. The cause I believe to be as follows: St. Kilda is such a precipitous island that boats can only land when the wind is blowing from the east. When the wind does blow from the east, the people in the island are seized with a kind of influenza cold; and this influenza is imputed not to the wind, but to the arrival of the boats.

I was told at Lerwick of another disease which was new to me. It is a peculiar disease of the eye, brought about by the presence of herrings. To guess at this disease would be almost impossible, but when the facts are known the reason becomes apparent. The scales of the herring are very thin, and like very thin glass. They fit very loosely into pockets in the skin of the fish. The women, in the operation of cleaning the herrings, handle them very quickly; the scales are rubbed off in flakes like snow, and are rubbed from the hands into the eyes; they then get under the eyelids, and can hardly be seen, being so transparent. The only way to get them out is for the operator to open the eyelids quite wide, and lick out the herring-scales with the tongue. Engine-drivers and people connected with railways, or travellers on railways, sometimes catch a speck of cinder in the eye; this gets under the lid, and, being almost invisible, can with difficulty be removed. Engine-drivers, I am told, are very clever at getting the ashes, splinters, &c., out of the eye by means of the tongue.

As we passed Fair Island a great number of sea-gulls came in the track of the vessel, to pick up what bits they could get. As the cook in preparing dinner threw the scraps over into the sea, it was very wonderful to see with what great ease these lovely birds kept up with the 'Jackal,' without apparently any effort. I luckily had some herrings in my pocket; these I cut up into bits and threw overboard for the gulls. It was very amusing to see how quickly the birds saw a bit of herring not larger than one's thumb floating on the white and ruffled waters caused by the paddles of the ship. The lot of them would make a struggle for it, and when one got it the others would hunt him and try to steal it from him. After the successful gull had swallowed his bit, the others would all fly back again at once up to the ship, even

though it had left them almost out of sight astern. Two
or three of the gulls came quite close over the ship's
wheel, and I could see with what ease they turned their
head as if it were upon a pivot, in search of food. Their
little black eyes seemed to say, 'Please don't hurt us.
Give us a bit more herring; we have a long way to fly
back home to Fair Island.'

While the gulls were off having a row over a whole
herring, I asked the captain's permission to try to catch
one of them. Wherever I go I carry fishing tackle.
Having tied two salmon lines together, I first of all
ground-baited with chopped herring and bits of paper,
with herring screwed up, and then tried them with a
Thames trout spinning tackle, baited with a portion of a
herring's tail. But it was no go; they would not bite.
They came close to it, but were too suspicious to make a
final swoop down upon it. I then tried a spoon bait, an
artificial minnow, and a sand eel, but in vain, the rascals
would not be caught, and all I got for my trouble was a
nice chaffing from the officers, one of whom tried to play
me a trick by putting on to my hooks a fresh-caught burn
trout. So in trying to gull the gulls I got gulled myself.

In the distance we saw several gannets at work. They
came splashing down into the water with tremendous
force. When soaring, the gannet's wings are extended to
the utmost. When he takes his header he forms his wings
into the shape of a W; this W is gradually closed, and
before he reaches the water the wings are shut up close to
the body, the loose feathers of the neck forming a fender
to the shoulder of the wing, so as to slip easily into the
water.

Instead of swooping like a gull, the gannet drops almost perpendicularly from a great height into the sea, causing the water to splash up. By an admirable structure the gannet is enabled to blow the whole of his body full of air, so that in fact he becomes an animated balloon, the skin also being divided into air cells. I am more convinced than ever of the wonderful adaptation of means to ends as seen in the structure of the gannet.

Captain Digby told me than on March 19, 1877, the 'Jackal' came across a lot of herring nets between Ailsa Craig and Ballantrae, on the Ayrshire coast. The nets were floating on the surface with a great quantity of herrings in them. Besides the herrings, there were several gannets caught by the neck in the meshes of the net. The gannets had dived, as usual, from a great height on to the floating herrings, had thrust their long-pointed beaks through the meshes of the nets, and so were drowned.

I was told quite a new story about gannets, which breed very abundantly in Scotland. When these birds are building, they steal materials for the nest one from the other. If the thief gannet is caught in the act, the bird to whom the property belongs gives the thief a good thrashing, which she takes quietly, and as a matter of course. If the thief is not detected stealing, she flies out to sea with the stolen property, and then returns looking very innocent, and pretending that she had got it away at sea. So we learn that there are humbugs among birds as among our noble selves.

Just after passing Fair Isle the sun went down, and it began to get very dark and cold. We adjourned to the

M

captain's cabin, and after hearing many interesting stories from our friend Bartlett, coiled up for sleep, Captain Digby kindly giving me permission to turn out with him when the look-out men reported the light off Sumburgh Head, the southernmost point of the Ultima Thule of Scotland, the Shetlands.

About two in the morning I heard the door of the cabin open gently, while at the same time 'Jack,' the captain's dog, gave a threatening growl. I was awake in a moment, and looking up, found that the cabin was dimly illuminated by a lantern. A wet-looking man, dressed in a suit of shiny waterproof, entered the cabin. This was the gruff-voiced boatswain of the middle watch, come to call the captain. I was out on the floor in the 'shake of a sheep's tail,' as they say in Oxfordshire, and hurried up on deck. The 'Jackal' was out in the ocean; it was dark, O so very dark! To quote the beautiful poetry of Ossian, who wrote his Homer-like poem nearly sixteen hundred years ago,—

Dark were the clouds of the sky : great was the darkness among
    the clouds of night.
Night had settled with all her clouds on the hill,
Gloomy and dark, like the gathering of the rain-clouds behind
    the meteors of heaven.
The night is gathered around, let us wish for the moon of
    heaven.

Except the watch on deck, and those on duty, deep sleep sealed the eyes of all those on board the 'Jackal.'

> Jamque fere mediam cæli nox humida metam
> Contigerat ; placidâ laxarant membra quiete
> Sub remis taciti per dura sedilia nautæ.

It is a curious fact that all men sleep soundest just before sunrise. This is the time when savages always make their attacks. The ship alone appeared neither to slumber nor sleep; she rolled her ponderous but graceful form with a majestic motion as she met the dark rolling seas of the ocean, and dipped her head as if acknowledging their superiority.

> Tollimur in cælum curvato gurgite, et idem
> Subductâ ad manes imos desedimus undâ.

Her engines alone were not tired; unceasing in their efforts, they drove her still through the vast, blue rolling waves. What would not Æneas of old have given for a gunboat when out on his exploring expeditions, with an account of which he so humbugged poor Queen Dido. 'Pius Æneas,' as he had the impudence to call himself, was not much of a sailor. He was a 'Soldier Officer,' and he and his pilot Palinurus made a nice mess of it when they managed to run their ship (what a curiosity she must have been!) high and dry on the rocks.

I went to the compass in front of the wheel, with a salute to the two silent man-of-war's-men who had command of the wheel, and looked at her course. Having ascertained her whereabouts, I was enabled to see how very steady she was going on the course the captain had marked out for her. There was a lovely bright star right ahead of the ship, and as she rose to the seas her bowsprit seemed to be attracted, as if by a magnet, to this star.

> Armatumque auro circumspicit Oriona.

The end of her bowsprit was like the foil in the hands of

an able fencer preparing for the attack.   It turned gently,
first to the right from the star, made a complete circuit
round the star, and then lunged forward direct at her
again.   Looking over the side of the vessel, I could just
make out the huge ocean billows over which the 'Jackal'
was riding with the ease of a sleeping sea-bird.   I confess
I looked very respectfully indeed at those big dark waves;
they seemed as though they had not quite made up their
mind as to whether they had King Neptune's orders to
come on board the 'Jackal' or not.   I gazed steadily at
them, and found that, as the ship heeled over, they simply
peeped over the ship's bulwarks to see who was on board.
They found on board the commissioners, looking after
Neptune's children—the herrings; so they let us pass
forward over their mighty shoulders.   For this I was
deeply obliged.

I found the captain in the chart-room, consulting
with the navigating lieutenant, who had piloted the
ship through the darkness of the night.   So nicely were
the reckonings made that I was told that in twenty
minutes' time we should see the light at Sumburgh Head,
and sure enough within a minute or two of the appointed
time I saw the great bright single eye of this island
Cyclops winking at us in the far distance—

Argolici clipei aut Phœbeæ lampadis instar ;

as much as to say, 'Come on, my boys, all right; only
don't come too near me, please!'

Sumburgh Head is just the place where one might
expect to find the cannibal Cyclops giant Polyphemus,
whose only eye Ulysses put out with a red-hot pointed

stick. One might almost expect Polyphemus to appear on the top of the cliff. If he had come, Captain Digby would, I am sure, have sent a war-rocket after him.

We sat down and watched. Gradually the dawn of the morning became more and more apparent. 'The warriors of the night moved on, the ghosts swam away on gloomy clouds;' by degrees the lonely and treeless mountains of Ultima Thule appeared on the sky-line. We were approaching good old Virgil's

Penitus toto divisos orbe Britannos,

It was indeed a lovely morning. I saw indistinctly, just as it was daylight, something right in the track of the vessel; another moment, and just as the figure-head of the ship, viz., the wooden portrait of a jackal, came over the objects, up went two guillemots, and scudded away as fast as wings could carry them. These fellows had been sleeping out at sea, and had not yet awakened till the 'Jackal' was near upon them.

As it gradually got lighter, I made out the form of Sumburgh Head, so beautifully described by Sir Walter Scott in the introduction to the 'Pirate.'

Shortly after passing Sumburgh Head I turned in again for forty winks, as I was aware we had a hard day's work before us at Lerwick. When I again turned out it was full day, and we were gradually drawing into the comparatively smooth water between the island of Bressay and the mainland. Lerwick is a splendid harbour. It is about a mile wide, and being three miles in length it affords ample and secure rendezvous for a large fleet. In the year 1650 the English navy, consisting of ninety-four men-of-war, lay for some time in the bay; and twelve years afterwards another fleet of ninety sail remained there for some days.

The moment the anchor was down off Lerwick the captain's boat took us ashore. It was early morning when we arrived, and there were not many people about. The first thing that struck me on landing was the great number of whale skulls lying about, being chiefly used as supports to keep the fishing-boats upright. I understand that whales come in here in considerable quantities in the spring of the year.

Healtaland, or Shetland, is a wonderful archipelago, consisting of more than a hundred islands. The sea-coast on the mainland is broken up and indented with deep bays, locally called 'voes.' In Cornwall, similar places are called 'zawns.' Round the majestic cliffs and towering headlands the turbulent surges caused by the currents of the ocean are called 'rousts.' In England, similar places are called 'races,' as the 'Race of Portland,' &c. The sheep, as well as the ponies, are very small in Shetland. The sheep give the wool from which the shawls are made. In the high latitude of Shetland the light of day at midsummer never totally disappears, and the smallest print can be read at midnight, when the lingering rays of the preceding day mingle with and give way to early dawn of the morrow. During winter the nights are proportionally long and dreary, and in the month of December the sun is not above the horizon more than five hours and twenty minutes.

Besides the herring fishery in Shetland, there are the 'greatlings' fishings, which means the great fish fishings with long lines. Among the fish thus caught are, I believe, the very large halibut, and another northern fish called the torsk—*Gadus brosme*, or *Brosmus vulgaris*. This fish somewhat resembles the ling, only it is thicker in proportion to the length. I unfortunately was unable to get a specimen in a fresh state; the nearest approach being a salted fellow, split, and without a head. So I could not ' make him up.'

All over Scotland I observed that the nets and long lines are frequently buoyed by dogs' skins. They catch Mr. Dog, kill him, cut off his head, and turn his skin inside out, hair inside; they tar the outside, then tie up his legs, and put a wooden plug into his neck, and blow him up quite tight by means of a plug in one of his legs. They tie the plug on to the buoy rope, and the dog's tail and hind legs floating on the surface of the water have a very curious appearance. For some reason they don't turn cats into buoys, and pigs are too expensive. The month of May is specially dangerous for dogs, as buoys are then wanted. Mr. Dog gets a crack on the head, is turned inside out, blown up and tarred, and in a quarter of an hour is anchored to a net out at sea. I think it would puzzle anybody, even a judge at a dog show, to swear to his dog when blown up without a head, and turned inside out. Captain Digby has on board the ' Jackal ' a wonderfully nice black dog, a faithful kind creature. I am afraid Jack (for that is his name) will end his earthly career as a buoy to a herring-net, so please look after poor Jack in the month of May.

On looking at the map of the north of Scotland I cannot help thinking that at some time or other the

Shetlands were joined to the Orkneys, the Orkneys to the
north of Caithness, Cape Wrath to the Butt of Lewis,
that is the extreme northern point of the Hebrides; the
island Barra, the extreme south of the Hebrides, to the
Mull of Cantyre, *viâ* the islands of Toree and Islay, and
that when the continent was broken up, on the west coast
a large inland sea was formed, divided into two, as it were,
by the isle of Skye, the northern sea being now called
the Minch, the southern sea the Little Minch. The conformation of this part of Scotland has great effect upon the
migrations of the herring, the season for herring fishing
on the west coast being very much earlier than on the
east coast.

I confess that before I got half-way through the herring inspection, I got quite tired of scenery, everlasting
mountains, and solitude.

I dislike much the words 'tourist' and 'picturesque.'
Towards the end of the journey I positively refused to
look at any more scenery of any kind. At Oban I saw
an omnibus and a four-wheeled cab, which reminded me,
to my delight, of my native home. I would suggest to
those hotel-keepers and others who make an easy living
out of the mountains, which, poor things, do not get any
share of the plunder, that the mountains should be all
properly numbered and labelled, like plants at a flower
show. I think that a little variety in the names would
also be advisable. It is always Ben this or Glen that,
every day and all day long. And allow me to inform my
readers that there are no hills in Scotland. A friend of
mine asked a bystander, pointing to the distance, 'Pray,
may I ask, what is that hill?' 'Hill, sir? It is not a

hill at all; it's a mountain,' was the answer. In the
same way, a visitor to a kennel of foxhounds said to the
huntsman, 'What a fine dog that is!' 'Dog, sir? It's
not a dog; it's a hound,' said the huntsman.

I must give my colleague, Mr. A. Young, due credit
for the admirable way in which he piloted us through
Scotland.

Mr. Young has a most extraordinary memory for
localities and figures. He has apparently the whole of
Scotland mapped out in his mind, and he astonished us
mightily during our journeyings by telling us off-hand
and with the greatest accuracy the height of almost every
mountain we saw, the depths and fishing capabilities of every
loch, the lengths and peculiarities of every salmon river,
and the names of the proprietors of most of the shooting
lodges and gentlemen's properties that are to be met with
so plentifully in Scotland. I cannot pretend to recollect
one quarter of what Young told us, but my general impression of these properties is that no one in Scotland has
less than 20,000l. a year, and that the proper thing to do
when one has made a fortune is to find out a desolate,
barren island where Robinson Crusoe himself would be
uncomfortable, or a lonely moor where there is nothing
but barren rock and heather, and where, as Colonel ——
informed me, the distance from civilisation is so great
'that he was obliged to give his chimney-sweep a bed.'
There, in these desolate places, do the rich people establish
their Lares and Penates.

I think I have found the reason why people who have
made fortunes go and live in desolate places, like so many
Robinson Crusoes. In his original state, man depends for

his existence on hunting, and hunts wild beasts and
birds, in order to obtain his necessary food and clothes.
When he has obtained all the food he can possibly want,
and every luxury he can possibly get, then what does he
do? Why, he immediately goes back to his primitive
state, and begins to hunt again. So you see the savage is
not very far removed from the Scotch or English rich proprietors and lessees of grouse moors and deer forests.

I fancy I have made a discovery. It is a new sport
for yachtsmen and those who are fond of large game
shooting; moreover, the shooting-grounds are not very
far from London.

When at Peterhead, on the crab and lobster inquiry,
my friend Captain David Gray, of the whaling ship
'Eclipse,' informed me that every year in the months of
July and August, when the herrings appear off Peterhead,
they are almost invariably followed by large Finner whales.
These fellows are often seventy feet long, aye, even bigger
than that sometimes, and they have hitherto been allowed
to hunt the herrings with impunity. The fleet of herring
vessels do not care to touch them, and they are not of
sufficient value either for oil or whalebone to render it
worth the while of the crews of the regular whalers to
go in pursuit of them. I understand that these whales
generally worry the herrings, not by rushing into the
shoal, but by swimming round the edge and driving them
together, just as a colley dog folds sheep. At Newcastle
one of these Finner whales managed to roll himself up in
a herring-net and get drowned; he came ashore near the
mouth of the Tyne.

In Captain Gray's yard, where he boils the whale oil,

I was fortunate enough to discover the mouth with the whalebone still *in situ* of one of these big Finners.

I have a little story to tell about this whale. Mr. Morris, of the Coastguard at North Berwick, about one hundred miles by coast from Peterhead, told me that a day or two previous to my visit there, a large whale had been picked up by some herring boats at sea, and towed ashore, where it was cut up and sold for oil. This whale had no head, and it was a great puzzle to the fishers to know where the head could be. I rather astonished Morris when I told him that it was in Captain Gray's yard at Peterhead. Captain Gray had informed me that fourteen days before my visit to Peterhead some herring fishers had found a whale floating dead at sea, had cut off his head, and let the body go adrift; the second lot of fishermen found it miles away.

Now I really do not see why these rascally herring-poaching Finners should not afford excellent sport to yachtsmen and gentlemen who often go immense distances to shoot big game. Peterhead is not far from Aberdeen, the Scotch express runs up there in about eighteen hours. Gray thinks the best way would be to shoot the Finners with a whale harpoon-gun (a weapon like a stumpy duck-gun), from a steam yacht, or if preferred, regular whale-boats might be towed by the yacht, the Finner harpooned, judiciously played on the whale-lines, and killed in the same way as the ordinary northern whale, which, by the way, does not require so much killing as the Finners. It must, however, be recollected that these Finners are bad to kill, as they will sometimes, when harpooned, turn about and fight

the boats, using their tail with tremendous force. Here,
then, there is an element of danger which, no doubt, would
add zest to the sport of some of our friends. There are
many sportsmen in England who have shot an elephant,
but very few who have harpooned a whale; besides this
it is to be recollected that the killing of these whales
would be a benefit to the herring-fishers, as it would
keep the herrings from being worried, and prevent the
nets being rolled up and carried off by Master *Physalis
boöps*, for that is his name—*boöps* because he has a little
eye like an ox.

For those who do not care to go out and kill a seventy-
foot whale, I have yet another plan.

At the meeting of the Yorkshire Salmon Fishery
Board at York, the fishermen made a formal complaint of
the great injury done to the salmon fisheries by the porpoises and grampuses coming up the Humber. These
hunt the salmon so closely that they leap out of the
water and go out to sea again to get out of their way; the
consequence is, the fishermen do not catch the salmon.
The hungry Cetacea follow the salmon up the Humber
as far as Goole.

A discussion took place as to the best way to kill
them, whether by net, harpoon, or explosive rifle balls;
finally, it was determined to offer rewards for their
destruction, and the tariff of reward was settled at one
shilling per foot, big and little. Some are herring-hogs,
four feet long; some are grampus, eighteen to twenty feet
long.

About July or August whale and porpoise shooting
may begin; and to those who wish to have the novel sensa-

tion of killing a whale, I expect it will be real good sport. The ladies, by the way, will be interested in this proposed whale-hunting expedition. I was told that good whalebone is worth from 800*l*. to 900*l*. per ton. The Finner whalebone is not valuable like that of the right whale, but still it is of some service. The whales, I think, will not thank me for writing the above lines.

NOTES FROM SCOTLAND.

JOHN-O'-GROAT'S house, the extreme north of Scotland, where I went in 1877 to obtain evidence from the crab and lobster fishermen, is a most interesting place. Not much seems to be known as to who the original John-o'-Groat was. I was, however, fortunate enough to come across an old fellow, who was up to his ankles in water, cutting his crop of oats; his name was Jock-o'-the-Burn. John-o'-Groat must, I should imagine, have been just such another character. I learn from the Thurso handbook, 'the tradition is that John de Groat was a Dutchman, who, along with two brothers, obtained by royal charter of James IV. land in the parish of Canisbay. In process of time there came to be eight different proprietors of the name of Groat. An annual festive gathering having been established to commemorate the anniversary of their arrival in Caithness, a dispute arose on one occasion among the Groats respecting the right of taking the door, the head of the table, &c.; and it is said that, in order to preserve harmony, old John built a house separate from all others, of an octagonal form, with eight doors and windows; and having placed a table of the same shape in the middle of the house, at the next anniversary he invited each of his friends to enter at his own door and sit at the head of the table, and so all were satisfied.' Such is said to be the origin of John-o'-Groat's house.

Another but more unlikely story is that the first Groat was a ferryman betwixt Caithness and Orkney, and that the fare across was fourpence or a groat for each passenger, and that the ferryman, whose name was John, got the sobriquet of Johnny Groat for this reason. There are many of the name of Groat in the county yet, and from local records they seem to have been a family of some consequence since the year 1496.

Close by the sea-shore there is a tumble-down cottage, which will answer the purpose very well of the original house of 'John-o'-Groat.' Near this house a substantial hotel has been erected. The Prince of Wales has visited it and the inhabitants of this part of the world are very proud of this *Ultima Thule* having been inspected by Royalty. I must confess that the view from John-o'-Groat's house is magnificent in the extreme. Immediately opposite is the island of Stroma; South Ronaldsha, and beyond that the other islands of the Orkneys can be seen more or less distinctly. To the eastward is Duncansby Head; although the sea was quite calm, the water off Duncansby was in a great state of agitation, and it appeared to me that a large tidal wave, like the tidal wave or bore on the Severn, was coming round the corner. This remarkable appearance was caused by two eddies or whirlpools, called the 'Bores of Duncansby.' These bores are at their greatest height at the flood tide. Off St. John's Head there is another set of bores; these are called the 'Merry Men of May;' these awful waves appear with the ebb tide. The consequence is that this passage is dangerous to ships passing through the strait, where the tide is said to run at the rate of ten miles an hour. Virgil's description, in the third 'Æneid,' of Scylla and Charybdis, exactly applies to John-o'-Groat's house :—

> Dextrum Scylla latus, lævum implacata Charybdis
> Obsidet, atque imo barathri ter gurgite vastos
> Sorbet in abruptum fluctus, rursusque sub auras
> Erigit alternos, et sidera verberat unda.

'Scylla guards the right side, whirling Charybdis the left, and thrice with the deep eddies of its voracious gulf swallows up the vast billows in the abyss, and again spurts them out by turns high into the air, and lashes the stars with the waves.'

To the westward from John-o'-Groat's is seen the Hoy Head, which is, I believe, one of the highest cliffs in Scotland. It is said to be 1,100 feet high. St. Paul's is 404 feet high, consequently this fearful cliff is nearly three times higher than St. Paul's. A story is told of an eagle's nest having been discovered far down a cliff somewhere in this neighbourhood. The sum of a guinea each was offered for the eggs; an Orkney man, determined to gain the prize, made a rope of heather, fastened his wife to the end, and let her down no less than 240 feet from the top of the cliff to rob the eagle's nest of the eggs. The rope was made of heather, as the clever wife suggested, if made of ordinary hemp it might chafe by the friction against the projections of the rock. The young woman performed this perilous feat of bird's nesting with success, and sold her eggs at the price offered. This adventurous pair are said to have collected, with their heather rope, a dozen eagles' eggs in one season.

I was informed that sixty eagles had been killed in the island of Lewis in seven or eight years, and that there were about seventy breeding-places patronised more or less by eagles in Sutherlandshire, many of them inaccessible to human beings. Grouse-preservers do not like eagles, computing that an eagle kills one grouse every day. In the Orkneys peregrines breed, and a very nice specimen was sent me from near John-o'-Groat's. The great Skua gull breeds in the northern Orkneys and Shetland. A gentleman living at Kirkwall informed me that a demoiselle crane (of all birds in the world) was shot in the Orkneys; he was, of course, most anxious to obtain the specimen, but was just too late to get it, as the man who had shot the bird had picked off its feathers and made it into soup.

I was also told a very funny story of the artfulness of common chickens. In former days it was difficult for visitors to get anything to eat at John-o'-Groat's, there being no butchers or bakers within miles. When visitors arrived it was the custom of the proprietor of the little inn to chase and catch a chicken, and pluck and roast him at once for the visitors' dinner. In course of time the chickens became very artful. They kept a sharp look-out, and when they saw a carriage coming along the road— they could see a long way down the straight road from the inn—they bolted, as the French would have it, *à toutes jambes*—with all legs—into the heather, and did not reappear until the visitors had eaten their bacon without the chicken and taken their departure. That birds learn

N

from experience is quite certain; when the telegraph wires were first put up between Berrydale and Hemsdale, the grouse were continually flying against the wires and killing themselves, and in one season the driver of the mail-cart picked up no less than forty brace of grouse that had been so killed. Of late years not a grouse has been found killed by the telegraph wires. They seem to have passed on the warning that telegraph wires were dangerous.

The sea-gulls at Wick are very tame; indeed, there are hundreds of them in the harbour, and they are never allowed to be touched in any way.

Apropos of sea-gulls, a very pretty sight can now daily be seen at Southport, in Lancashire. The gatekeeper of the long pier advertises that the sea-gulls will be fed daily at twelve o'clock. Their feeding-time at my visit had long passed, but nevertheless there were hundreds of gulls floating gracefully on the water at the end of the pier. The young woman at the refreshment-room close by sells bags of biscuits to feed the sea-gulls. It was most interesting to watch the actions of these pretty birds when the food was thrown into the water; a great scramble at once took place for it. I threw in a whole biscuit; a gull flew away with it, with some six or eight after him, and a battle ensued. In half an hour or so, many hundred gulls had assembled. This is the prettiest sight I have seen for a long time.

A friend of mine residing at Thurso complains bitterly of the effects of the Sea-Bird Preservation Act: he says that the gulls, especially the black-backed gull, do an enormous amount of mischief to the salmon fisheries. These fellows watch the shallows, and eat the smolts; he has taken no less than five smolts from one gull : in his opinion there are no salmon poachers in the world so bad as sea-gulls; they practically destroy more human food in the form of salmon than all the other salmon poachers in Scotland. The sea-gulls will also eat oats. They spit up the husks of these seeds in balls like owls' pellets; they also destroy the turnips, inasmuch as they bore holes in them; the water gets in, and the frost following, kills the turnips. The gulls have been known to destroy in a six-acre field as many turnips as would feed three cows. I understand that hares prefer swedes to turnips, and that it is not a bad plan to plant swedes to induce hares to leave the turnips alone : this is on the same principle that the butler advises his master to put strong ale in the cellar if he wishes to stop the table-beer from evaporating.

I noted several other matters during my journey of inquiry in Scotland which I should like to record.

The first thing that struck me was that everybody in Scotland seems to be educated. At about nine in the morning, at every place, both town and village, the children may be seen 'away to school,' and they seem rather to enjoy the prospect of learning lessons—quite a contrast to the state of things in England some sixty years ago, when the late Bishop Shuttleworth began his celebrated verses on the ' Progress of a Clergyman ' thus :—

> The fatal morn arrives, and oh !
> To school the weeping lad must go.

The lad, however, goes to school, is ultimately rewarded,

becomes a college tutor, and winds up with the aspiration—

Oh, make me a bishop, or at least a dean !

Dr. Shuttleworth prophesied his own fortune; he became Warden of New College, and then Bishop of Chichester.

But all Scotch lads cannot become bishops or deans. Backed, however, by education, they mostly get promoted —as old Dean Gaisford once thundered out at the undergraduates of Christ Church, Oxford, in his celebrated sermon on learning—to ' positions in life to which considerable emoluments are attached.'

Education also accounts for the answer of an individual to the King, who asked what he should do for him for services performed. His answer was, ' Please, your Majesty, make me a Scotchman.'

Of an evening, in that charming city of Edinburgh, can be seen at the corner near the post-office—

A little crowd,
That bawls so loud,
It really runs quite through ye ;
It's all the charity girls and boys
A-singing Alle-luia.

These little wretches are not, however, singing a hymn of praise, but are bawling out the halfpenny evening papers. Very few, if any, of these urchins wear shoes or stockings; but the sole of the foot gets harder the more you use it, and there are no shoemakers' bills to pay. They are mostly scantily clothed, but seem well fed and happy. I understand none of these urchins are allowed to appear with the papers under their arms for sale unless they have been to school in the morning.

I saw a little incident that would make a capital picture for an artist. In one of the jewellers' shops in Princes Street there was a magnificent tiara, with bracelets, earrings, &c., of lustrous diamond brilliants. Two little mites of children were racing to sell their halfpenny papers, when all in a moment the glitter of the diamonds struck them; they pulled up short, and stood aghast at the objects to which they were so little accustomed, gazing at them with all eyes and great wonderment. Here is a picture, 'Poverty and Riches.'

I was fortunate enough to be at the railway station when the train arrived with a number of fishwives from Newhaven. They were all dressed in blue serviceable serge: some were young, some old. They all had their creels or baskets of fish with them. I observed that it required two, and sometimes three railway porters to lift these heavy creels on to the women's backs. The creels are so made that the weight rests along the length of the spine, and is balanced, as it were, by a band that crosses the forehead.

The distance these women will walk, and the weight they will carry, are astounding. I was told of an old fishwife, living at Dunbar, who every morning sets out on a journey of from six to nine miles round the country to sell her fish, carrying sometimes as much as one hundredweight on her back. So accustomed is this fine old lady to carry weights on her back, that when, having sold her fish, she is returning homewards, she picks up heavy stones from the road-side, and puts them into her creel;

finding, I suppose, that a weighted creel is easier to carry than an empty one.

In the evening the fishwives come into the streets, and, putting down their creels, cry, 'Caller O! Caller O!' which, being translated, means 'Fresh oysters.' I interviewed one of these oyster ladies, a charming old woman. She complained bitterly of the price of oysters, and the difficulty she experienced, as a widow, in keeping her bairns in clothes and food. So you see the much-mooted oyster question affects not only the London clubhouses and the rich, but also the extremely poor. There is a famous song put into the mouths of these poor 'Caller O' women :—

> Wha will buy my caller herring ?
> They're no brought here without brave daring.
> Some call them lives of men.
> Wha will buy my caller herring,
> Fresh drawn frae the Forth ?

I have received, through the kindness of an Edinburgh lady, a very pretty song, called 'The Oyster Girl.' I would advise my young lady readers (if any) to get this song. The melody is very pretty, and the chorus, 'Caller O!' sweet and far-sounding, like the Swiss jodel songs with which the shepherd girls on the Alps awake the echoes to call their cows home.

By association with the fisher-people I have, I think, found out the meaning of that very common expression in Scotland, 'They call him.' If you ask a peasant in Scotland, 'Who is that?' the answer is sure to be, 'They call him' So-and-so. Now, the fisher-people intermarry among themselves. The consequence is that the same surnames in a village get very much multiplied. Hence the origin of the term 'Tec names,' such as 'Jock of the Burn,' 'Sandy,' &c., in cases where almost everybody bears the name, say for example, of 'Buchan.'

Among the Scotch, there is, I find, often a vein of the comic. I asked a boy at a railway station, 'When will the train start?' 'She'll just start when ye are all ready,' was the quick answer. A gentleman living near Peterhead one morning ordered his machine (by the way, why are all possible kinds of carriages in Scotland called machines?) at ten. He kept his old servant out in the wet holding the horse till twelve. On coming out two hours after his time he said, 'John, I fear I have kept you waiting.' John simply touched his hat, and grinning broadly replied, 'I'll no contradict ye, sir.'

One of the most interesting facts I came across in Scotland was the remains of fire-worship at Burghhead, near Forres. A very ancient rite is there still carried on, called the clavie. On the last day of the old year, old style, which falls on January 12, a large tar-barrel is set on fire, and carried by one of the fishermen round the town, while the assembled folks shout and holloa. If the man who carries the barrel falls, it is an omen of misfortune to him or his family. The circuit of the town having been made by the man with the burning barrel, it is placed on a large stone on the very top of the neighbouring cliff, and more fuel is added. The sparks, as they fly upwards, are supposed to be witches and evil spirits leaving the town, the populace hoot and execrate them accordingly. The fire-barrel is then placed on an ancient Roman altar to finish its burning out; this altar is called the douro. As the barrel falls in pieces the fisher-wives rush in, and endeavour to get a lighted bit of the wood; with this light the fire on the hearth of the cottage is at once kindled, and it is, I understand, lucky to keep this same fire going all the year round. Bits of the charcoal of the clavie fire-barrel are also collected and suspended in the chimney, to keep away witches and evil spirits.

It appears to me that this curious ceremony of the clavie and the douro are the remains of fire-worship.

I examined the douro, and also a curious Roman well, and some rude ancient Roman sculpture in the harbour-master's office, built into a wall near the douro.

I am informed that up to a very recent date, the carrying of a tar-barrel was also a regular custom with the lads of Stromness on Christmas and New Year's Eves; and when the tar in the barrel got spent, the barrel was carried to Brinkie's Brae, and there burnt. Sometimes a boat with tar on fire in a pot inside of it was substituted for the barrel, and drawn through the streets by many willing hands, who sang sea songs as they passed along.

NOTES FROM YARMOUTH.

I VISITED Great Yarmouth in October 1875, to procure some particulars for my official report on 'The Fisheries of Norfolk.' [1] When I had been there in June the sea was almost as calm as a sheet of glass, and little wavelets gently washed upon the beach, the sands of which were quite hot to the touch. The visitors were basking on the shingle, or being photo'd by the photographer on the beach, and the pleasure-boats were merrily dancing about: *Vela dabant læti et spumas salis aere ruebant.* On looking out of the window of the Royal Hotel on this October morning I found the weather entirely changed from what it was in June. An autumnal gale, which had for some days been threatening, had come into port from the north-east. The great 'white horses' came rolling in from over the Scroby and other sandbanks outside, and reaching the shallow gracefully curled themselves over, and then suddenly broke up with an awful thud. They then formed themselves into light squadrons of air-bubbles innumerable, which rushed up the beach with a Balaclava-like charge, rattling the pebbles and shingle, and making a terrible din as the waves hurled

[1] The Norfolk Fisheries Act, now in operation, was founded on this report.

them ashore, or swept them violently seawards. The
thought struck me that this boiling of the great waters
was a happy provision of the Creator to aërate His ocean,
for—

The sea is His, and He made it.

If the sea were allowed to remain stagnant several days
together, the water would become decomposed, lose its oxy-
gen, and be unfit for the sustenance of fish and the myriad
forms of animal life, 'the things creeping innumerable,'
which inhabit its vast waters. Storms, therefore, though
often terribly injurious to human life and property, are
necessary in the economy of the universe. Without them
we know not what catastrophe might happen in the ocean
world. It might even be 'all up' with the herrings.

As I came out of the hotel the wind came round the
corner with such violence that it was positively difficult
to progress. Dense sand-clouds came dashing in from
the shore with terrific violence, and in many places sand
covered the roadway so thickly that the carriages had
to go slowly through these newly formed obstructions.
However, we went out to the end of the pier, and it was
very beautiful to see the huge waves roll in with their
white-crested foam, and charge the piles of the pier till
the whole structure shivered again.

I immediately thought of Virgil's description of a
storm which caught poor old Æneas, after he and his
army (like the Russians at the Crimea) had got a hiding
at Troy. What a fool he was to let that wooden horse,
filled with his enemies, Greek soldiers, into the city!
Æneas could not have been a good observer, especially of
horses.

And first of all, ladies and gentlemen, you must know that in olden times lived, and may be even now living at the bottom of the sea (especially in the North Sea opposite Yarmouth), King Neptune, the lord of the sea. The following beautiful description of the king's submarine palace and horses has been recorded by friend Homer. I give the translation in English, as the Greek may be a little difficult to some of my readers :—

'Presently King Neptune descended from the rugged mountain, rapidly advancing on foot, and the high hills and woods trembled at Neptune's tread. Thrice, indeed, he strode forward, and with the fourth stride reached Ægæ (*i.e.*, Yarmouth), the place he sought. There lofty mansions, resplendent with gold, ever incorruptible, are erected for him in the depth of the sea. There he yoked to his chariot the brazen-footed horses swiftly flying with golden manes, but himself he clad in gold, took his golden lash, beautifully fabricated, and mounted the chariot. He drove over the billows; the whales, exulting around him, rose on all sides from their recesses to hail their king. The seas stood asunder for joy, and the chariot flew very rapidly, nor was the brazen axle wetted beneath; so his horses bounding on bore him to the ships of the Greeks' (*i.e.*, the Yarmouth and Gorleston fleet of herring-smacks).

'There is an ample cave in the abysses of the deep sea between Tenedos and the rugged Imbrus' (*i.e.*, out in the 'Silver pits' between Norway and Scotland, where the soles live, so well known to the Yarmouth trawlers). 'There Neptune, the shaker of the earth, stopped his horses, and loosing them from the chariot, cast beside

them ambrosial fodder to eat, and round their feet he
threw golden chains invincible, insoluble, that there they
might wait their king's return.'

Virgil takes up this idea very beautifully.   The cave
where Neptune pulled up his four-in-hand is the cave of
Æolus, the king of the winds:—

> Hic vasto rex Æolus antro
> Luctantes ventos tempestatesque sonoras
> Imperio premit ac vinclis et carcere frenat.
> Illi indignantes magno cum murmure montis
> Circum claustra fremunt.   Celsa sedet Æolus arce
> Sceptra tenens, mollitque animos et temperat iras.

'Here in a vast cave King Æolus controls, with imperial sway, the turbulent winds and blustering tempests,
and confines them with chains in their prison.   They
chafe indignant with loud roar around their mountain
barriers.   Æolus, seated on a lofty throne, wields his
sceptre, and therewith calms their fury and moderates
their rage.'

It appears that Madame Jupiter, that is, Juno (she
must have been a disagreeable mawther[1]), had a spite
against poor Æneas for some reason or other, so she went
to Æolus, and, woman-like, humbugged him with the
promise of a bride, one Miss 'Deiopœa' (rather a nice
girl, I should think, from her name).   Juno then persuaded
Æolus to let his pack of winds out of their kennel, and so
turn all Æneas's fleet into 'Vanguards,' and send them
to the 'bottom of the deep blue sea.'   The following is
the description of King Æolus starting his winds for the
race across the ocean :—

[1] Yarmouth for ' young woman.

Hæc ubi dicta cavum conversa cuspide montem
Impulit in latus ; ac venti velut agmine facto
Qua data porta, ruunt et terras turbine perflant.
Incubuere mari totumque a sedibus imis
Una Eurusque Notusque ruunt creberque procellis
Africus, et vastos volvunt 'ad litora fluctus.
Insequitur clamorque virum stridorque rudentum.

'Thus having said, whirling the point of his spear, he
struck the hollow mountain's side; the winds, as in a
formed battalion, rush forth at every vent, and scour over
the lands in giddy whirls. They ply the ocean furiously,
and at once, the east and south and stormy south-west
winds plough up the whole deep from its lowest bottom,
and roll vast billows to the shores. The cries of the seamen succeed, and the cracking of the cordage.'

Well, then in came Æolus' mighty winds to have a
turn at the good people of Yarmouth, and a very beautiful sight it was. Presently a big steamer appeared in
the offing, and up went a flag on the staff opposite the
Sailors' Home, and in an amazingly short time the
sharp-eyed signalman made out her flag with the telescope. Her letters were W. D. R.; the books showed
that she was the 'Bradspeth. In a few minutes more
it was known in London that the 'Bradspeth' was passing
Yarmouth. The telegraph, close to the beach, is doing
wonders for the trade of Yarmouth. Every ship as
she passes Yarmouth shows her number by means of flags.
By referring to the book in the signal-house it can be
immediately seen who she is, and the news appears in the
shipping papers the next morning.

Among the noticeable features of Yarmouth are the
'look-outs.' These are scaffolds, with a platform on the

top, from which the men on duty can see an immense distance out to sea. When we were standing on the pier I saw a crowd begin to collect on the shore at some little distance. Of course, I ran to see what was the matter, and was shocked to see, just washed ashore, a poor lad who had been drowned when bathing a few days back. I was so sorry for the poor lad, and thought of his father and mother when they heard the news. A bystander told me that no less than twenty-three poor sailors were once washed ashore by one tide from a wreck outside.

Many shipwrecks occur every winter. The lifeboat bell clanging loudly in the midst of a gale of wind in the dead of a winter's night, to signal the 'turn-out' to the beachmen from their slumbers, is a sound which if once heard will never be forgotten. I should like some musician to write a song, 'Hark! 'tis the Lifeboat Bell.'

From October to May the big lifeboat is kept on the beach close to the water, to be ready at a moment's notice; the rest of the year it lives in its stable. If the boat is launched for saving life in reply to signals of distress at sea during the night-time, a certain fee is always payable. If the boat is launched in the day, half the amount is claimed. The smaller 'surf-boat,' as it is called, also receives regular fees for launching to save life. The sands near Yarmouth are terribly dangerous.

Year after year, more especially during the time of the equinoctial gales, very disastrous shipwrecks take place; indeed, it is estimated that of the wrecks in each year off the coast of Great Britain, more than half occur off the eastern coast. There are various sands which protect the Roads: Scroby lies opposite the town, and is the principal one in extent; the others are Newarp, Cockle, Barber Corton, Newcomb, and Holm Sands. The entrances to the Roads are by gatways, the principal of which are St. Nicholas' and Hewitt's.

From the Britannia Pier we could see some vessels at anchor, rolling and pitching about in a most fearful manner; so much did they roll that it was easy to see down their cabin stairs, and the wonder was that the men were not washed out of them.

Fog are very nasty things in the North Sea. When going through Yarmouth Harbour I heard a most dismal sound; this noise was our friend Captain Emerson, of the Trinity Board, making hideous diapasons with his new patent steam fog-horn.

I must not omit to mention that excellent institution, the Sailors' Home, on the beach. In this admirable institution there is every possible convenience for the care of shipwrecked sailors. A most excellent place it is, and well worthy the support of visitors and the public in general. During the past year no less than 138 shipwrecked sailors were relieved, making the total number received since its establishment 3,986.

In the yard of the Custom House I examined a capital mermaid on duty at the foot of the signal post. She is life-size, and represents a really very pretty woman; the fish's tail is capitally made. This mermaid answers exactly to Horace's description,—

Desinit in piscem mulier formosa superne.

One of the most curious features in Yarmouth is its 'Rows,' and in this respect it resembles no other town in

England. The 'Rows' are straight, long, and narrow, with houses on either side; the residents have been known to shake hands from opposite windows. They are paved with large pebbles from the beach.

I understand that these Rows were invented by the fishermen who were the first inhabitants of Yarmouth; they used to hang their herring-nets in long rows on the beach. After a time they built the huts alongside the beach; the houses in time took the places of the huts; this, then, was the origin of the Yarmouth Rows.

It was necessary, of course, that some provision should be made to get heavy goods down to the houses in the Rows. In Yarmouth, therefore, there exists a kind of cart which, I believe, is unique. Two long and strong timbers form the shafts for the horse. Immediately behind the horse's tail boards are inserted between the shafts, and then comes a platform somewhat in the shape of an easy chair, the seat sloping, and without arms. The whole of this rude, but yet very convenient kind of vehicle, is supported by two wheels cut out of solid wood, and joined together by a wooden axle, which run inside as in a railway carriage. Wheels of this kind are of very ancient origin, and if I recollect right the war chariot of the ancient Romans ran upon solid wheels just like these Yarmouth carts, which are called *trolls*. The fact is, it is a very difficult thing indeed to make a wheel or a barrel. The only thing that beat Robinson Crusoe was the manufacture of a cask, and I dare say there are very few of my readers who know how to make a watertight cask.

When the trawlers come in laden with fish they transfer them to very large boats rowed by several men, and thence into trolls, which are backed into the water. These boats are very strong, and admirably fitted to fight the surf, which sometimes breaks with terrific force. The poor horses must suffer much in drawing the heavy-laden trolls through the deep shingle; surely, for humanity's sake, a platform or tramway of some kind might be devised and put into operation.

The Church of St. Nicholas at Yarmouth is most interesting. The organ is said to be inferior only in power to the celebrated organ at Haarlem. When completed it will be one of the best, if not the best, in England. Over this venerable organ is a gilt figure of a bishop, with mitre and crosier. To this venerable wooden prelate I took a great fancy. This Yarmouth bishop is very like in face to our founder of Winchester College and New College, Oxford, William of Wykeham.

When visiting this beautiful church at Yarmouth, the visitor cannot fail to be struck with the numerous records of officers and men of merchant and other ships who have been drowned in the great North Sea, itself not so very far from the walls of St. Nicholas.

Behind the door of the church, at the west end, is an enormous bone, which looks exactly like a huge arm-chair. The parishioners of Yarmouth do not seem to know much about this bone; and at first it gave me some little trouble to find out what it really was. Ultimately I made out quite suddenly that it is part of the skull—the occipital bone and part of the parietal—of a large sperm whale, probably washed ashore near Yarmouth, and converted into a relic for the church. The vicar, the Rev. Mr. Venables, could not tell me what it was, but I have cut up the skull

o

of a common porpoise to represent this balænarian chair in St. Nicholas's Church, and prove that my diagnosis of its nature is correct.[1]

Yarmouth is a very healthy place, and I advise any who do not know whither to go for a holiday to patro-

[1] The following note is from Lubbock's *Fauna of Norfolk*, 2nd ed., p. 16 :—

'No recent occurrence of the sperm whale (*Physeter macrocephalus*, Linn.) on the Norfolk coast is on record, but Sir Thomas Browne says, "A spermaceti whale sixty-two feet long [came on shore] near Wales [about 1646] ; another of the same kind twenty years before [June 1626] at Hunstanton ; and not far off eight or nine came ashore, and two had young ones after they were forsaken by the water" (Wilkin's edit. iv. p. 326). In December 1626, according to Booth's *History of Norfolk* (ix. p. 33), a great whale, fifty-seven feet in length—from his excellent description evidently a male sperm whale—was cast on shore at Holme-next-the-Sea ; and lastly, Mr. Arthur Bacon, of Yarmouth, writes to Sir Thomas Browne, on May 10, 1652, of the sperm whale cast on shore there (i. p. 369). In St. Nicholas' Church, Great Yarmouth, is the basal portion of the skull of a whale of this species. It is placed near the door at the west end of the church, and used as a chair. Mr. C. J. Palmer, of Yarmouth, informs me that in the churchwardens' accounts for 1606 there is a charge of eight shillings for painting this skull, which fully establishes its great antiquity. The full-grown males of the sperm whales are said to be generally solitary in their habits, except when migrating from one place to another; and it seems probable that the majority of those which occur singly on the British shores are these solitary males, which have wandered from their true habitat, the warm sea of the tropics. But when they visit us in numbers, as mentioned by Sir Thomas Browne, they are most likely adult females, or young males, which associate in separate herds.'

These wandering parties would, as a matter of course, be more frequent when the species was more numerous, and when once entangled in the shallows of the German Ocean, want of sea room and of suitable nourishment would soon bring about their destruction. The statement by Swinden (p. 885, edition published 1772) is as follows :—' Near this door, under a niche, stands a large old jaw-bone of a whale. It formerly was used for a seat at the church grate (*gate?*) under the old Guildhall.' Comparative anatomy was not understood then as it now is, or this would not have been mistaken for a *jaw-bone*. It is the portion of the skull upon which the lower part of the brain rests.

nise Yarmouth. So healthy is this interesting seaport, that I understand from my friend Dr. Norman that the gravedigger some time since became insolvent through want of professional occupation. When brought up before the County Court he attributed his insolvency to better drainage of the town, and the supply of water from Ormsby Broad, but more especially to the scarcity of doctors as compared with former times, when he first entered upon his professional duties. 'Gentlemen,' said he, 'a poor fellow then had some chance of a living; now I have only buried twelve and a half the last fortnight, so I leave you to guess how I have to get a bit of bread in these here hard times.'

The trawlers of the North Sea have, above all men, opportunities of finding out much that is going on in the subaqueous treasure-houses of the ocean. This ocean is not only the habitation of myriads of living creatures, but is also a cemetery containing the bones of creatures that lived in past ages.

Amongst the treasures of the deep often brought up by trawlers or their nets, the bones of elephants frequently occur. In the museum of the Sailors' Home at Yarmouth there is a very interesting collection of the bones of elephants, dredged up between the English coast and Heligoland, off the mouth of the Elbe.

At no very ancient geological period England was certainly united with France, and it is supposed by some that the Thames did not at that time flow into the sea at the place where it now does, but that the river broke through the ridge of chalk, somewhere to the north of Reading, and emptied itself into the ocean in the estuary of the Humber.

At the same time it is the opinion of some that a mighty river larger than the Rhine drained the European continent.

These two rivers probably brought down into the sea the bodies of dead elephants. This, I believe, is the usual explanation of their bones being found in the North Sea : but elephants' bones are found abundantly in other parts of England, at Woolwich, Sheppey, the London gravel beds, Oxfordshire, Abingdon, Arundel, and many other places. It may be that the North Sea now covers tracts once shaded by forests, the home of these huge beasts.

Yarmouth, as we all know so well, is one of the chief fishery ports in England. There are 400 to 500 smacks marked Y. H. registered at this port, and besides these a fleet of Scotch and other boats come here every autumn for the herring fishery ; the value of the fish landed each year at Yarmouth is very great—but I am not writing a fishery book, so must not be tempted into details.

Not only does the sea at Yarmouth yield fish, but also even, sometimes, ready-made money, for when looking over the Britannia Pier, during the gale, I noticed many men and boys anxiously waiting the coming in of the big waves. Every now and then one of them would rush into the boiling wash and snatch up something out of the shingle. I ascertained that these people were looking for money, which was being washed out from the shingle composing the beach. One man got as many as six sovereigns the day I was there, others smaller sums ; the theory is that visitors drop the money out of their pockets when lying on the shingle.

Nearly every year coins are found on Yarmouth beach.

From sixteen to twenty sovereigns were found lately near the pier ; they were all of modern date. This is a matter worthy of further investigation. I don't think the theory of visitors dropping their sovereigns will quite do.

I also heard a new theory why the weather was so bad at one time. An old salt was smoking his clay and looking out discontentedly seawards. On being asked the cause of the bad weather the old man gave the following account :—

' Ye see,' he says, ' it's all along of the sun ; the sun, he have a shiny side and he have a dark side, and now he turns his dark side to Yarmouth. I have a friend in the town they call a hastronomer as pilots the stars, and he says the old sun got foul of the comet, he got jammed up in the meshes of this 'ere comet's tail. Then directly after there come a heclipse, and the sun, he has never been hisself not never since ; he ain't well, and can't do his waark [work] not nohow.'

Amongst the many charitable institutions which Yarmouth boasts is the Fishermen's Hospital, a quad-rangular building near St. Nicholas's Church. It was built by the Corporation in 1702 at a cost of 621*l.* Since its erection various sums have been bequeathed ; these now produce 49*l.* 10*s.* per annum.

Seeing some poor old weather-beaten men basking in the sun, I thought I would see what evidence they could give me about the herring fishery when they were young. I was fortunate enough to obtain evidence from Mr. Silvers, aged 85, and from Mr. Colby, aged 71, who had both served nearly all their lives as man and boy in the North Sea. The answer from both these veterans was, that there are as many if not more herrings caught now than 70 or 80 years ago, and this in spite of the increased number of boats and nets. I was very much struck with the manners and appearance of old Mr. Silvers; in spite of his age, hale, hearty, and contented, with a regular fisherman's eye, which no one accustomed to deep-sea fishermen can mistake. He told me some of his history, which was as follows :—

'I was born in 1790, and have been a sailor and fisherman from a sprat to a whale all my life. When I was about thirteen years old I was 'prenticed to a cooper, and after being with him some time he sent me out for a short voyage in a vessel he freighted, as I was a strong lad. When I came back I went on larning my trade till I was just seventeen. One cold winter's night in the year 1806 —Trafalgar was fought Oct. 21, 1805—I was a-standing in a public-house in Yarmouth, called the " Horse and Gig,' with two other boys; a blind fiddler who was there was just a-going to tune up for us, when in rushed the press-gang and took the lot of us. We was took off in boats to a man-of-war lying in Yarmouth Roads, and kept aboard all night, and brought before the officers in the morning. Those who had a protection were never kept, as there was a law against it. A protection is this: If you was bound a 'prentice in those days to any trade, that protected you from being taken; for you was obliged to serve your time till the seven years indenters was out.

'That fiddler he was let off at once, as, being blind, of course he was no use; and my master, he come aboard in the morning, thinking he could get me off as being a 'prentice, but he happened to say I had been to sea in his vessel, so the officers said that was enough, and I could not now be protected. I had six hours to go ashore and bid my father and mother good-bye, and then I had to go to my ship and serve in the King's service.

'I was away six years from old Yarmouth. A lot of us was taken prisoner by the Danes; we were marched three hundred miles through their country to the prison, where I was thirteen months, almost starved I was. After being there all that time, I was let go; the English admiral gave up two Danish prisoners for one Englishman. Then I joined my ship and soon came home. After that I went away with Admiral Young in the Victoria. One day when I was a-walking on the deck I see a gentleman a beckoning of me, so I went up to him, and it was my old master, Captain Hutchinson, who had a schooner of eighteen guns called the "Pigmy." He said to me, "Why, Silvers, how ever came you here?" So I told him what I had been doing; and he says, "Well, would you like to come with me, or stay where you are?" In course I said, "Well, sir, I would rather be with you than any one." So he managed with the admiral, and on I goes aboard the schooner. We started for Gibraltar, and left there during the 'Merican war, landing at Plymouth with the Government mails.

'Well, I runned away that very day, and I went to Exeter, from there to London, and then on to Yarmouth; but when I got here I was as bad off as ever, for the pressgang was out, and I daren't stop, or they'd have nabbed me sure enough. So off I goes to Hull, and from there I goes a fishing to Greenland for three years after whales and ile. I know'd the pressgang couldn't catch

me there anyhow. When I returned from Hull again the
'Merican war was over, and peace proclaimed, so I had
to remain in Yarmouth ; and then I went out in fishing-
boats for owners, after herring. I have helped kill many
a whale. We used to get half-a-guinea a fish, and 50s.
per week. It will take the Arctic Expedition all their
time to get to the North Pole, and when they get there
there is nothing but ice and rocks. I never was higher
than 72° myself. But them press days was terrible, that
they was. Why, they once took our Mayor of Yarmouth
(he was a rum-looking old chap), when he was a standing
on the jetty. They didn't care. One time a whole lot of
carpenters went together, and when the gang came ashore
the carpenters took and chopped the boats all to bits,
In course, they was took up, and sent to Norwich Castle.
When they was tried in London they was sentenced to
twelve months' imprisonment in the castle, and one of
the poor fellows died there.'

Mr. Silvers showed me how he made tea, an ounce of
which lasted him a week in a general way. 'Gentlefolks
do not taste half the goodness of tea,' he said ; 'they
don't boil it enough. Why, the tea-leaves that gentlemen's floors are swept with would make rare, beautiful
tea for me.' Half-a-crown a week this old man lives on ;
and he proudly said he did 'everything for himself, except
once in three weeks, when he gave a woman threepence
to "lap up the water" off the floor, while he scrubbed it
with a brush on the end of a pole.'

'You see,' he added, 'I can't go on my knees now, I
haven't been active for twelve years, for I got a shot in
the leg when I was in the sarvice, and as I grew older I

felt it the more. The only thing I wish for is to have
some one come and see me sometimes. I haven't a rela-
tion in the world; but I don't wish to complain. I sit
here and read when I have anything, and a book that a
kind lady sent me I have read over and over again.
When I can't do that I sit and think over old times, as I
do when I am restless o' nights. Please God, come next
4th of August I shall be eighty-five, and a good deal have
happened in that time to think over.'

After leaving my old friend, I could not help thinking
of the old saying, 'Not one half of the world knows how
the other half live.' This poor old man in his lonely
home, with but comparatively few comforts, is far more
contented than hundreds with every luxury. Not a
murmur does he utter, and not a wish to be better off,
but with his cheerful disposition and good heart sees, or
endeavours to see, 'in each dark cloud a silver lining.'

Those who wish to have a real treat would do well
to take my advice and go by Great Eastern Railway
to Yarmouth to inspect the herring harvest, which begins
at that port in the month of September. For some
days an increased number of tug steamers and smacks
may be noticed either coming in or going out of
Gorleston Harbour. These are the drifters bringing in
their fish from the great North Sea. These powerful
tugs tow the herring-boats alongside the Yarmouth
fish quay, and of all sights in England this quay is at
this season one of the most wonderful. The quay is
admirably built for the purposes it is intended to fulfil.
The merchants' offices are all on one side, faced by a
solid stone pavement, with a road only intervening be-

tween them and the Suez Canal, as I call that portion of the Yare which flows past the town, and in which the herring-smacks are brought alongside.

The market begins every morning in the season at ten o'clock. Large bodies of men, as strong as lions, are employed in unloading the smacks. As the herrings are caught at sea they are put down into the hold and mixed with salt; arriving at the quay, they are sent up in bulk on to the deck, and are there counted.

The counter takes two herrings in each hand and very quickly puts them into the basket. The men get three shillings a last for 'telling'—that is, counting the herrings. Four herrings are called a 'warp.' From the basket the herrings are emptied out into large baskets called 'swills.' Each swill contains 500 herrings of long tale—that is, 132 for 100—a very ancient measurement. A last of herrings contains 13,200 fish.

I found the pavement of the fish-quay almost covered with these swills full of herrings, and it seemed wonderful to me how ever they were going to be disposed of.

Presently a man comes along with a bell, and the fish-buyers turn out to the place where the sale is going to take place. The auctioneer takes his seat with each foot on a swill, a red note-book and pencil in hand. He begins at once, with his loud cheery voice, 'What shall I say for this lot?' I see no sign and hear no bid! Somebody has made a bid, for he begins most rapidly, 'Eleven—eleven—eleven—eleven; ten—ten—ten—ten—ten; eleven fifteen—thank you; look at 'em again—a splendid lot of fish—don't lose the lot for a crown; twelve—twelve—twelve—at last twelve fifteen.' The little pencil hits the book, and the lot is sold—to whom, it is impossible for *me* to say.

The purchasers stand round in perfect silence, but though pretty quick in the eye I cannot see their bids. A movement of the eye, a slight turn of the head, or other mysterious sign incomprehensible to the public, is quite enough for the auctioneer to take the bid.

No sooner is one lot sold than he puts up another. I give him a nudge, pretend to wind him up (on his great broad back) like a clock with a key, and he puts on the steam in reality then; and the wonderful way and clever chaff with which he leads on his bidders to buy is most amusing, putting the famous auctioneer of our ancestors, Robins, quite in the shade. The prices vary according to the quality of the herrings and demand in the market. One lot was knocked down at 16*l.* 15*s.* for twenty swills.

The fish first out of the hold are the most valuable; those last out do not fetch so much money, as they are salter. The herrings on sale were North Sea herrings, very large fine fish. I examined the milts and roes, and found they were not quite in spawning condition, but very nearly so. A shoal was just then reported a few points west by north-west, direct from Yarmouth, near the Doggerbank.

The result of my earnest consultations at Yarmouth enables me to classify the herrings somewhat as follows: Spring herrings, long-shore herrings, midsummer herrings, and deep-sea herrings, the latter of two kinds. But this is such an intricate question, I cannot go into it here.

The process of curing is as follows: the swills full of

herrings are brought to the curing-house and turned out
on the floor; the men then mixed them about with shovels,
while another man scatters salt plentifully over them.
The herrings are then placed in a heap and allowed to
remain a certain time, then washed in a huge tub, then
spitted (a process called 'riving'). Spits are sticks perfectly round. The stick is passed through one gill; and
each spit, which carries twenty-five herrings when full,
is hung up on what is called a 'horse' for a time. The
fish are hung up in such a way that they can all be
stripped off very quickly. The smoking-house consists of
a large room; upon looking up to the ceiling may be seen
a great number of racks, called 'grills;' the space between
the racks is just the length of the spits. A man climbs
up to the very top of these racks, another places himself
halfway down, another man is on the floor, and the spits
with the herrings are passed from one man to the other,
and immediately hung up until the place is quite full of
herrings suspended by their gills. Fires of oak and oak
sawdust are then lighted on the floor below. The oak is
chop-and-lop from the forests, and is sold by the cast;
each bit of wood has a peculiar marking on it. Here,
again, we have a strange measurement: in the sale of
wood 1,000 stands for 600. The red herrings are smoked
six or seven weeks, to give them a good deep red colour.
During this process some fall off the spits; these are
called 'plucks' and 'tenders,' and are collected and
hung up again by the tail on what are called 'tenter
baulks.'

Real Yarmouth bloaters are herrings very slightly
salted, and smoked for three or four hours only. In this

process they puff up somewhat, hence they are called 'bloaters.' When the fish are quite prepared, they are quickly taken off their spits and packed into barrels ; a small barrel contains 200, a large barrel 660. They are packed with their heads outermost, and in order to save room they are occasionally pressed under a heavy iron screw, somewhat resembling the apparatus for making cheese. The herrings cured at Yarmouth in this way are mostly sent to the Mediterranean by fast steamers.

The question of salt is of great importance. That which I saw was very hard, and in beautiful crystals resembling snow. This salt came from Nantwich, in Cheshire, and is brought to Yarmouth in steamers.

After inspecting the curing-houses we calculated how many industries must be put into action before the barrelled herrings leave Yarmouth. Thus : 1, boats and rigging, &c. ; 2, nets ; 3, salt ; 4, steam-tugs ; 5, salesmen and staff ; 6, baskets and swills ; 7, carrying carts ; 8, washing the herrings ; 9, spits ; 10, riving and hanging ; 11, oak for smoking ; 12, packing ; 13, barrels ; 14, freight, besides employment to a vast number of smacksmen. Thus we see of what importance red herrings are to Yarmouth, and to how many people and trades they give employment. Surely we English should be most grateful to Providence for giving our country such a rich harvest of the sea. I wish I could persuade some of our influential M.P.'s to come down to Yarmouth and see the immense amount of capital and labour involved in the herring fisheries.

We held our official inquiry at Lowestoft in the 'Fisherman's Shelter.' This is a most excellent institution—a large wooden building with plenty of air and light, roofed inside like a new church. There is every accommodation for fishermen; excellent tables, good seats, and, above all, good food—cheap, very cheap. A man can get meat, bread, cheese, cocoa, tea, and coffee there for a surprisingly small price. I myself had lunch there off some capital American beef, that was really first-rate. This institution is greatly, if not altogether, indebted to Colonel Leathes, of Herringfleet Hall, for its foundation, and the admirable way in which it is now kept up. The fishermen can come in and out in their working clothes, and get warmth, excellent food, cocoa, &c., much better than they could at any public. In bad weather especially is the Shelter patronised by these brave North Sea fishermen. Smoking is allowed, which adds greatly to its success.

A curious fact which came to my notice at Lowestoft is the acclimatisation of lobsters about the pier. Some years ago a box full of live Norwegian lobsters, the property of a local fish merchant, got adrift and was broken up; there were in this lot several 'berried hens,' *i.e.*, lobsters carrying eggs under their tails. The lobsters escaped, and have now permanently established themselves among the rocks. This is a good hint to those who wish to try lobster cultivation elsewhere, and there are many places admirably suited for the experiment.

I saw that the teredo is making havoc with the wood piles of some of the harbour structure. The rascals, in spite of copper nails, get in and will scoop out the piles till they become as hollow as chimneys. The fishing-smacks going in and out of the harbour were beautiful to see. A tug was continually going to and fro from the inner harbour, saving the men's time and labour by tugging the boats either in or out. The quantity of trawl fish on the quay was something amazing, and how it is that the North Sea is not trawled out may be a wonder to many. Still, we must recollect that if England was cut out of a map and placed on the North Sea, drawn to the same scale, England and Scotland could be sunk in the North Sea, and space still be left over. Again, supposing the trawling vessels to be represented by balloons, and the soles, &c., by human beings, the ballooners would be a long time before they could trawl up all the men, women, and children in England and Scotland.

I think I have said elsewhere that a trawl net fished almost immediately behind another trawl net would often catch even more fish than the first net. I think this might be illustrated by what I saw at Yarmouth. There was a wedding at the big church of the place, and when the people saw the carriages going to the wedding they all began to run after the carriages. During the wedding the crowd assembled, and then came the trawl net, as represented by the carriages, into the thick of the crowd to take away the bride and bridegroom, and their friends; but the more carriages that came, picking up a certain number of the wedding party from the crowd, the thicker the crowd became.

I was much amused at a large red-faced fisherman's reception of the bride; he established his monstrous self right opposite the window of the bride's carriage waiting at the door of the church. He was dressed fisherman fashion—tarpaulin hat and jersey. Move, not he! There he stayed with his great ugly head right inside the carriage till the bride moved off from amid the charity children, old women, babies, and the whole turn-out of the poorer parts of Yarmouth, to whom a gratuitous exhibition such as a wedding is a great amusement and delight.

Yarmouth fair happened to take place when I was there. Of course I went into the shows. The best thing by far was the Hairless Horse. Yes, he was perfectly hairless, as bald as a billiard ball. His hair had not been shaved, he had never had any. Some part of the skin was white, the rest black: the white was very white, like the skin of a sucking pig; the black was the black of the edible Chinese dog, also called the 'India-rubber Dog.' There was also on view a living skeleton—certainly a skeleton something awful to look at. He was said to be thirty-four; he might have been any age. He was awfully thin. His wrist would pass through a gauge of one inch and one-eighth. I asked the skeleton what he lived on. He said, ' Rump-steaks and porter.' Anyhow, he certainly did not grow fat on it. I went also to see a ' Petrified Mummy,' about which the showman of course had a long yarn to tell. This was an old friend that I am continually coming across at penny shows—viz., the ' Abogine.' The history of the ' Abogine ' is as follows: He is a dried Australian native, thrown in as a bargain with some shells, spears, &c., in a lot, and bought by a dealer. The shells, &c., were sold, but not the dried Australian, and the dealer got quite tired of his bargain. At last he called him an ' Abogine,' and chopped him to some penny showman for some monkeys. The poor ' Abogine ' does not get on; showmen can't make money out of him. The

' Abogine,' of course, means ' aboriginal native,' only the word has been a little twisted.

There were a tremendous number of roundabouts in the fair. Why the women, children, and men do not get giddy and fall out of these model boats and rocking-horses, I can't tell. The sailors were great at the swings, and, I must say, were sent up fearful heights, higher than any landsmen could or would go.

LONDON BIRDCATCHERS.

PISCATOR et Auceps visited in August 1878 my friend Mr. Higford Burr, at Aldermaston Park, Reading. Piscator is myself, Auceps a professional London birdcatcher, Mr. Davy, whose name is well known to ornithological collectors both in London and elsewhere as a dealer and as a first-class authority on everything pertaining to British birds.

I proposed to Mr. Burr that I should bring Davy down to Aldermaston, that the party staying at the house might see the process of catching wild birds, an art about which Londoners know but little.

Arriving at Aldermaston in company with the Squire, Mrs. Burr, Sir Austen Layard, then Minister at Madrid, Lady Layard, Dr. Hooker, Mr. Fergusson, &c. &c., we at once started to pitch the net at a place selected by Davy. He told the head keeper he wanted to find a place where the birds came to drink ; so, guided by the Squire with his big walking-stick, we at once proceeded to the fish-house, where the Squire breeds his great lake trout, in one of the wildest parts of the forest. The forest at Aldermaston is one of the most beautiful in that part of the country ; the oaks in it are of very great antiquity, some as old as, if not older than those in Windsor Park. The Squire takes

great care of these venerable oaks, and doctors them up in
their extreme age. Passing through the forest, it was interesting to watch Davy, as he trudged along with his
call-birds and net in 'the pack' on his back through the
thick ferns, looking up into the trees, and giving different call-bird notes as he went on. His diagnosis of
the forest was not, however, very promising. 'Not
much here, sir,' he said, 'except owls and woodpeckers.'
And just at that moment, as luck would have it, a woodpecker began to holloa. 'Hark at him,' he said ; 'that's a
spotted woodpecker ; there ought to be several kinds of
woodpeckers in this forest.' 'Yes,' said the Squire, 'there
are, and I never allow the keepers to shoot them under
any pretence.' The Squire well knows how very useful
these unpaid servants the woodpeckers are in the management of forest trees.

Just by a gate which led us through the high iron deer-
fence Davy suddenly halted, and said, 'Mr. Buckland, sir,
there's an owl's nest in that tree.' 'If there is,' I said,
'Davy, there should be some pellets at the bottom.' So
the Squire and myself routed about among the grass, and
in a few minutes we found some eight or ten owls' pellets.
These consist of balls which look like matted hair. After
the owl has eaten a mouse, he spits up the hair and the
bones in one mass, all the flesh being digested. I have
just dissolved out one (only one) of these pellets in water.
I find in it the almost perfect skull of a shrew mouse with
the most lovely little teeth, and also half the skull of a
common mouse. The bones of the shrew are indeed
most delicate. I know no other bone the structure of
which is so beautiful, and, at the same time, so light.

The Squire's owls not only keep down the mice, but at night they give us a most lovely serenade, to my ears far more interesting than the singing of any prima donna at the Italian Opera. 'Should not wonder if there isn't some young owls in that nest,' said Davy. 'Up you go, then,' said I, 'and look.' 'There's been young owls here,' said he, after he had examined, ' and I can't tell, they may be in the nest now,' as he showed me a lot of the down of the young birds. He then explained the proper way to take young owls. The owl's nest is often deep down in a tree; it is necessary to wait till the owls get to a certain size; the best way then to catch them is to roll up a stocking or ball of worsted, fastening on a piece of string and letting it down into the nest; the birds immediately turn on their backs and claw at the stocking; they have not sense to let go, and up they come.

The old oaks in Aldermaston Park are very favourite breeding-places for owls, and the Squire does not allow them to be shot.

The next morning, after breakfast, Mr. Davy reported to the Squire and myself that he had been out very early to see what the park produced in the shape of birds. He reported numbers of thrushes, blackbirds, jackdaws, starlings, and rooks, but he had not seen a magpie. He had heard one or two jays, abundance of green woodpeckers, and a few of the summer soft-meat birds, such as the flycatcher, willow-wren, chiff-chaff, and a common shrike. There was not a small seed-eating bird to be seen either in the forest or the park. The only way Davy could account for their non-appearance was that the park and forest lands had been kept clear of seed-bearing weeds. He was certain large numbers of all kinds of birds had been bred in the Squire's forest and in the gorse, but having brought out their young they had now left for their feeding-places.

The Squire gave Davy permission to lay his nets wherever he chose. He selected a spot close to the end of a most beautiful shaded avenue. The process of laying the nets is somewhat as follows:—Two nets, twelve yards long, and when open covering the ground for twenty feet in width, are neatly laid down on the ground. To the far ends of the nets are attached staves. The distance Davy stood from the nets to work them was about eighteen yards. It is impossible to describe the rough yet very excellent machinery by which a pull on the rope held by the bird-catcher will make these harmless-looking nets instantly spring into the air and catch the birds either on the wing or on the ground. They act so quickly that the eye can scarcely follow. Anything on the wing crossing the nets within four feet from the ground will be shut in instantly. It is better to catch the bird before he has time to settle. If birds touch the net with their feet they are off instantly.

The next process in birdcatching is to put out the 'brace bird.' A brace bird is taken from a cage ; this bird always wears his brace with a swivel attached, whether at work or no. The brace consists of a piece of string made into a kind of double halter. It is put over the bird's head, and the wings and legs are passed through ; in fact, when I saw Mr. Davy brace a bird I was strongly re-minded of a nurse dressing a baby. When the brace is on the bird, the feathers fall over it and it cannot be seen. The brace bird is then put on his 'flurr stick;' this is a

straight stick, which by means of a hinge on its lower end
and a string is made to rise and fall at the will of the
birdcatcher. Then when any bird is seen coming the
flurr stick is gently pulled up, the brace bird all the
while standing on the stick is made to hover and to show
wing, *i.e.* flutter as though about to settle on the ground:
this, of course, is to attract the wild birds to the place.
Mr. Davy then proceeded to arrange his call-birds. These
birds when put out begin to sing, especially if they hear
another bird of the same kind in the distance. The wild
ones, being attracted by the decoys, are shown by the
brace birds the place where they are wanted to go. No
bait is used for the birds; they simply come to the decoy,
and imagine from the call that they, the decoys, are
feeding there.

The brace bird that Mr. Davy put on the flurr stick
had been at work for three years almost daily. He had
been the means of catching thousands of other birds, especially sparrows, ordinarily called 'Jims.' Mr. Davy says
the call-birds get very artful: sometimes they will give a
note of warning or fighting to the wild birds; thus a linnet
will set to hipping, that is calling 'hip, hip, hip,' several
times. This note of the call-bird causes the linnets
coming in a flight instantly to dash away in all directions.

The goldfinch will oftentimes set to 'gidding,' that
is, saying 'gid, gid, gid,' several times in succession.
This has the same effect as the 'hipping' of the linnet.
The birds are off in a moment. Mr. Davy's call-bird
goldfinch was a very good one, and Mr. Davy put his
song into words. By listening attentively I could make

out that the goldfinch did really say the following words. There are two songs of the goldfinch ; one is

Sippat-sippat-slam-slam-slam-siwiddy.

The other is—

Sippat-widdle-widdle-slam-siwiddy kurr-hurotle-chay.

Goldfinches are now becoming very scarce, because the cultivation of land is exterminating the thistles. This year, for the first time, the birdcatchers have gone for them to Ireland, and have sent large takes of goldfinches thence into the London market. During this autumn goldfinches were more abundant ; this may be attributed to the provisions of the Bird Preservation Act. At the end of the year the goldfinches lie up in quiet feeding-places, and remain there as long as the food lasts ; they will not be seen on flight again until April.

The song of the linnet is thus written by Mr. Davy—

Hepe, hope, hepe, hepe,
Tollaky, tollaky, quakey, wheet,
Heep, pipe, chow,
Heep, tollaky, quakey, wheet,
Lug, orcher, wheet.

This is the song of the wild linnet.

The toy linnet is a bird that has been taught to sing by the titlark, woodlark, or yellowhammer ; they are educated at an immense amount of trouble. The linnet is taught 'in-and-in,' 'in-and-in,' *i.e.* by constant repetition ; and only a very few take the perfect song. The song begins thus :—

Pu poy, tollick, tollick, eky quak.
E wheet, tollick, cha eyk, quake, wheet.

This is one stave of the song. Then follow in due order the following staves :—

> Phillip, cha eke, quake, wheet.
> Call up, cha eke, quake, wheet.
> Tollick, eke, quake, chow.
> Eke, eke, eke, quak chow.
> Cluck cluck, chay, ter wheet tollick, eke quake, wheet.
> Echup, echup, pipe chow.
> Ah, ah, ah ! J-o-e.
> Eke quake, chow rattle.
> Tuck, tuck, wizzy ter wheet ;
> Tolliky, quake wheet.

This is the finish of the toy linnet song. When the above song is put together by a properly trained bird it is just like a flute.

To get these birds to take the song they must be taken from the nest very young, before they get the call of the parent birds.

Perfect toy linnets are worth almost any sum of money —15l. to 20l. would be given readily for a thoroughly good one. Broken song-birds are only worth 30s. to 50s. each. A broken song-bird will not make his stops in the song as given above ; he will run one stave into the other. Good toy linnets are very scarce, and their trainers are getting old and dying off.

Towards the middle and end of November the birdcatchers always expect what they designate the ' November flight of linnets.' This great flight generally takes place between the 15th and last day of November. The men lay their nets before daybreak. As soon as it is light the birds appear. They come in flocks of from two to three hundred; the call-birds 'charge,' and give the catchers notice that the birds are coming before they can be seen by the men.

Very large takes of these migratory linnets have been made; as many as five dozen have been taken in some years at one pull of the clap-net. Although so many linnets are captured annually, there has been no general diminution noticed in their numbers. The greater number of these birds are bred on the wild gorse lands, especially in Scotland. They are very prolific, and have three to four nests each season, producing from fifteen to twenty young.

When this linnet migration from the north takes place the birdcatchers are certain that some wild weather is coming behind them. Observers will find this right. The linnets when arriving at the south of England disperse themselves over the stubbles, 'clover lays,' and 'fed-offs;' they eat large quantities of charlock and other wild seeds, which otherwise would be injurious to the farmer. The large takes of these birds in 1878 glutted the bird market. Before the flight cock linnets were worth from four to five shillings a dozen, they soon dropped in price to from eighteenpence to two shillings.

Mr. Davy also had a bullfinch, and it was quite wonderful how this bird would answer him at almost any distance. The call consists of a low, plaintive, melancholy whistle. If any wild bullfinch came within the call of this clever bird he would never let him go away, but keep continually working at him. This bullfinch is always worked in an open-top cage, so that he can either be used inside the nets or for birdliming purposes.

The best time for catching bullfinches is in the black-
berry time, viz. September and October. They also eat
privet berries and dock seed, but they never begin on the
privet berries until after the frost has touched them.

Birdliming is a more sporting mode of catching birds
than netting, and is thus practised. The bullfinch catcher
finds his game principally by his own call. He walks
along suitable lanes and margins of woods, continually
calling with his mouth; this is called 'whooping;' it is
the challenge or call-note of the bullfinch, and sounds very
much like 'whoop, whoop, whoop.' In some parts of the
country bullfinches are called 'whoops.' After a time the
man finds his game by a bird answering his call. He immediately puts down a call bullfinch in a cage, and a twig
already limed near the cage. After a time the decoy 'gets
hold' of the wild bird by his call; the man then ceases,
leaving the bird to finish his work. The wild bird, being
of a pugnacious disposition, challenges the caged bird, and
alighting on the stick he is done for immediately, being
held fast by the lime. It is not an uncommon thing for
a single-handed man to take two dozen bullfinches in a
day; fresh-caught 'bullies' realise to the catcher twelve
shillings a dozen for cocks and three shillings a dozen for
hens.

Cock bullfinches are in some parts of the country
called 'soldiers,' on account of their crimson breasts.
'Bullies' are taught to pipe by being taken very young
from the nest, and having one tune constantly hammered
into their heads either by a bird-organ or by whistling.

Numbers of birds, however, will not take to the song,
in spite of great attention being paid to their education.

The Germans are very clever in teaching bullfinches to pipe. A trainer would think himself very fortunate if four out of twelve ' bullies ' became pipers ; they are worth three and sixpence each ; a perfect piper is worth from three to four pounds.

The nets being spread and the birds put out, we adjourned to the end of the ' pull-line,' in hopes the birds would come, and waited patiently. The silence in the forest was very remarkable. Bully kept on answering Mr. Davy when he chose to talk to him. Davy also talked to the goldfinch and the linnet, and I think Mr. Davy sings the linnet's song better than the linnet himself. He assists himself in trapping linnets by the use of a small whistle. We waited most patiently in silence for the birds to come and be caught. But as Mr. Davy anticipated, nothing came to be caught, not even Jims (sparrows). At last a poor little robin was fool enough to come : in an instant the nets were over him to show us how they acted. Poor little Bobby was taken out of the nets and handled most carefully, and was marked on a feather by the Squire so that he should know him again, I had the curiosity to put the robin to my ear to listen to his heart. The rapidity with which his poor little heart was going was amazing ; is was perfectly impossible to count the pulsations, the sound was like a locomotive letting off her steam. This was caused by the sudden surprise of the moment. Birds cannot change their faces or show any symptom of alarm, or the Bobby would probably have looked white about the gills.

The question has arisen if a robin could be brought to talk. Mr. Keilich, the naturalist, tells me that he knew of a robin who said, 'Pretty Bob; pretty Bob. Come and kiss Bobby.' But Mr. Davy says he has never heard of a robin talking.

The blackbird is a great mimic, or rather mocking-bird. If taken young he will go through one or two songs. Davy had one that would whistle 'Pop goes the weasel,' and 'Hey, jim along, jim along Josey; hey, jim along, jim along Joe.' He would sing at any time at command. Mr. Searle, my secretary, says he heard a blackbird in the Mile End Road sing the principal parts of the Huntsman's Chorus.

If any one wishes to try the experiment of training a blackbird, he must raise one or two young ones from the nest. As a rule, two out of three will take the song taught them. The blackbird is very pugnacious, and this is a drawback to his being kept in an aviary with other small birds.

Wormwood Scrubs was once a celebrated place for catching birds, especially starlings. Mr. Davy has caught there from two to three dozen at one pull of the net. The nets must be laid so as to begin catching at dawn. By eleven o'clock starlings are 'fed up' and are off; they go for shelter into the woods, to get out of the heat of the sun. Five or six dummies—*i.e.* stuffed starlings—are placed near the nets to attract the wild birds, and also one live bird on a 'flurr stick.' The autumn is the best time to catch starlings. They are very artful. It is necessary to 'take a cut' at them—that is, pull the net sharp the moment they get within reach of it. They will often hover over the net, not making up their minds to go in. This is the time to 'cut them in.' The birds about in

August, being mostly young, are not 'up to the game'—
that is, the net work—but they will very soon learn it and
get artful.

Starlings are extensively used for trap-shooting. The
price varies from five shillings to six shillings per dozen.
Directly after the breeding season Mr. Davy would take a
twenty-dozen order at two days' notice.

Sparrows are also much used for shooting purposes.
Large numbers of them leave London after harvest and go
upon the stubbles to feed ; by September there are hardly
any sparrows in London. They return again during the
winter months when ploughing begins. After many
have been caught and their number thinned they become artful, and the moment they see the net they
cry 'Jim, jim, jim,' and are off. An old Jim is as
cunning as an old man, from seeing his pals so often
caught in the net. Sparrows are a great pest at the
Zoological Gardens, entering into the houses, and especially the warm houses in the winter. They are not
at all shy, but enter into almost all the houses where
the animals and birds are fed, helping themselves to the
most delicate morsels and luxuries. In the winter the
sparrows are caught by bat-folding. Bat-folding is
commonly used in the country for catching all kinds of
birds.

Mr. Davy in his time has supplied large numbers of
gentlemen with pigeons (blue rocks) for trap-shooting.
These pigeons are bred in many parts of the country by
thousands in dove-cots, and bought up by the dealers.
Any kind of sharp-flying pigeon is also used when the
price of blue rocks is objected to. Blue rocks vary from

16*s.* to 24*s.* per dozen, common kinds from 12*s.* to 15*s.* Davy has supplied twenty-two dozen or 264 birds a day. After they are shot and brought home, the birds will always fetch 6*s.* per dozen. If in good condition there is always a ready sale.

Pigeons are very pugnacious. If two cock pigeons are put in a cage together, they will fasten on to each other by the beak, and cut away with the wings until one is completely mastered.

Scotch larks are abundant in England; they locate themselves on the clover and grass lands, where they are taken by thousands on dull nights with trammel nets. At the beginning of the winter they are sold dead indiscriminately, both cocks and hens, just as they are caught. By the end of January the catchers can find ready purchasers for the live cock birds. The price of cock larks then rises monthly up to the end of April. In January they fetch four shillings a dozen, in April there is a ready market at twelve shillings a dozen.

Wood-pigeons are very numerous in the early winter, and large numbers are then sent to the London market. They are then in the very finest condition, and are regular 'lumps of meat.' They are very good for table when stuffed with sage and onions and roasted like ducks. When the severe weather sets in, the damage that is done to the farmers by wood-pigeons is great; they destroy large quantities of swedes and turnips, spoiling more than they eat. These birds peck out the heart of the green part in the centre of the turnip; in doing this they make a deep hole, the water then gets in, and the turnips are destroyed by the first frost. In years when there are no beech-nuts, the wood-pigeons make more inroads than ever among the turnips. Wood-pigeons also do much damage to the vetches grown for early lamb-feeding.

The siskins, chaffinches, bramble-finches, and haw-finches that come in the Michaelmas flight, and locate themselves where food is abundant, disappear before winter and the birdcatchers cannot find their whereabouts. In all probability they will not show up again on flight until the middle or end of February. Fieldfares, redwings, and missel thrushes then arrive in large quantities, and are to be found about the environs of London so long as they can get food; they are very wary birds, but the moment frost and snow set in they are easily approached. The redwing of all the thrushes is the most duck-hearted; he will soon succumb to the cold, even when the berry food is abundant; he cannot exist long without 'ground food,' that is, worms and insects.

As it was very hot we sat down in the shade to rest, while Mr. Davy gave us a yarn about his birds. It was unusual for a thrush to be in song so late, viz., August 17, as at this time these birds are in full moult. August, in fact, is the dullest month in the year for song. Nearly all the birds, being 'sore in moult,' hide away in damp shady places. Mr. Davy has put the song of most birds into words. He repeated the words of a thrush's song, and I found by carefully listening that the bird does actually sing the following words :—

> Knee deep, knee deep, knee deep,
> Cherry du, cherry du, cherry du, cherry du ;
> White hat, white hat.
> Pretty Joey, pretty Joey, pretty Joey.

My readers should learn these words by heart, and listen to a thrush singing. They will find the thrush pronounces the above words as nearly as possible. Repeat them all, even when no bird is present, rapidly in a bird-like manner, and see the effect.

It is very difficult to word a blackbird's song. Mr. Davy can imitate a blackbird's song so well that he can bring Mr. Blackbird up to him to be caught, but he cannot put his song into words.

Having got on to the language of birds, Mr. Davy gave us some more examples. I give his reading of the song of the nightingale. The song is commenced in ' wheeting and kurring,' which may thus be written :—

> Wheet, wheet, kurr, k-u-u-r-r-r.

The song after that continues,—

> Sweet, sweet, sweet, sweet,
> Jug, jug, jug, jug, jug,
> Swot, swot, swot, swotty.

They keep on these notes a long time, finishing up with ' swotting and kurring.' The song must be pronounced with great inflexions—crescendo-diminuendo, I think the lady pianists call it; especially modify the ' sweet, sweet,' and pronounce it in a plaintive manner. The ' jug, jug, jug ' is quick, like a dog barking.[1]

[1] The following note has been kindly sent me :—' The " wild bird," whose liquid warble our Poet Laureate, in his " In Memoriam," recognises as characteristic of both joy and grief, had some two hundred years ago his much-loved song reduced to words and letters by a well-known and very learned Jesuit, Marco Bettini. This production was at that time deemed a most successful one, but about a hundred years ago a German naturalist named Bechstein made what many call an improve-

I hear the peasants in Brittany translate the nightingale's song thus :—

> Le bon Dieu m'a donné une femme,
> Que j'ai tant, tant, tant, tant battue
> Que s'il m'en donne une autre
> Je ne la batterais
>   Plus, plus, plus
> Q'un petit, q'un petit, q'un petit.

The wagtails have different calls. The call of the black-and-white wagtail is ' Physic, physic, physic,' quickly repeated, and with a whistle Davy can make them come close up. Listen to the first wagtail you hear, and you will find he invokes the aid of the medical profession.

As there were no small seed-eating birds in the park, Mr. Davy then gave us a lecture on birdlime. He first of all gave us the process of making it. There are two ways of making birdlime. The first is to get a quart of linseed oil and boil it down to a little over half a pint. The process of making it is dangerous. The oil gets so

---

ment on Bettini's " Song of the Nightingale," and I forward you a copy of it :—

> Tiouou, tiouou, tiouou, tiouou
> Shpe tiou tokoua ;
> Tio, tio, tio, tio
> Kououtio, kououtiou, kioutiou, koutioutio ;
> Tokuo tskouo, tskouo, tskouo
> Tsü, tsü, tsü, tsü, tsü, tsü, tsü, tsü, tsü, tsü, tsü
> Kouorror, tiou, tksoua, pipetk souis
> Tso, tso, tso, tso, tso, tso, tso, tso, tso, tso, tso, tso, tso,
> Tsirrhading,
> Tsi, tsi, si, tosi, si, si, si, si, si, si, si, si,
> Tsorre, tsorre, tsorre, tsorreki,
> Tsatu, tsatu, tsatu, tsatu, tsatu, tsatu, tsatu, tsatu, tsi
> Blo, blo, blo, dlo, dlo, dlo, dlo, dlo,
> Kouiou, trrrrrrrrretgt,
> Su, su, su, ly, ly, ly, li, li, li, li.'

very hot that a pipkin is obliged to be used. When boiled down the oil must be poured into cold water, and is then very apt to fly up in the face and scald badly; the stench of it is almost unbearable.

The birds principally caught with birdlime are gold-finches, bullfinches, woodlarks, and chaffinches.

Mr. Davy told us he would make the other kind of birdlime in our presence, if the Squire would allow him to cut off a bit of holly bark from a tree. Davy chose a thick old tree; he cut a piece about four inches square from the outer bark, and divided it into three. He gave the Squire one piece, myself one piece, keeping a piece him-self, and told us to put it in our mouths and chew it. The taste of the bark was of an agreeable bitter—the bitter cup of the chemist's shop. In about five minutes the holly bark, being thoroughly crushed between the teeth, began to be very tenacious, and in about ten minutes the birdlime was produced. It is wonderfully sticky stuff, and it is difficult to rub off the hands, and much more so off the moustache; in fact, at the end of the operation it was difficult to talk. This, then, is a new discovery for the Pharmacopœia. It will be a capital thing for a lady or gentleman who talks too much, if you can only once persuade him or her that holly bark is a tonic which would do them good. In about five minutes it would shut up their chatter.

It is not an uncommon thing in London for clever thieves to place a small portion of birdlime on a walking-stick; the confederate then takes away the barmaid's attention, and the man with the stick takes the coin from the bar. Another trick is to place a small portion of birdlime on a silver coin and give it to the barmaid, and it is amusing to see how she tries to throw it into the till; or, in fact, get rid of it out of her hands at all.

The birdlime we made from the Squire's holly bark turned out very good when it was quite finished. Davy triumphantly showed it to the Squire, and assured us it would 'hold a duck or a parrot; he would not get away unless his feathers came out.'[1]

Mr. Davy had got to this point of his lecture when the gong at the mansion sounded for luncheon, and of course we went back at once. At luncheon I was obliged to give an account of our morning's proceedings, and we all began to 'talk bird.' Sir A. Layard informed me that the swallows leave Venice about St. James's Day, July 25, and the day after they leave the mosquitoes begin. He also told me that in this year all about Verona the locusts came in millions, devouring everything before them, and they were followed up by vast flocks of the roller (*Coracias garrula*), which devoured them in numbers. He also said that when making his discoveries at and about Nineveh the natives used to catch quail in a wonderfully clever manner by throwing a casting-net over them.

He regretted we had not yet introduced the gigantic partridge, the ourkakich, the royal partridge of the Per-

---

[1] The following is a recipe for making birdlime. Peel off the bark of the holly in July, and remove the outer rind, the brown epidermis; put the bark into boiling water in an earthen vessel, and let it remain about a fortnight in a damp place. Then take it out and bruise it well until it becomes a paste. This wash in cold water, to separate all extraneous matters, and leave it for four days, when a sort of scum will appear on the surface. Take off the scum, and the birdlime is fit for use, and will hold a duck as firmly as the famed Polytechnic cement does china.

sians, or Caspian snow partridge. I also learned a new plan they had in Madrid to turn birds into politicians; they dye pigeons various colours, and let them fly when any fun is to be made or politicians are to be annoyed. Doves are also dyed and turned loose when any particular *prima donna* sings at the theatre; the doves being dyed with her favourite colours.

As the name Davy came into conversation, some one asked what was the meaning of the sailor's phrase, 'Davy Jones's locker.' A gentleman present, who had been in India, immediately told us, to our great delight, that 'Deva Loka' is the 'Goddess of Death' in Hindustani. Some English Forecastle Jack must have heard this expression, and put in the word 'Jones' to make it sound right.

The best time for seeing the nets in full operation is at daybreak on commons, waste lands, or seed-growers' grounds. After ten o'clock in the morning the catching ceases to a great extent, for the birds having fed 'lay up.' Towards evening the birds again work the feeding-places, but the birdcatchers have generally then left the ground.

The captured birds are carefully taken out of the net and immediately placed in cages called 'store cages.' The doors of the cages are at the top, and made with the leg of a stocking fastened on: a usual wooden door would not answer, as the birds might slip out when fresh additions were made. All kinds of British birds, from a wren up to a rook, can be taken in the pull net.

During ordinary weather the nets are worked by decoy and 'flurr birds' on the open lands. During the hot weather the nets are worked on the margins of brooks, lakes, or ponds.

Birds will go for miles to a clear-running, gravelly-bottomed stream. An experienced catcher on passing a suitable place can tell it immediately; the signs are that the shallow water on the edge of the pool is muddy, and the tracks of the birds are visible in the mud. Birds frequent the water for drinking, washing, and moulting purposes about midday during the hot weather.

By this mode of netting, which is called 'the water-trap,' many British birds which will take no notice of call-birds are captured. Among these are taken the black and white flycatcher, woodpecker, jays and magpies, doves, woodpigeons, blackcaps, butcher-birds, lesser and larger pettichaps, thrushes, blackbirds, and all the titmouse tribe.

SIR WALTER SCOTT'S HOME AT ABBOTSFORD.

I MAKE it a rule invariably to buy the local guide-book of every place I have to visit. When at Melrose, in September 1879, on an official inquiry into the salmon disease in the Tweed, I found to my delight in the guide-book that Abbotsford, Sir Walter Scott's residence, was not very far off; so I made up my mind to go and visit it, as there was just time so to do before our court began the next day. I was so interested in what I saw, that I now venture to describe the appearance of the home of this illustrious Scotch baronet.

An old college scout at Christ Church, Oxford, one 'Cicero Cook,' held an aphorism that a man's character could be told by the books and surroundings in his study. At Sir Walter Scott's house, therefore, I expected to find a reflex of the thoughts of the great novelist.

The house itself stands at the bottom of a steep declivity which leads from the main road. It is built close to the Tweed, and the Gala water falls into it just below. The general appearance of the house is that of an old castle but built with modern stone, after a design suggested by the antiquarian mind of Sir Walter Scott, who evidently treasured up many things which otherwise would have perished. For instance, the old Tolbooth, of Edinburgh, having been demolished in 1817, the stones of the portal were given to Sir Walter Scott, and rebuilt into a doorway which bears the following inscription :—

> 𝕿𝖍𝖊 𝕷𝖔𝖗𝖉 𝖔𝖋 𝕬𝖗𝖒𝖎𝖊𝖘 𝖎𝖘 𝖒𝖞 𝖕𝖗𝖔𝖙𝖊𝖈𝖙𝖔𝖗,
> 𝕭𝖑𝖊𝖘𝖘𝖎𝖙 𝖆𝖗 𝖙𝖍𝖆𝖞 𝖙𝖍𝖆𝖙 𝖙𝖗𝖚𝖘𝖙 𝖎𝖓 𝖙𝖍𝖊 𝕷𝖔𝖗𝖉.—𝕸𝕯𝕷𝖁𝖁𝖀.

I had to wait a few minutes in the ante-hall before the guide came to conduct us over the house.

In this little room were several very curious prints, especially a picture of a sea-fight, the 'Wolverine,' Captain Montague, taking some French luggers ; a desperate fight between the Russian and Cossack cavalry, 1800 ; and a procession in Edinburgh ; also a trunk made of tiger-skin, probably a present to Sir Walter years ago.

The first room we were ushered into was Sir Walter Scott's study, the furniture of which is left exactly as when Sir Walter died.

The table on which he wrote is an old-fashioned affair, but has many drawers and many wings, just the table to suit a man who had a great many papers to deal with. The arm-chair is covered with leather, the sort of chair into which a busy man would delight to throw himself back and think. Near the fireplace is a piece of furniture made from portions of the Spanish Armada, with this motto : 'Afflavit Deus et dissipantur.' The tables in the dining-hall at Westminster School are made from portions of the wreck of the same Armada. All round the room there are numerous shelves with books, and halfway up the room a gallery with more books, very like what we have at the Athenæum Club. It may be possible that Sir Walter took the hint from the Athenæum, which was founded in 1824, and of which Sir Walter was one of the first members. Behind the chair is a cupboard devoted to Sir Walter's pipes and sticks, and I was delighted to find out that Sir Walter Scott smoked.

Among the books I noticed bound copies of the French newspaper, the 'Moniteur.' I could not think why Sir Walter had such a collection of the 'Moniteur' until Mr. Walpole, who was with me, told me he thought Sir Walter Scott had bound them because they would contain Napoleon's bulletins, and were the official repository of French despatches in those days. In return for his kindness I told Mr. Walpole that I should be only too pleased if I could find any book in the library relating to his family, so I looked about sharp, and within five minutes I caught sight of two—namely, 'Orford's Works' and 'Memoir of Horace Walpole.'

The next room to the study, the drawing-room, is a wonderful place. At one end of it stands an admirable bust of Sir Walter by my godfather, Sir Francis Chantrey.

In a bay-window is a table containing many interesting relics, as follows :—Portrait of James Stuart, born June 10, 1688, died at Rome, 1766. The purse of Rob Roy, also the Skein Dhu (English, black knife or dagger) belonging to Rob Roy. The tumbler used by Burns. Tam O'Shanter's snuff-box. Napoleon's portfolio, ornamented with golden bees ; this, if I mistake not, was presented to Sir Walter by the Duke of Wellington, probably at the time when he was writing 'The Life of Napoleon ; ' the Duke's autograph accompanies Napoleon's portfolio. A lock of Lord Nelson's hair. A lock of the Duke of Wellington's hair.

In this room there are some ebony chairs; these were presented by King George IV.; also some other very handsome old furniture.

In the next room, the dining-room, is a picture of Sir Walter Scott, taken about 1815 by Raeburn, a famous portrait painter. Standing by Sir Walter are represented two hounds, one Maida, the Luffra of the 'Lady of the Lake,' and another hound called Menus.

A portrait of an old lady struck me as wonderful, and I admired it still more when I was told it was Sir Walter Scott's mother. There is also a fine portrait of King James I., and a marvellous bit of work, namely, Camrood s painting of the head of Mary Queen of Scots, the day after this unfortunate lady was beheaded. I was transfixed by this picture, as the features of life seemed to have been suddenly frozen by death into the cold pale face; particularly well did I observe that the lips were pursed up—probably the facial expression of the very last moment of this unfortunate lady. I understand that there is a painting of the head of Mary Queen of Scots in the museum at the old Castle of Heidelberg; this is doubtless a copy of Camrood's masterpiece. The whole of this room is papered with some wonderful and very handsome Chinese paper, said to be all hand-painted.

The walls of the passage leading out of this room are hung with the most interesting relics. A pair of pistols found in Napoleon's carriage after Waterloo, very handsome, handy weapons, engraved ' Versailles.' King James VI.'s hunting flask. The spurs of Prince Charlie. Rob Roy's gun, with the initials 'R.M.C.' The iron mask worn by Wishart, the martyr, at the stake, to prevent his

addressing the people.   The money-box of King James IV.
Bruce's candlesticks, with a most admirable arrangement
for keeping up the candle always to burning point; and
the magnificent tusk of an elephant.

But what much pleased me was a pen-and-ink drawing
of Queen Elizabeth dancing.   It *must* be a good likeness
of the Queen because it is so like the monument in Westminster Abbey, the bust of which, in my deanery days at
Westminster, it was my special province to keep clean.
The Queen is represented as dancing by herself, apparently
unconscious that a lot of gentlemen are quizzing her.
The faces of these worthies can just be seen grinning
through the curtains.   If Queen Elizabeth was not pretty,
the want of facial beauty was, as is very frequently the
case, compensated by an exceedingly pretty foot and
ankle.   Her Majesty wore clocked stockings, and a lovely
little pair of shoes, which, according to the present mode
of measuring ladies' *chaussures*, would be the size called
' small twos.'

This sketch of Queen Elizabeth dancing was, I afterwards learned, made by Charles Kirkpatrick Sharpe, a
great ally of Sir Walter in his antiquarian pursuits, and a
poet and artist, to commemorate a well-known incident.
The Queen, in order to let her expectant successor, James
VI., know that he would have to wait a little longer, set
herself to ' dance high and disposedly,' giving Cecil a hint
that he might let the Scotch Ambassador, Sir Robert
Melville, be an unseen witness of the performance.

In Lockhart's Life of Scott, a letter from Sir Walter
to Mr. Sharpe, at Christ Church, Oxford, is given, dated
Edinburgh, December 30, 1808, which commences as

follows :—'My dear Sharpe,—The inimitable virago came safe, and was welcomed by the inextinguishable laughter of all who looked upon her caprices.' Scott used to expatiate with delight on this drawing to all who visited him at Abbotsford.

The doors of the hall were then suddenly thrown open, and a most interesting place it is. All along the walls are hung cuirasses, helmets, and swords of, I should say, almost every age and period. Above the armour are coats-of-arms, and a double line of escutcheons displays the heraldic bearings of the Scotts, Kerrs, Elliots, Douglas, and other border clans, these reminding us of the flags of the Knights of the Order of the Bath hung up in Henry VII.'s Chapel, Westminster.

The following inscription runs round the walls of the hall :—

> These be the coats armories of the clanns,
> And chief men of name,
> Who kepit the marches of Scotland
> In the auld time for the king.
> Trewe men war they in their time, and in their defence
> God them defendpt.

At the west end of the room are a helmet and cuirass of the French Life Guards ; also the finest head I ever saw of the fossil red deer, forming a capital pair with a magnificent skull of the extinct British ox (*Bos urus*). There were many other objects to which I should like to have given my attention, but my time was limited, as I had to return to Melrose.

I afterwards visited Sir Walter Scott's tomb at Dryburgh Abbey. It is a plain granite tomb in the ruins of what once had been a chapel. It bears a simple inscription indicating that Sir Walter was buried there on September 26, 1832. This, therefore, is the last resting-place of the greatest literary man since Shakespeare's time—historian, antiquarian, poet, novelist, and above all, a really true and good man, an ornament to the country of his birth, Scotland.

SALE OF MANDERS MENAGERIE AT THE
AGRICULTURAL HALL, ISLINGTON.

IN August 1875 I attended the sale of Manders' Menagerie at Islington.

To those fond of practical natural history and living animals a sale like this is a very great treat. Here we meet all our animal-dealing friends—a new profession which has sprung up in our own time. These gentlemen collect at vast expense the inhabitants of the desert and forests, and exhibit them to the public: thus we all get acquainted with the wondrous forms of life which exist in climates where we ourselves never have been, and probably shall never go.

The following is a list of the chief animals sold. I have affixed the prices they fetched :—

Two splendid Lion Cubs, eighteen months old, born at the Agricultural Hall, 150*l*.

A splendid Lioness in Cub, expected to cub by the time of sale, if not previously, 150*l*.

A spotted Hyena (female), 5*l*.

A very fine breeding Lioness, about five years old, 30*l*.

A Leopardess, 30*l*.

A fine young male Panther, 12*l*.

A handsome South American Jaguar (female), 30*l*.

A ditto, 32*l*.

Two Tasmanian Devils, male and female, 6*l.*

A very fine Wombat, 5*l.* 10*s.*

An American Racoon. Five small monkeys, and a Cat, 3*l.*

An American Racoon, 8*s.*

Mongoose in cage—finest specimen in England, 1*l.* 2*s.*

A remarkably fine variegated Mandrill or red and blue Baboon from Abyssinia, the only specimen in England, 105*l.*

A black Canadian Bear (male), 1*l.* 6*s.*

A fine Russian or Grizzly Bear (male), 1*l.*

A very handsome Zebra, the largest in England, 30*l.*

A fine South African Gnu or Horned Horse—very rare (male), 51*l.*

An American Wolf.

A very fine spotted Hyena (male).

A silver-haired Jackal (male), from India.

A young black Donkey (female).

The right of using the title of 'Manders' Royal Star Menagerie.'

A brown golden-colour Java Hare (male), 2*l.*

A black Opossum, great rarity, 11*s.*

Three handsome white- and red-nosed Cockatoos, 1*l.* 10*s.*

A handsome Macaw, yellow and blue, 4*l.* 4*s.*

A ditto, red and blue, 4*l.*

A valuable orange-coloured crested talking Cockatoo, 7*l.*

Three white- and red-nosed Cockatoos.

A very fine Pelican, 4*l.* 5*s.*

A very fine Camel, 7*l.* 10*s.*

A ditto, 7*l.*

A ditto, 20*l.*

A ditto, 20*l.*

A Camel Calf, about four months old, 21*l.*

A handsome female Llama, 16*l.* 10*s.*

Two Milch Goats, 3*l.*

A sheep, 1*l.* 5*s.*

I bid for the Russian bear.   He had the moth in his

coat, and had not good teeth. I had intended to make him into a skeleton, but then I should have had to kill him, and I can't bear to pain, much less kill, anything, and if I had not killed the bear he might have killed me, so I 'let him slide.'

Bob, the bear's good-hearted keeper, nearly shed tears over the low price of this big bear. 'What, Johnny,' he said, 'don't you know your own Bob?' The bear made a grateful 'Ahr! ahr!' as much as to say, 'Bob, hang it all, I'm worth more than a pound even for bear's grease.' 'Bless your heart, Mr. Buckland,' said Bob, 'Johnny and I have had many a dance together round his cage, and he has nursed me in his lap oftener than my mother, ain't you, Johnny, my lad?' Poor Johnny! I wish somebody would buy this poor old bear. I thought to myself, let us sub-scribe and present him to good, kind-hearted Bob, who has known him so many years.

The big mandrill, Jerry, was a rare fine monkey; his nose was the colour of the blue the washerwomen use; he had a most diabolical low forehead, like the demons in Fuseli's pictures, and awful teeth. He would be worse than a tiger to meet in single combat. How they ever got him out of his cage, where he had lived so long, I can't imagine. Bob said he was fourteen years old.

The director of the Bristol Zoological was very sweet on the lioness. His lion at Bristol was a widower, and was looking out for a second wife. A great many lions have been bred at Bristol, and the cubs are always healthy, and their coats, parents and children, 'like the satin of a well-groomed racehorse.' At Bristol they have hit upon the right mode of feeding lions. Instead of everlasting horseflesh, these Bristol lions often get a treat of a goat just killed. This is their natural food; they eat them up, hair, bones, and all, and thrive.

The auctioneer tried to make the buyers think that if they bought the lioness in cub, they would have the chance of her kittens. 'No,' said Bob, 'them as buys her won't get no kittens; she'll eat the lot; she's the wust mother out.' I thought of buying the wolf and jackal, and turning them down in a certain foxhunting county I know, for the hounds to have a bit of a change in their sport. I told Bob about this; he answered, 'Run, sir! that wolf will never run; and he will eat his own weight of sheep in a night;' so I did not buy him.

I had not, however, seen the last of Mr. Wolf. When out on a salmon fishery inspection at Taunton, I went with Mr. Bartlett to see a wild beast show then in the town. One of the most attractive of the performances was the 'Dwarf and the Wild Beasts.' There was a big cage containing three or four largish bears and a wolf. The dwarf, a very funny little fellow, with a hoop in one hand and a stick in the other, walked boldly into the cage, and placing the hoop before each bear in turn, hit him a smack and made him jump through the hoop. The wolf followed the dwarf wherever he went, showing his white teeth and with a perpetual snarl on his face; Bartlett and myself did not like it: the wolf evidently meant mischief to the little man. When Mr. Dwarf came out of the cage, we asked him how he got on with the wolf. 'Well, sir,' he said, 'I'm a bit afeard on him, he follows me about so close like, and he has nipped me twice.' By this time I expect the poor little dwarf has been set upon by the wolf, and finished off by the bears. When we suggested this possibility to the owner of the wild-beast show, he simply replied, 'Shouldn't wonder at all, sir, if it did happen; but look here, sir, what a fine advertisement it would make!'

Poor Mrs. Manders told me that Topsy, the young black donkey was the offspring of a mule. I should have liked to cast her head, but Miss Topsy was too free with her pretty heels to make me love her. I expect she is in a coster-monger's cart by this time.

The first camel, a magnificent beast, hung fire a long time. The first bid was two shillings; then I bid three shillings for fun, and the third bid was four and sixpence. I myself then bid a sovereign, and was very nearly getting him—to my horror, as I thought what ever would Mrs. B. say if I brought a gigantic live camel back to Albany Street! He was a splendid animal. He ultimately brought 7*l*. 10*s*. Bob told me that the beast was dangerous, and would bite tremendously if he had a chance; he had 'nipped' several of his keepers in Bob's time.

The auctioneer did not warrant the camel's temper, which was naturally bad, as most of those present knew quite well. I do not know who was ultimately the pur-chaser. It was somebody, however, who did not know how to manage him, for a few days afterwards Mr. Camel turned rusty, and this is the account of his exploits from the 'Ipswich Journal':—

'PANIC AT A MENAGERIE AT FRAMLINGHAM.—A collec-tion of wild animals was exhibited here on Thursday even-ing last. Feeding-time had arrived, and a considerable number of the visitors stayed. Operations had just com-menced, when an accident caused the greatest terror and

R

confusion to those outside as well as those inside the menagerie. *A camel, a vicious animal,* which had been bought at the late sale of animals in London, and had arrived by train, was standing between two caravans, when suddenly the camel seized the man in charge by the wrist, threw him down, and bit him severely. His cries for help, and the falling down of a board during the endeavour to extricate him, filled the spectators with terror, as it was thought one of the lions had escaped from its cage. Women and children screamed, and the confusion was great. Luckily none of them were hurt.'

I began to wish then that I had bought this dangerous camel, for I should have much liked to dissect him, and to have made a preparation of his wonderful stomach, in which he is said to be able to carry supplies of water all stowed away in little bags ready for use when water fails during his travels across the desert. The great John Hunter had his doubts about this story, and it would have been a great chance for me to have further investigated this point.

I should have had no difficulty in disposing of his body; his skin would have made a carpet, and my cat's-meat man would have bought the flesh and sold it in pennyworths to the London cats on his beat.

PLAYGROUND FOR THE LIONS AND TIGERS AT THE ZOOLOGICAL GARDENS.

It is very pleasing to see what great interest the public now take in living animals. So strong is this feeling, and so great is the knowledge spread abroad about the habits and structure of animals, that artists have to look smartly to their laurels, for if the artist delineates an animal wrongly, he is pretty sure to be found out either by myself or some other naturalist, and justly criticised for his want of proper observation.

Of all created animals, none are so graceful as the large Carnivora. No animals, at the same time, are less patient of captivity; and doubtless these big active cats, that are not born in a den, feel their want of the once-tasted liberty very much. From the days of Mr. Broderip, F.R.S., who, so far back as 1847, wrote that charming book, 'Zoological Recreations,' a desire has been felt that a building should be made large enough to allow these beautiful animals to be observed under conditions when they would have free use of their admirably constructed limbs, and I can recollect the idea being discussed by my father and Mr. Broderip.

After much deliberation and planning, the new lion house at the Zoological Gardens was built in 1878. Space was judiciously left for the erection of large outdoor play-grounds. These playgrounds are large dome-shaped, palatial cages. In the centre of each are artistically arranged groups of tree trunks and rockwork, upon which the animals may disport themselves at will. There are sixteen dens in the lion house, and four playgrounds at the back, so that every set of animals shall have their proper turn in the playground.

The transfer of the large, powerful wild beasts from their old dwelling to the new house was a task requiring very great care and organisation, and a thorough know-ledge of the habits of the animals. It must be recollected that these large Carnivora cannot be taken up by the ears and handled like tame rabbits. They are, moreover, very suspicious, and terribly frightened if there is anything about in the least like a trap.

In former times the usual method of making animals move from one den to another was to set fire to some straw and thus start them, or else to throw a rope round their necks, and when half strangled drag them into the den. Mr. Bartlett wisely preferred to employ persuasion rather than force. A large box, called a 'shifting den,' six feet eight inches long, twenty-four inches wide, and about six feet high, was placed opposite the door of the cage. It was, of course, very strongly built. The animals at first were very shy of going into this box, and were therefore kept hungry, and a tempting bit of meat was put between the bars at the far end of the cage. When an animal entered the box or trap an atten-dant keeper pulled a cord and the slide fell down, making a prisoner of him. This shifting den was, in fact, like a large mouse-trap, with the only difference that it was not self-acting.

Several days were occupied in removing the animals. As it was very desirable that they should be in no way frightened, orders were given to various keepers in the gardens to come to the old lion house directly the bell rang. The trap was then set by the keeper Misselbrook, and everything kept quiet. When the beast, attracted by the bait, had gone into the shifting den, the bell was rung, the keepers at once came up, the trap was placed on a truck and wheeled away, as quickly as was consistent with safety, to the new lion house. Some animals bore their journey better than others. The big young lion was the worst of all. Most of us know how difficult it is to handle a common cat, even when in a bag, and if this be a difficult job, how much more so to handle a lion mad with rage and fear? The male tiger was also very furious. Several of these animals were born in menageries, and had never been trapped before. It was found more difficult to trap and carry these than those which had been caught wild.

It is a curious fact that lions born in travelling menageries are generally stronger than others. In former times the cubs at the Zoo were often born with cleft palates, so that they could not easily suck. Since the mode of feeding has been changed, the cubs are born without any deformity. For some reason lions and tigers breed better at Bristol than anywhere else.

The transfer of the animals from the indoor dens to the playground outside was also a difficulty requiring ingenuity to overcome. A wide passage runs between the dens and the playgrounds : each den in the house has a doorway at the back; immediately opposite this door is a corresponding door in the playground. If, therefore, a communication were made between these two doors, the animals could easily transfer themselves from one place to the other.

An iron box was therefore constructed, both ends of which could be left open or shut at will. This box was mounted on wheels, so as easily to be shifted along the passage by means of a tramway; and thus a through communication was made between any two of the doors as required.

In June 1879 the Carnivora were let out for the first time. On going into the lion house and standing in front of the tigers' den, it was readily seen how admirably the tunnel plan answered. The wondering tigers ascertained that the door at the back of their den was wide open, and being open, that it communicated apparently with the open air. The tigers naturally, therefore, took advantage of what they probably thought to be a chance of immediate escape.

The first tiger that went through the tunnel belonged to H.R.H. the Prince of Wales—a happy coincidence, for is it not right that a tiger's palace should be publicly opened by a royal tiger? This tiger was a cautious gentleman. He approached the tunnel with the greatest caution, testing its stability with his huge paw at every step. Seeing that the tigers were about to come out, I speedily took up a position in front of the open-air playground.

The spectacle of the four tigers coming out into the open was really grand. First, there appeared the head of a tiger; he surveyed everything outside for a minute, and then cautiously came out, creeping along, cat-like, without the least noise, bringing to my mind the answer of Dean Swift, who, upon being asked the meaning of ' walking circumspectly,' answered, ' Have you ever seen a cat walking on the top of a wall studded with broken glass bottles ? well, that is walking circumspectly.'

It was indeed a beautiful sight to see these lovely gigantic cats, the four tigers, gradually emerge one by one into their new large open playground. By a little imagination one might easily fancy that the scene was situated in the middle of India, and that the tigers were coming out from their fastnesses to seek their food.

When they arrived at the open, it was very beautiful to watch them crouch down, making themselves appear as small as possible. Finding nothing to hurt or alarm them, they curiously examined the trunks of the trees and rockwork placed there for their especial benefit. They trusted to their sense of smell and touch for objects near them, and to their sense of sight for objects distant from them.

One of the greatest ornaments the tiger's head possesses besides the regulation V mark over the eyes, which is observable in all thoroughbred tigers, is formed by the long, graceful whiskers, situated for the most part on each side of the upper lip. To the lower end of each whisker is adjoined a very large bulb of nerve-matter, and from this bulb of nerve-matter a nerve goes directly to the brain. This nerve is, in fact, a telegraph wire, and the whiskers are the office at which news is received. If an ordinary cat be examined, and her lips taken between the fingers, these bulbs of nerve-matter will be readily perceived, and if one of the cat's whiskers be gently pulled the effect upon the cat will be instantaneous. When the tiger is crouching for, or gradually creeping up to its prey in the jungle, these whiskers warn it to keep to the right or left, and tell it that the coast is clear or obstructed, so that when the animal's eyes are fully occupied watching its prey, the whiskers act as watchful sentries to guide it.

When the four tigers were loose in their playground, and the door closed behind them, they at once began to play, and very beautiful were their movements as they ran after each other, tumbled, and gambolled like young kittens, their coats looking like satin in the warm sun.

All of a sudden, a new and, to them, a most interesting object made its appearance. This was a young and very white zebu calf of a few days old, which came out of its shed in full sight of the cage only a few yards off.

The moment the Prince's big tiger saw it he crouched to the ground, and remained stationary watching the innocent-looking baby zebu. He was all fixed and statue-like, perfectly motionless except the very tip of his tail, about two inches of which kept jerking from side to side, signifying great anxiety, expectation, and readiness for immediate action. Presently the other three tigers perceived that their comrade had seen something. They also instantly assumed various attitudes of contemplated attack, indicating their intense desire to kill this young zebu calf and eat him.

This group of four magnificent tigers, all intent upon one and the same object, was grand in the extreme. It was also very interesting to observe that the mother of the young zebu seemed to know instinctively that her calf was in danger, as she appeared to warn it in her own peculiar way.

I left the four tigers still looking at the zebu calf, when we adjourned to watch the lions come out into their playground at the other end of the four large iron cages.

These lions seemed to be of a somewhat different disposition from the tigers, more courageous, but not so active. When the door was opened, the two lionesses came out, but not so the old lion. The ladies of the family first inspected their outdoor den, and then retired through their tunnel. I ran round into the house, and found the old lion sitting, looking rather sulky, and evidently much disinclined to move. One of the lionesses then went up to her lord and master and patted him slightly on the face, as much as to say, 'I have looked over our new house; it is a splendid place; so come out and see it.' But the noble brute would not stir, nor do anything else, but in a condescending way, to oblige the ladies, he just peeped through the tunnel.

The idea of letting the large Carnivora roam comparatively loose at their free will has thus at last been realised; and the public will, without doubt, pass a vote of thanks to the Zoological Society by acclamation.

I protest against the idea that every animal is to be killed by man without check or hindrance. Tigers, though frightfully destructive, are not always the ferocious beasts they are represented to be. A sportsman wanting to kill a tiger intrudes on his retirement in his private jungle, and makes the beast savage. When the beast is wounded it turns on its pursuer and is forthwith termed 'a ferocious brute.' A man would become a ferocious brute if he was persecuted by all the world. I like to let all things live, for everything has its use.

I have no practical experience of tigers except in the state of captivity. I observe that caged tigers are not always in a state of ferocity. They will bask in the sun, and seem as happy as a cat before a fire, and I have no doubt that if we could see the tiger at home in his own jungle, we should find that he enjoyed life as much as any pussy-cat can.

I protest against the wanton destruction of wild animals by sportsmen. It is almost impossible to take up any book on foreign sporting without reading of scenes something as follows : An animal, we will say a bear, is seen quietly enjoying himself or having his dinner. The sportsman immediately contemplates the destruction of the bear. He fires a bullet into him, and breaks the bear's leg, giving the poor animal intense agony. The bear then charges the man who has injured him, and if he survives the attack, the sportsman in his book describes the bear as a ferocious brute. I don't think anybody can blame the bear for taking his own part. If the man had left the bear alone, and not begun the row, the bear, on seeing the man, would have most likely sneaked away as quickly as possible.

I believe that if a tiger were not hungry, and not looking out for his food, he would, if he heard the approach of men coming into his home among the underwood, hide or try to sneak away, and if the men passed on nothing would happen. Tigers must, of course, live, and if they are hungry would as soon kill a man, woman. or child, as any other animal. Even in this case I almost doubt if the animal can be called ferocious, as he is only following the instincts of his nature, and we do not apply the term 'ferocious' to a cat when she is killing a mouse. If a dog were to come into the room where a cat had kittens, she would fly at the dog; but this cannot be called ferocity; it is only natural instinct to defend her young; but if a cat came into my room where I am now writing, and flew straight at my face, without any provocation on my part, then I should call it a ferocious cat. Tigers have their uses, and I understand that in districts where tigers are killed down, the wild pigs and deer have so increased that they do much damage to the crops of the natives. One thing, I think, is quite certain, that the balance of nature according to the law of 'eat and be eaten' is so admirably adjusted that it is difficult for man to interfere without disarranging the whole order of things.

TIGER FIGHT AT THE ZOOLOGICAL GARDENS.

In November 1879 a severe fight took place between two of the tigers at the Zoological Gardens—an event, I am glad to say, not very common.

It is customary to place tigers that are likely to pair in the same den. For some time two tigers, the female being a Chinese tiger, and the male a native of Malacca, were mated in the same den. They agreed very well until the day in question. They were playing together quietly, when by accident (I suppose) the lady tiger suddenly struck one of her sharp claws through the septum of the gentleman tiger's nose, tearing it completely through. The male tiger immediately pulled back his head with a jerk, and the lady's claw in consequence cut its way out of the tender skin of the nose, naturally causing great pain and bleeding.

Not liking this sort of courting, the male tiger turned upon and pitched into his sweetheart, rolled her over, and gave her a good thrashing; there the matter would have ended, but as he was walking away, the lady unwisely, and wishing to 'have the last word,' followed him and bit him in the thigh. War to the knife was then proclaimed. The male, the stronger of the two, rushed at her, rolled her over, pinned her by the throat, and the two fought most desperately. The sharp, sabre-shaped, razor-edged canines of the male tiger made a terrible wound in the female's neck, and there was plenty of blood lost on both sides.

Hearing the fight going on with the tigers, the lions at the other end of the house thought that they too might as well have a bit of a fight on their own account. They bristled their manes and hair, lashed their tails, swore a good deal, but luckily did not pitch into each other, although a Frenchman writes, ' *to quiet them*,' to use his own expression, ' I ran up and down ; I made great noises ; I agitated my hat ; I waved my handkerchief to disturb them, but they were agitated by so strong anger, that my efforts were of little effect.'

After the tigers had grappled with each other like two fighting cats, they luckily came near to the bars of their cage, and Sutton, the keeper, who thoroughly understands the management of these big Carnivora, contrived to make the male tiger let go his hold, and got him into one of the sleeping compartments in the den. The lady, who really began the quarrel by scratching the gentleman's face, lay still for some time and bled a great deal, which bleeding probably saved her life. After a while she was induced to creep into her own sleeping den at the back, and though of course her nerves were considerably upset, she was soon all right again, but will no doubt be more careful for the future to carry on her domestic quarrels without such free use of her sharp nails.

N.B.—The best way to stop tigers, cats, dogs, monkeys, or even men and women fighting is to squirt water strongly into their faces. The effect is marvellous. Try it.

POLAR BEAR CUBS.

In December 1871 a beautiful little polar bear cub arrived at the Zoological Gardens from the Arctic regions. It was presented to the society by Mr. Smith, on his return from a voyage to the high latitudes in his private schooner 'Sampson.' He brought home this little bear with him. The sailors christened the little beast Sampson in honour of their vessel. He was a jolly little fellow, about a year old, as far as we could judge, and was installed in a private den next door to the original polar bear, which everybody knew so well, and which came to the Gardens in September 1846. I am sorry to say that Polar Bear No. 1 did not welcome his young relative, Polar Bear No. 2, with such cordiality as one might expect at Christmas-time, for I saw him run at and snarl at him like an ill-tempered old beast as he was. Sampson was about the size of a large Newfoundland dog, but more short and stumpy, with a splendid shaggy coat of long yellow hair, and his general appearance reminded me of an animated door-mat. When he stood on his hind legs he looked like a fat boy with an ulster coat on. As the old polar bear was about six feet in length, and about three feet two inches high, it was not safe to let out the cub into his den, as the cub would have had no chance if the 'old man' pitched into him.

The natural history of the polar bear is very interesting, for there is a great deal in his economy which is well worthy of study, as proving the grand old rule that the structure of every animal is admirably suited to the climate in which he lives and the duties he has to perform. What can be a more wonderful example of the adaptation of structure to the mode of life than that which we find in the polar bear ? In the first place his coat is white. Most Arctic creatures are white ; doubtless because white is a bad conducting colour. Again, the hair of the polar bear is exceedingly long, and yet it does not easily become wet. After he has been in the water the animal has only to shake himself, just as we trundle a mop, and he will dry in a few seconds. If this were not the case, when at home the poor polar bear, after a dip in the water, would soon be a mass of ice.

I have the foot of a polar bear now before me. I find an admirable provision in this foot for preventing its owner slipping on the ice. As an old woman ties a bit of list on the bottom of her shoes to prevent slipping in frosty weather, so we find a somewhat similar provision in the bear, the sole of whose foot is nearly as hairy as the top of his head, only the hairs on the foot are thinner and longer.

A polar bear has to walk nearly all his life upon nothing but snow and ice. If, therefore, he had not natural snow-shoes, his life would become a burden to him. If we watch the polar bear walking at the Zoological Gardens, it will be seen that he goes with a kind of shuffle, lifting his feet but a little way off the ground, so that he can get over the ground quickly, and without fear of a slip. It has been aptly written, 'The paths of the bear, when he ranges in quest of his food, are mostly on the ice; and he has frequently to stand upon ice while by main force he hauls his food out of the water; and that food consists often of living animals, which of course make all the resistance in their power. But the vast size of the bear's paws enables him to stand on a broader base than even the elephant, while the great length of his neck gives him the power of reaching to a considerable distance. His claws are neither so long nor so crooked as those of the land bears; and, from their form, they are digging claws more than climbing or prehensile ones. These agree with his habits. He is not a climber, and he cannot well be, for there is not much to climb in the places of his habitation save rocks and icebergs. The form of the claws enables him to dig his food from under the snow when such an operation is necessary; and the texture and colour of his coat render him proof to all the vicissitudes of seasons and weather.'

As we find lions, tigers, leopards, &c., in warm climates, who keep in check the superabundance of the herbivora, so we find in the Arctic regions that the polar bear keeps in check the seals and walruses, for these animals form the chief food of the great Arctic carnivore, though he will eat fish as well when he cannot get a good plump seal or an aldermanic walrus.

The seals have air-holes in the ice, and Mr. Bear catches them ' on the hop ' when the poor things come up to breathe; he also stalks them when on the ice floes, coming up as quiet and almost as invisible as a white cat hunting rats and mice when deep snow is on the ground. I must say I should like to see a battle between a polar bear and

a walrus, though I think the sharp canines of the bear
would be a match for the walrus's ivory pike-like tusks,
should he once get within biting range.

The seal seems to be the chief food of the bear, and
in capturing it he exercises great ingenuity and patience,
rivalling the Esquimaux in the manner in which he will
sometimes sit for half a day watching it, and if unable to
take his prey by approaching it on the ice, getting quietly
into the water to leeward of his intended victim, gradually
nearing it by a series of short dives, and at last coming
up just under the spot where the seal is lying. If this
manœuvre is successful there is no chance for the seal, as
by rolling into the water it falls into the paws of the bear;
while if it lies still, its pursuer, by a powerful spring,
pounces upon it on the ice. If, however, the seal per-
ceives the bear in time, and escapes by a dive into the
water, Bruin's indignation knows no bounds, and is most
ludicrous to behold. When approaching a seal on the
ice, the bear doubles his fore paws up under him and
pushes himself along by means of his hind legs until
within easy distance for a spring, and consequently the
upper part of his fore paws gets rubbed quite bare.

During the winter, when hard driven by hunger, the
bear does not scruple to attack a man; and many hunters,
while engaged in visiting their seal-nets, have been un-
comfortably surprised by feeling a smart blow on the
shoulder, and finding a rough old bear standing over them.
It is said that the only way of escaping in such a case
is to feign death, and to shoot the bear while watching
you. A native of Upernavik, however, who had just
pulled up a seal in his net, received a pat from a bear, who

took no further notice of him, but at once applied himself to the seal and commenced to devour his favourite food.

What lots of things must be going on in the Arctic regions that we know nothing about, and, I regret to say, are not likely to know! In most, I am afraid all, books of Arctic travel, we read accounts of polar bears being seen; then comes the old story—'out with the rifles'—and away somebody or other goes to kill the poor beast. 'Somebody or other' possibly misses the bear, who, of course, charges, and perhaps nips his enemy pretty smartly. The shooter comes home and writes, 'The ferocious brute then felled me to the ground, and made his teeth meet in my arm,' &c., &c., 'Ferocious brute,' indeed! I think the boot is on the wrong leg. The bear is at home, the shooter is a stranger, and if he chooses to insult Mr. Polar Bear on his own estate, he must take the consequences.

I now give an old, but yet I believe a true story, to show how cruelly these poor polar bears are used.

When a certain frigate, which went out to make discoveries towards the North Pole, was locked in the ice, the man at the mast-head one day gave notice that three bears were approaching towards the ship. 'They had, no doubt, been invited by the scent of some blubber of a sea-horse that the crew had killed a few days before, which had been set on fire, and was burning on the ice at the time of their approach. They were a she bear and two cubs, nearly as large as the dam. They ran eagerly to the fire, and drew out of the flames part of the flesh of the sea-horse that remained unconsumed, and ate it voraciously. The crew from the ships threw great lumps of the flesh of the seahorse, which they had still remaining, upon the ice. These the old bear fetched away singly, laid every lump before her cubs as she brought it, and, dividing it, gave to each a share, reserving but a small portion for herself. As she was fetching away the last piece, the sailors levelled their muskets at the cubs, and shot them both dead; and in her retreat they wounded the dam, but not mortally. Though she was herself so dreadfully wounded that she could scarcely crawl to the place where her young lay, she carried the lump of flesh she had fetched away, as she had done others before; tore it in pieces, and laid it before them; and when they did not eat, she laid her paws first upon one and then upon the other, endeavouring to raise them up, uttering the most piteous moans. When she found she could not stir them, she went off, and when she had gone some distance looked back and moaned; and that not availing to entice them away, she returned, and smelling round them, began to lick their wounds. She went off a second time as before, and having crawled a few paces looked again behind her, and for some time stood moaning. But still her cubs not rising to follow her, she returned to them again, and, with signs of inexpressible tenderness, went round, pawing them, and moaning. Finding at last that they were cold and lifeless, she raised her head towards the ship, and uttered a growl of despair, which the mariners returned with a volley of musket balls. She then fell between her cubs, and expired in the act of licking their wounds.'

This was a nice bit of cruelty. Reader, do you not agree with me?

I understand polar bear's flesh can be eaten, but that it tastes rank and fishy. The liver is reported to be

s 2

poisonous. Polar bears pair in July and August. They
are said to hybernate about Christmas-time, and to come
out in April ; they get under the snow, and make a kind
of nest deep down in a snow-heap, and go to sleep till
the weather softens. I know not how far this is the fact.
There are but few naturalists in the Arctic regions in the
depth of winter, when the bears would be hybernating.
It is now more generally believed that only the female
while with young retires during the cold season.

Polar bears often grow to an enormous size. I find a
record of one which measured eight feet seven from the
snout to the root of the tail, and weighed 1,600 lbs.

My friend Captain Gray kindly presented me with a
magnificent skin of a polar bear. It is a lovely white
colour, and the fur as thick as an Axminster carpet. It
measures eight feet in length, and eight feet across the
fore paws, and seven feet six inches across the hind paws.
The beast which wore the skin must have been an enormous animal, yet they are sometimes much larger.
Captain Gray writes me as follows :—

‘Bears attain a very large size. I shot one in 1870
eleven feet from nose to tail, and eleven feet across the hind
legs. I would not say that this was by any means the largest
I have seen, but it was the most perfect I ever came across.
Males before they attain this size are generally destroyed
in encounters amongst themselves. Bears are great swim-
mers, and it takes a smart pull in a whale-boat to come up
with one if it is any distance away. They only use the fore
paws in swimming ; the hind legs are at rest, and stretched
out behind them. They can dive, too, like a whale, down
at one side of a piece of ice, and up at the other, when

pursued, or hunting for food. I was very much amused on one voyage at a certain bear; he was upon a sheet of very thin ice, and when he came to a place which could not bear him, he lay down flat, stretching out his legs both behind and before, and pulled himself along by his fore paws, thus covering as great a surface of ice as possible; and when he did fall through, which he did frequently, he dived for some place where he found firmer footing.'

It has often struck me as curious that the polar bear should be represented by a group of stars which keep their silent watch, during the long dismal Arctic winter, over the very place where he reigns supreme. Everybody knows the constellation of the 'Great Bear' and how that his two foremost stars indicate the position of the pole-star. The Phœnicians gave this constellation the name of Dubbe et Chaber, or the 'Great Bear'; the Hebrews and Arabs called it Dub Achber, the 'Great Bear,' and, above all, is not the bear-keeper Arcturus mentioned in that most marvellous and grand Hebrew poem, the Book of Job, in the following soul-moving lines?—

> And he setteth a seal about the stars,
> Bowing the heavens himself alone,
> And treading on the heights of the sea;
> Making Arcturus, Orion, and Pleiades,
> And the chambers of the south.

I am told by a missionary who has been living among the Esquimaux and Indians in North America along Lake Athabaska, the Great Slave Lake, the Mackenzie River, and Buckland Mountains (so named after my father by Sir John Ross) on the border of Alaska, that the Esquimaux have discovered that in the fur of the polar bear there is a peculiar repellent power of snow; thus when people come in covered with snow, it is the custom to brush the snow off their fur dresses with a piece of polar bear skin. The philosophy of the fact is not apparent, but still it is a fact that in these far distant countries, polar bear skin clothes-brushes have long been used as snow-brushes.

In November 1876, Sir Allen Young, who had lately returned from the Arctic regions in the s.s. 'Pandora,' called upon me, with the medical officer of the ship, Dr. Horner, and asked me to prescribe for a young polar bear (then at the Zoological) which they had brought home in the 'Pandora' as a present for his Royal High-ness the Prince of Wales. The following morning the death of the bear was announced, and Captain Young allowed me to make a cast of him. Mr. Searle, therefore, went to the gardens, and brought the poor bear in a sack from the dissecting-room to Albany Street. I found making the mould a matter of very great difficulty and labour, but I finished it, and there is now in my museum a most perfect cast of a polar bear; almost every hair is perfectly marked, and the features of the poor beast are marvellously lifelike. This young bear measured five feet in length, and weighed from two to three hundred pounds. Dr. Horner has kindly given me the following memoir of the pet of the 'Pandora':—

He was captured off Cape Horsburgh, North Devon, in the north-west of Baffin's Bay, while swimming in the water in company with two other bears. Nothing but their three heads could be seen from the ship, making off as fast as pos-sible, every now and then looking anxiously round to see if mischief was intended. A boat was lowered, which, with a little hard pulling, soon overtook them, when the old mother and also one of the young ones were despatched by a shot in the head. Our little friend was only captured after considerable difficulty, for he showed no intention of letting the noose which was held out to him drop quietly over his head, but ducked and dodged round the boat, making the most frantic efforts to become an inside passenger, and bellowing loudly the whole time. When secured, he was dragged to the ship, and after being allowed to expend a little of his superfluous energy in trying to board her, was hauled on deck, and firmly chained to a staple. He soon recovered from this operation, and lost no time in showing his temper had already been spoilt, and that the only sugar-plum to which he was partial was the calf of man.

He was considerably larger in size than the other young bear, a female, which led the captain to suppose that he must have been only the adopted child of the old bear, who had perhaps swopped him with another of her sex for one of her own offspring. At all events, when she was being skinned and cut up, he showed the greatest interest in the operation. At night he had to be contented with the skin of his mother, to which he clung affectionately, and went to sleep.

The next morning he was in as bad a humour as ever, and would listen to no one who did not offer him a piece of seal's blubber.

A few nights after this, Bruin managed to get loose, and had he not been detected in the act he would probably have had the quarter-deck to himself in a very short time.

He had a small cage rigged up for him over the

officers' mess-room, with just space for him to turn round. Here he remained during the rest of his journey to England, making himself extremely disagreeable at times, though on the whole behaving himself as well as bears can be expected to do under such trying circumstances. Like other folks, he had his likes and his dislikes. He had a strong partiality for an old Esquimaux dog called King, whose greatest pleasure was to steal bits of his food from between the bars of his cage, or have a bite at one of his paws should it chance to be exposed. If Bruin seemed at all down in the mouth, the sight of old King would revive him at once. Like all children, little Brownie could not get on without playthings, and for lack of anything better he would rattle his chain with his paw till he tired of it, and then set to and roar for hours together, amusing no one but himself, but rather to the discomfort of those who were in the room beneath him. It was curious, too, to notice how noisy and irritable he always became when the ship approached land or was in the neighbourhood of ice. He evidently smelt their presence, for he would put his nose between the bars, and sniff with as much satisfaction as if it were eau de Cologne. One great drawback to having him on board was that he frightened all the seals away, for they have no greater enemy than a bear; so that after he became a passenger the larder was seldom decorated with that luxury, seal's meat.

He was just at that troublesome age, too, when young bears cut their teeth, so that he liked something hard to bite. This was shown by his gnawing through several bars of wood in his efforts to bring forward a troublesome tooth, but it took a long time coming through. His age must have been about six months, if born in March, as is usual among bears. He was fed chiefly on seal's blubber, but was a little dainty at times, when he would only consent to drinking the oil. For a change he would be allowed a little seal's or bear's meat, or perhaps a bird now and then.

It is the custom among whalers to call these bears 'Brownies,' not because they are brown, but because they are white. We therefore christened our captive in the orthodox manner, and called him Brownie. However ill adapted a name it seemed at first, it became him well enough after he had been on board a month or so, in spite of his having a wash-down every morning as regularly as the decks.

The warmth of this more southerly climate did not suit him at all. He could do nothing but lie down and pant, and lick ice or drink water all day if the sun came out. 'My constitution won't stand this,' he used to say. 'I can't even cut my teeth properly;' and, poor fellow, he was quite right, for they were the death of him. He had a fit of an epileptiform character the second day after reaching England. He was a few days afterwards transported to the Zoological Gardens, where he moped and pined away, eating nothing except two herrings for the space of about a week. He felt the parting with poor old King more than anything. Poor Brownie! he could not last long at this rate, so he died one unlucky Friday.

The tale of Ursa Minor is now told. He was a noisy but well-meaning sort of baby, and had he lived he would, no doubt, have been an honour to his country and his race.

DESCENT OF
THE LION FROM NORTHUMBERLAND HOUSE.

On July 2, 1874, I was fortunate enough to witness an event which, though carried out without display or ceremony of any kind, was yet truly historical. The poor old lion who had braved the battle and the breeze at the top of Northumberland House, Charing Cross, for no less than 125 years, descended from his exalted look-out, to be lost to sight (as far as the wayfarers at Charing Cross are concerned) for ever.

I was most fortunately passing to the Home Office, Whitehall, when I spied our dear old friend the lion swinging in mid-air. Scaffold-poles had been erected over him; a strong rope three times round a pulley ended in a hook, and the poor lion was gradually and slowly going up, and up, and up. His venerable body was enveloped in sacks, and chains (to which the pulley was fastened) surrounded him. As he swung in mid-air he looked round—a great, long look round—for the last time, the very last time.

At last his paws were well off the stand, and he began to descend very slowly. The poor brute cried, I am sure he did. If he did not, I felt inclined to shed a tear for him, he looked so utterly miserable and crestfallen; and so he well might. Just as his noble face was eclipsed by the parapet, I fancied I heard him roar a roar of agony, indignation, and despair. I took off my hat and waved him a last adieu, but I had not seen the last of him. After a while he reappeared in his descent, with his noble face gazing out between the walls of the arch, at the top of which he had so long stood a silent but splendid sentry. As the men steadied him in the air he swung once heavily forwards, and positively made a low bow by dipping his head forward to myself and the crowd standing by the fountains. He then descended bodily out of sight, and the crowd dispersed with a melancholy look about them. I was pleased to see this, as the lion is the emblem of England; and we English do not like to see lions going downwards—they should always be going upwards.

I then with a sorrowful heart copied the inscription under the lion, as I saw a man begin work with a pickaxe at the top of the parapet, and the inscription might not be there the next morning. It ran thus:—

ALG: D: S 1749. C: N: REST

Under this, on the east side, was a monogram of the letter A with an S twisted into it; on the west side the letter N with a P: below this was a crest, viz. a coronet with five spikes, carrying round balls, and underneath a half-moon; on the other side was a coronet of different pattern, with three strawberry leaves and a phœnix rising from the flames;—the former was the earl's, the latter the ducal coronet.

As I was walking away very melancholy I felt that I should just like to pay my respects to the poor old lion.

I knocked the big knocker at the gates, and gave the porter my name and business. The porter, who recollected me, at once conducted me on to the roof, where I found the old lion looking like a grand Egyptian lion of the Pyramids.

I measured the lion, and the result is as follows : From tip of nose to end of tail, eleven feet seven ; tail, four feet three ; height at shoulders, five feet five ; round the mane, six feet ; weight, about one and a half tons.[1] The body is lead, the tail copper. When closely viewed this noble lion is not pretty ; his features, especially about the lips, nose, &c., are very deep-cut cavities, and the mane is coarse ; the legs also appear rather clumsy ; but this shows the talent of the artist who made him, for he knew, of course, that his lion would only be seen from the street below ; he was, therefore, obliged to cut in the lines pretty deep; the result, as Londoners for one hundred and twenty-five years past well know, being an immense success. If the lines had not been well marked, the lion from below would have looked sleek and cat-like, and not like the noble British lion he is. There were three coats of paint on the lion ; one was bright blue. He was painted blue in 1822 by the then Clerk of the Works.

The inscription, when interpreted, runs as follows :—

ALGERNON, DUKE OF SOMERSET, 1749, (AND THE) COUNTESS
NORTHUMBERLAND RESTORED.

---

[1] I give for comparison the measurements of the old lion that died at the Zoological Gardens May 1872 :—Nose to tip of tail 9 ft. 1 in., nose to tip of ear 1 ft. 7 in., across upper portion of mane 2 ft. 5 in., tail 3 ft. 2 in., round forearm 1 ft. 3 in., tip of foot to top of back, 2 ft. 10 in., at withers 2 ft. 7 in.—a fine fellow who died of old age, known to be twenty years old.

The Duke began, his daughter finished, the restoration. The lion represents the *blue* lion, the crest of the Percy family, Earls of Northumberland. The stone on which the lion stood, and into which his paws were fastened with long iron rods leaded in, represented the *chapeau d'honneur* of the crest.

Northumberland House was first built by Henry Howard, Earl of Northampton, in 1603; and the fourth side of the square was added in 1636. The front was restored when the lion was put up in 1749.

The lion was carefully lowered to the quadrangle below, and then taken to the Duke of Northumberland's residence at Sion House, where, after 125 years' service at Charing Cross, he has begun life again. He was packed up in a low cart, such as are used for carrying marble slabs, and was then wheeled away in state down Whitehall, I following behind, explaining to the crowd of people who collected to stare at the lion's face, as he glared at them out of the straw packing in the cart, who and what this noble lion was. Dear old Northumberland lion! good luck to you and the noble family you have represented so many years, and whom I trust you will continue to guard in health and wealth, peace and prosperity, for centuries to come.

LORD BUTE'S BEAVERS.

In August 1872 the Marquis of Bute wrote to me as follows: 'I am anxious to obtain some live beavers to turn out in the Isle of Bute. I thought the climate in Wales, which is hot, close, and exceedingly wet, would not suit them so well as the clear and sharper, albeit mild climate of the west of Scotland, where I have streams running through pine woods, which I think would suit them well.' I wrote to North America and many other places to get beavers for the Marquis. At last we managed to procure, in October 1874, four—one pair from France and one pair from America. They were carefully packed and sent to Scotland, but unfortunately they did not live very long. In December 1874 the Marquis wrote me as follows: 'The beavers, when they were originally turned into their enclosure, all took to the water, burrowing under the banks, and have hardly been seen since. The original and biggest pair, which came from France, disagreed with the smaller pair from America, growling and flying at them when they met. They established themselves in the swampy part of their demesne, damming up the river, an operation which they have had to renew, more than once, owing to floods. The traces of their work are apparent all about, in cutting down trees, for

which purpose they avoid, except in one case, the Coni-
feræ, I suppose because of the taste. Holes became
manifest, and also a great round heap of sticks near the
water, which we discovered a few days ago was the roof of
their house, the dwelling part being a chamber excavated
in the earth, and approached by at least two long passages,
one of which opens under the water of the stream, and
the other on to the land, but both under the water-level
of the swamp. This residence is occupied by the French
pair, or one of them. It was suspected that one or more
had escaped, and a day or two ago the usual gnawing and
damming phenomena were found on the moors, a good
way from the enclosure, in a little hollow where there is a
stream with a quantity of whins and some small alders or
birches. And now I hear one is found dead, I suppose in
the neighbourhood of the last-mentioned spot. I believe
it is one of the Americans.'

Shortly after this two dead beavers arrived from the
Marquis; one, the larger of the two, I began to dissect at once, and the following are its dimensions:—
Extreme length, three feet four inches; tail, ten inches;
weight, about twenty pounds.

The hind feet were five inches long and four inches
wide. There is a strong web between each toe. The two
innermost toes have a second nail fitting accurately into
the primary one; the edges of these are very sharp. The
animal probably uses these nails for cleaning his fur.
The other toes are rounded and broad, so as to enable the
animal to scratch.

The femur or thigh-bone was four inches long, and
over an inch wide in the widest part.

The fibula is thrown out behind the tibia in the form of a bow; the heel-bone is also curiously arranged so that the beaver can easily sit up on his haunches.

The clavicles or collar-bones are very large, measuring in this specimen two and a half inches long, and one-fourth of an inch across. The muscles of the fore-arm are exceedingly strong. These muscles and collar-bones give the animal very great power where the use of a fore-arm is required. They use their fore-arm to push along in front of them logs of wood and other building materials, thus transporting their heavy weights by water, not land. The collar-bone is also of very great importance to the animal in its building operations.

I was much astonished to find the œsophagus or gullet so small. It is not large enough to admit the little finger. The same strange conformation may be observed in the œsophagus of the otter.

The stomach is very simple, and not large for the size of the animal: it contained a large quantity of gnawed wood or bark. There is a remarkable gland situated at the junction of the œsophagus and the stomach; I do not know its use, unless it is to secrete a fluid to help dissolve the woody material which goes into the stomach. The small intestines are very long and small; the larger intestines are exceedingly capacious. The colon is the size of a quart pot. The whole of this part was gorged with gnawed wood.

The brain is very large and highly developed; this one would expect with such an exceedingly intelligent animal as a beaver. The brain is about the size of a large walnut, and weighs one and a half ounces. No nerves are specially developed except the olfactory; the foramen in the skull for the nerves going to the whiskers, which is so large in the seal and otter, is exceedingly small in the beaver.

There are twenty-six vertebræ in the tail; the sides of these vertebræ are very widely expanded, so as to form a secure attachment for a very peculiar cartilaginous substance which forms a substructure of the tail. This cartilaginous substance is interlaced with numerous tendons, which work the tail, and is covered with a rather thin skin, thickly studded with scales. The tail itself measures ten and a half inches in length and five and three quarter inches in width. There are eighty-three scales counting down the centre line in a longitudinal direction, and twenty-two counting in a cross direction. The whole mechanism of the tail and hind legs forms a most admirable support to the beaver when building his house, the wood for which he cuts with his splendid chisel-like teeth. I am quite against the idea of the beaver using his tail as a trowel; the animal uses it as a prop to support his heavy body while engaged in gnawing, and also as a rudder, especially when diving or rising to the surface. These uses can easily be seen in the beavers at the Zoological. The arrangement of the pelvis bones and tail reminds me very much of that seen in the fossil mylodon, the gigantic creature which gained its living by pulling down boughs of trees when in a sitting attitude.

The teeth are as sharp as chisels, the outside being of an orange colour. The upper teeth measure three-quarters of an inch, the lower one inch: both are wide.

T

The beaver is a typical rodent, or gnawing animal, and its teeth are most beautifully adapted for the carpenter's work it has to do. The following is a capital account of the beaver's carpenter's tools :—

' His cutting teeth are two in each jaw, very large and strong, and standing so far clear of the lips that the animal can easily gnaw or cut a hard substance without the least danger of injury to these. The structure of these teeth, though common to most of the order, is peculiar and well worthy of notice. On their front sides these teeth are broad and flat, not white, like the teeth of most animals, but of a brownish yellow or chestnut colour. They have along the front surface a plate of very hard enamel, which covers the bone or principal substance of the tooth, just as a piece of steel may be seen covering the iron on the cutting edge of a chisel, which is both sharp and not liable to be broken. The body of the tooth is compact, but not very hard bone, and it is strengthened by a projecting ridge on the posterior surface, in the same manner as hoes and various other tools are fortified by a ridge extending from the socket which receives the handle. The tooth is thus formed upon the most skilful mechanical principles, both in the distribution of the materials and in the form. Bone, though not so hard a substance as enamel, is tougher, just as iron is tougher than hardened steel. The softness makes it wear faster than the enamel, and the toughness makes the tooth less easily broken. If the whole tooth had been enamel, it would have in time got blunted by the cutting edge wearing down faster than the rest; but the bone wears with less action than the enamel, and thus the enamel always stands highest

and forms a cutting edge, while the bone supports it
behind like the basil or sloping edge of a tool. Thus the
cutting tooth of the beaver is a chisel; and whether the
carpenter's chisel has been made in imitation of it or not,
the same arrangement of iron and steel as there is of bone
and enamel in the tooth, is the best possible for a chisel
of all work. There is one property in the chisel of the
beaver, however, which no art of man can give to the
chisel of the carpenter: the incisive or chisel teeth in the
beaver have not roots consisting wholly of bone, as in the
teeth of most animals, and as in the grinders of the
beaver itself; they are inserted deeply in the jaws, but
in a peculiar kind of socket, a socket which exists only
during dentition in other teeth. These sockets continue
gradually to produce the tooth in such a manner as
that both bone and enamel grow at the root as fast as
they are worn down at the point, and consequently
the chisel teeth remain in good condition during the
whole life of the animal. Their chisel edges are directly
opposed to each other, so that when the animal bites it
bites clean, just in the same manner as a workman
cuts a wire or other small piece of metal with his cutting
pincers.'

Many curious things are told about beavers' teeth.
Thus: 'Wherefore the biting of this beast is very deep,
being able to crush asunder the hardest bones, and commonly he never looses his hold until he feeleth his teeth
gnash one against another.'

Anxious to make as much of this large specimen as
I could, I propped up the beaver in position, and then
made a cast of him, which is now in my museum, and

which I am happy to say came out exceedingly well, recording the outlines and characteristics of this remarkable animal better than any stuffing can do. The markings on the tail came out splendidly.

I made a most careful examination of the 'castoreum,'
and afterwards a splendid preparation of it. The castoreum is secreted by two glandular bodies, each about an
inch and a half long. These I ascertained, by means of a
bristle, communicate with a pouch, which appeared quite
flaccid. I introduced a blowpipe, and was delighted to find
that there existed an immense pouch. The moment it was
full I cast it, so as to preserve its exact shape, and found
that when fully extended the pouch measured eleven and
a half inches long over the bend, and eleven inches round,
and would contain about a pint of water. I have not
the least idea of the use of the pouch. The castoreum
itself is a resinous kind of secretion, and when burnt has
a highly aromatic odour.

Two kinds of castor are met with in the drug trade;
the best is from Russia, Prussia, and Poland, but is now
scarcely to be obtained. The pods are large and firm, and
their contents dry, of a red-brown colour, pulverulent, but
somewhat tough, of a strong and peculiar odour, and a
bitter nauseous taste. The castor ordinarily sold is imported from Canada. The pods are usually flatter, smaller,
and moister than the former, and their contents so miscellaneous as to baffle all attempts at description. The
matter which they contain is commonly of a yellow or buff
colour, of a resinous appearance, and a faint odour.
Sometimes it is soft, viscid, and fetid in the extreme;
sometimes unctuous, and sometimes black and inodorous.

The yellow resinous kind is usually preferred, but it is difficult to say on what grounds.

Castor has been extolled as a safe and effectual anti-spasmodic in typhus, hysteria, and epilepsy; but its uncertain composition and quality, and its extremely high price, are objections to its use. Moreover, its virtues are of a very doubtful description, and it seems uncertain whether any real benefit has followed the use of the drug in its most genuine form. It has been administered in doses of from ten to twenty grains, the tincture is also prescribed as an addition to anti-nervous mixtures.

As regards the use made of this castoreum by the animal himself, Lord Bute made the following observations:— 'Two of the animals were for a long time shut up in a part of the battlements of the castle at Cardiff, where I had a temporary pond built for them, and could watch them very well, which I did. They would often come out and sit upon the edge of the water, *grooming* their coats with their forepaws. The action was something between a cat washing, and a monkey scratching itself. They would scratch their heads, and then rub their faces with both paws. The effect was extremely grotesque, very much heightened by the creatures' imperturbable look of stupid gravity. On these occasions I always observed a peculiar action, which I never doubted was that of taking the castoreum on their paws and lubricating their bodies with it.'

In November 1874 a third dead beaver was sent me by the Marquis, who wrote: 'Another of the beavers is dead. It was seen quite well apparently, as late as Sunday morning, when it was working at a tree which it had just succeeded

in felling.   On Tuesday it was found dead.   The only one,
therefore, which is, as far as I know, alive, is one of those
which escaped to the moors.   It is exceedingly provoking,
and to me quite inexplicable.   The climate here cannot
be worse than that of Canada; the inclosure in which
they were is very large, indeed, they never seem to have
visited six-sevenths of it; the variety of trees offered to
their ravages is very great, and they took to the alders,
and, to a certain extent, the oaks, quite freely.   Perhaps
your *post-mortem* may enable you to give some solution.
I am very loth to abandon the effort to acclimatise
them altogether.   I have just had a conversation with
the gamekeeper, who has taken much interest and trouble
in the matter.   His opinion is, first, that the beaver which
escaped on to the moors is dead, as no new traces of
work appear; second, that the two French beavers were
too much domesticated, and accustomed to be fed, particularly with special food, such as bread, corn, willow bark,
&c., to be able to shift for themselves in a wild state; and
third, that if the American (and wilder) ones had not
escaped, they would have lived; and that, with attention to
these points, one need not despair yet.'

The third beaver, which I was so sorry to find on my
dissecting-table, measured three feet three inches, and
weighed twenty-two pounds and a half.   There were no
marks whatever of external injury.   On taking off the
skin I found there was little or no fat, and that the
animal was very much out of condition; there was no food
in the stomach, but a quantity of gnawed vegetable matter
in the intestines.   Knowing that the Marquis would be
anxious to have as much information as possible on the

cause of the poor beast's death, Mr. Bartlett came down to give his opinion. He considered, as we could find no *post-mortem* appearances, except slight inflammation of the lungs, not sufficient to account for death, that it was possible that something had been wrong with the food on which the beaver had been living. He feeds his own beavers at the Zoological upon boughs of poplar and willow, of both of which they are very fond. He also gives them carrots, biscuits, and Indian corn.

The loss of these valuable animals was unfortunate, their usual price being between seventy and eighty pounds per pair.

In January 1875 Lord Bute obtained eight more beavers through Mr. Jamrach. These eight beavers were originally captured in North America, and were then sent to Germany, where they were kept for three months in a stable. Mr. Bartlett inspected the beavers with me before their purchase, and we were satisfied they were in good condition. As, however, the boxes in which they were confined were very dilapidated through long travel, and the weather excessively cold, we determined to give them a rest, and allow them to have a good sleep and a wash before sending them on to Scotland. Mr. Bartlett, therefore, offered to take them in at the Gardens, and turned them out into two beautiful dens close by the wombats, just behind the kangaroo sheds. Having given them a few days' rest, I inspected them again. The keeper turned them carefully out from their warm bed of straw, at which they seemed exceedingly indignant. The biggest of them, a very fine animal, sat up on his haunches, and made a curious noise, something between a grunt and a growl. All of them slapped their tails violently on the brick pavement, giving a sharp crack. This probably is a warning signal in time of danger.

It is difficult, if not impossible, to ascertain the sexes of these animals. There were, however, two big ones, five of a moderate size, and one very little one. They were all sent to the Isle of Bute, *viâ* Glasgow. We advised that a kind of pigsty should be made for them, in which a warm nest of straw should be placed, and that they should then be allowed to gnaw themselves out. If they could find a better place to build their own nest in the open, they would do so; if not, they would come back to sleep in the nest which had been made for them. Thus they would gradually be able to make themselves comfortable in their new home. Their food should consist of Indian corn, carrots, biscuits, and more especially willow boughs, of which they are exceedingly fond, and without which they will hardly thrive.

About the same time Lord Bute sent me the following interesting and welcome intelligence:—'A very unexpected episode has taken place here with the beavers. You remember that *two* of the original four escaped to the moors, and though the body of only one of them was found, both were believed to have died. But it is not so. The other animal has turned up in a large pond surrounded with trees, close to a farm about one and a half or two miles from where he had last been seen. His labours are quite gigantic considering his size and his being alone. He has felled a poplar with a girth of between three and four feet, and is taking it piecemeal to his head-quarters in a swamp at the other end of the pond, where are already collected many large branches, almost logs. He seems to feed eagerly upon the water-plants in the pond, which is large and altogether well adapted for his residence. The whole thing is very curious, as showing that the creature is able to live and flourish in a perfectly wild state in this country.'

Companions were afterwards found for the solitary beaver.

In September 1877 I was fortunate enough to have the opportunity of examining Lord Bute's beavers in the beautiful home he had prepared for them. H.M.S. 'Jackal,' in her cruise anchored at Rothesay, and the morning after our arrival, Captain Digby, the officers of the 'Jackal,' my colleagues and myself, chartered a carriage to pay a visit to the beavers.

At some little distance from Mount Stewart House there is a lonely pine-wood. Through part of this wood runs a natural stream. In the centre of the wood a stone wall has been built, in such a manner as to keep the beavers perfectly quiet and undisturbed.

As far as could be ascertained by the curator of the beavery, there were twelve beavers. There were certainly one or more young ones in the big house which these most intelligent animals had erected. These when born are about as large as rats; and from their size and other observations the curator thinks that beavers have two litters of cubs in the year.

On entering the inclosure one might easily imagine that a gang of regular woodcutters had been at work felling the trees all around them. Woodcutters had in-deed been at work very busily, but they were not biped labouring men working with sharp axes, but fur-clad quadrupeds, armed by nature with exceedingly sharp, powerful teeth.

The original stream, which flows gently down a slight incline, is now divided out into one larger and two smaller ponds, by means of dams or weirs, which the beavers have built directly across the run of the water.

It is difficult, if not impossible, to see these wonderful dam-makers at work, as they generally, I hear, are out at night, and are very shy beasts. From the structure they have made, it is evident that they work with a design, I may even say with a definite plan. The trees have been cut down in such a manner that they shall fall in the position in which the beaver thinks they would be of the greatest service to the general structure, generally right across the stream. The cunning fellows seem to have found out that the lowest dam across the river would receive the greatest pressure of water upon it. This dam, therefore, is made by far the strongest. They seem to have packed, repaired, and continually attended to the tender places which the stream might make in their engineering work.

A fact still more curious—the custodian of the beavers pointed out to us a portion of the work where the dam was strutted up and supported by the branches of trees extending from the bed of the stream below to the sides of the dam—forming, in fact, as good supports to the general structure as any engineer could have devised.

The beaver's hut, made by themselves, looks like a heap of sticks or waste firewood, and presents nothing

to attract much attention. Of course I could not disturb
it, but it appeared to be composed of tree boughs and
barked sticks. In 'Land and Water,' March 28, 1868,
a drawing is given of the 'beaver's home,' as seen by a
correspondent who had an opportunity of taking a beaver's
house to pieces; here is his report. 'The beaver's home
looks like a huge bird's-nest turned upside down, and is
generally located in the grassy coves of lakes, by the edge
of still-water rivers or artificial ponds, and less frequently
by a river side, where a bend or jutting rocks afford a
deep eddying pool near the bank. The house rests on the
bank, but always overlaps the water in which the front
part is immersed, and, as a general rule, the bottom of
the stream or lake is deepened in the channel approaching
the entrance by dredging, thereby assuring a free passage
below the ice.'

He then described the architectural design of the
beavers' house. It was a large house; nearly eighteen
feet in diameter at the water line, and nearly five feet
in height. 'On the outside the sticks were thrown
somewhat loosely, but as we unpiled them, and examined
the structure more closely, the work appeared better, the
boughs laid more horizontally and firmly bound in with
mud and grass. About two feet from the top we unroofed
the chamber, and presently disclosed the interior arrangements. The chamber—there was but one—was very low
scarcely two feet in height, though about nine feet in
diameter. It had a gentle slope upwards from the water,
the margin of which could be just seen at the edge.
There were two levels inside—one, which we shall term
the hall, a sloping mud bank, on which the animal

emerges from the subaqueous tunnel and shakes himself;
and the other, an elevated bed of boughs ranged round
the back of the chamber, and much in the style of a
guard-bed, *i.e.*, the sloping wooden trestle usually found
in a military guard-room. The couch was comfortably
covered with lengths of dried grass and rasped fibres of
wood, similar to the shavings of a toy broom. The ends
of the timbers and brushwood, which projected inwards,
were smoothly gnawed off all round. There were two
entrances; the one led into the water at the edge of the
chamber, and let in the light; the other went down at
a deeper angle into the black water. The former was
evidently the summer entrance, the latter being used in
winter to avoid the ice. The interior was perfectly clean,
no barked sticks (the refuse of the food) being left about.
These were all distributed on the exterior, which accounts
for the bleached appearance of many houses we have seen.
In turning over the materials of the house I picked up
several pieces of wood of but two or three inches in length,
which, from their shortness, puzzled me as to the reason
of so much trouble being taken by the beaver for apparently so small a purpose. My Indian, however, en-
lightened me. The side on which a young tree is intended
to fall is first cut through—say two-thirds—then the other
side one-third a little higher up. The tree slips off the
stem, but will not fall prostrate, owing to the intervention
of branches of adjacent trees. So the beaver has to gnaw a
little above to start it again, exactly on the plan adopted
by the lumberman in case of a catch amongst the
upper branches, when the impetus of another slip dis-
engages the whole tree. The occupants of the house were

out for the day, as they generally are throughout the summer, being engaged in travelling up and down the brooks, and collecting provisions for the winter consumption.'

Mr. Bartlett and I closely examined the markings of the beavers' chisel-like teeth on the trees which they had cut down. These trees were oak, larch, pine, birch, and willow. The young ones, judging from the markings of their teeth, are not such good workmen as their parents, and one would almost imagine that it was necessary for them to go through some sort of education in cutting down trees. It is very interesting to observe how the beaver goes to work to cut down a tree. Attacking one side, he cuts, by means of his sharp chisel, a regular notch in the tree. One side of this notch is flat, like a saw-cut; the other side is brought down to the saw-cut by an angle; in fact, he cuts down the trees by the same sort of incision as we ourselves employ to cut a stick out of the hedge. Mr. Bartlett informs me that he has seen the beaver put his head so far into the notch that he was afraid the weight of the tree from above would crush down upon him and smash his head; but Mr. Beaver is a better carpenter than this. Mr. Bartlett has seen him at this stage of the proceedings come out and go to a little distance, sit on his hind legs, and inspect the tree with the air of an engineer looking at a scaffold in process of construction. When the beaver has gnawed his notch as deep as he dare into the tree, the cunning fellow will test its stability by standing on his hind legs and pushing the tree, to see the degree of firmness of the portion which holds the two pieces of wood together: but how is he to separate this bit which unites the wood? He simply leaves off gnawing the big notch he has made. He then goes to the other side, where the bark and wood have not been touched at all, and gnaws away until down comes the tree.

The beavers are most industrious little animals. These water carpenters have converted the place into a regular subterranean city, for they have burrowed out the earth in such a manner as to form streets, galleries, highways, and by-ways. These runs, I imagine, are made primarily for the purposes of safety, and secondly that the homes or dams may be connected together, so that the families living in the different huts may be able at will to visit their friends.

These animals were at one time very common in North Wales. There is a valley running up from Bangor towards Snowdon, called Beaver's Hollow (Nant yr Afangewm). The more modern name is Nant Frangon; the river Ogwen runs through the vale. There are several Llyn yr Afanges (Beavers' Pools) in different parts of the country; and Giraldus Cambrensis, who wrote in 1188, says that beavers were found in considerable numbers near one of the Cardiganshire rivers. Hywel Dda made a law fixing the price of the *Llost lydan's*, or broad-tailed animal's skin, at 120 pence, a high sum for those days, but we must recollect that the skin of the beaver was one of the chief articles of finery and luxury in dress that the Welsh then possessed.

Mr. Kinahan, of the Geological Survey of Ireland, wrote me thus :—

' Some Irish lake-basins may possibly have been formed by beavers' dams. This suggestion, however, is merely conjectural, and prompted by the form of some of the lake-basins. Against it is the fact that although the beaver is known to have been an inhabitant of Wales during the historical period, yet we have been unable to find in the Irish annals any record of its existence. . . . There does not appear to be any real native Irish word for beavers. In O'Keelly's dictionary we find " *Dobhran-leasleathan,* a beaver," but he seems to have taken this from the Scotch-Gaelic, as no mention of beaver is known in any Irish MS. *Dobhran* means water-animal, and *leasleathan* broad-tailed. The Welsh, for beaver is similar, namely *llostlydan,* broad-tail.'

As regards the existence of beavers on the Continent, my late learned friend Signor Valetta informed me that Dante (who died 1321) mentioned beavers as then existing in the Danube. He called them *bevero,* and implied that they eat fish. The Italian name is now *castero.* Signor Valetta wrote me thus :—

' Dante mentions the beaver in Canto xvii. of " Inferno," as a comparison with the assumed posture of Geryon (a monster represented by mythologists as having three bodies and three heads), on the precipitous bank of the infernal abyss. Dante and Virgil have arrived on the border of a dismal unfathomable chasm which falls straight to the Well of Giants, and hence to the centre of the earth. As the bank is steep, and there is no practicable descent, and descend they must, Virgil bids the poet ungird himself of a rope which tied his waist, and give it to him. This rope was symbolical of penance, humiliation, and repentance, being the rope worn by the Franciscans, to whose society it seems the poet was affiliated. Virgil throws the rope down the abyss, and at this bidding the monster comes up to carry them.down, and waiting for them places his claws on the bank, and swings with the hinder coil in the air. Here comes the comparison :—

> Come talvolta stanno a riva i burchi,
>> Che parte sono in acqua, e parte in terra ;
>> E come là tra li Tedeschi lurchi
> Lo bevero s' assetta a far sua guerra ;
>> Così la fiera pessima si stava
>> Su l' orlo, che, di pietra, il sabbion serra.

which may be thus translated :—

' " As sometimes boats are so placed as to stand part in the water and part on shore, and as there amongst the glutton Germans the beaver sits down to wage its war, in the same way sat Geryon." '

Then Mr. Valetta says that the commentator on Dante, Brunone Bianchi, affirms 'that the beaver sits down to wage his war against *fishes*,' and all other commentators follow in his track, from which it is evident that the commentators aforesaid, although doubtless very learned classical scholars, were certainly not naturalists. The beaver is not a fish-eater, never was, and never will be. He is a typical rodent or gnawing animal ; his incisor teeth are formed like chisels to cut down boughs ; his molar teeth to eat vegetable substances only. It is about as sensible a thing to say a beaver eats fish as to describe a rabbit or a guinea-pig eating fish. Dante himself, when he had finished this line, was evidently puzzled to write what the beaver was waging war against, and showed his discrimination in not affirming a fact of which he was not cognisant. This mistake about the beavers eating fish has been lying dormant for about six hundred years, and it is pretty nearly time that the mistake should be rectified.

REMARKABLE ACCIDENT TO A RED DEER IN WINDSOR PARK.

His Royal Highness Prince Christian has been kind enough to allow me to place on record an event which I believe to be unique in the annals of forestry, viz. a curious catastrophe to one of the red deer of Windsor Park, which will be of the highest interest to all owners of deer parks, whether at home or abroad, to the proprietors and lessees of Highland shootings, to naturalists, and the public in general.

It may be remembered that in January 1879 we had some very severe weather, with snow and frost. On January 16, one of the keepers who has charge of her Majesty's deer in the royal domains, was going his rounds, when, to his great amazement, he suddenly came upon the scene represented in Fig. 2, namely, a magnificent red deer lying on his back, with his leg tightly fixed in the forked branch of a whitethorn tree. This unfortunate animal presented the following appearance :—He was lying on his near or left side, the tip of his right shoulder was supported against the trunk of the tree. The chest and fore-part of his body were clear of the ground, suspended by his right or off-foot between the fork of the tree. A closer examination showed exactly what we see

C.BERUEAU.DEL.

C.FLERRERS.

FIG. 2.—ACCIDENT TO A STAG IN WINDSOR PARK.

v 2

in Fig. 3, except that the body of the animal is (in the engraving) no longer attached to the foot. The keeper attempted to remove the foot, but found it so tightly fixed that with all his force he was quite unable to do so. The appearance of the stag's foot was as follows :—The shank bone was fractured and splintered diagonally. The fractured bones had made their exit by a cut right through the skin, thus causing a compound comminuted fracture. The portion of the bone below this fracture—tough and strong as the red deer's shanks are—was shattered into minute fragments the size of dice. The bone was again fractured at its lower part, and the thick skin entirely lacerated through. The large sinews at the back of the bone, as well as the wire-like sinews that work the toes of the foot, were elongated and pulled out, and in fact everything was broken right off except two very slender sinews and a small portion of the skin. The total length of the portion of the deer's leg caught in the tree was seventeen inches ; from the fracture to where it was torn off, eight inches. The leg was caught by the branches of the tree about four feet from the ground, and the lowest boughs carrying leaves were about nine feet from the ground. The deer was dead, and it is not known how long he had been held a prisoner by his foot.

As there were no eye-witnesses of the occurrence, it becomes somewhat difficult to account for this extraordinary event. It is probable, however, that in consequence of the weather the animal was short of food, and that in his wanderings he had observed above his head something edible on the lower branches of the thorn tree, perhaps leaves, moss, or lichens, on which deer feed in snowy weather; or possibly some ivy, of which deer are very fond. There was some ivy on the tree about nine feet from the

FIG. 3.—FORE-LEG OF THE STAG CAUGHT BY FORKED BRANCHES OF A THORN TREE.

ground, and the forked branch which caught the deer's leg was four feet from the ground, so that he could not reach the leaves when standing on all-fours. He therefore probably raised himself upon his hind legs, and when stretching himself upwards and forwards, the hoofs of his hind legs slipped from under him; or else, when letting himself down again, his right fore-leg slipped suddenly between the forked branches of the tree, and was instantly held there tight. (See again Fig. 3.) The animal then probably began immediately to struggle, but the more he kicked and fought the tighter the wrist of his foot got wedged in; in fact, when the preparation was brought to me the foot was so tightly fixed into the notch of the tree that it could not have been more jammed if it had been hammered down, and then a long screw passed right through it.

In his struggles to get loose (he was a fine, heavy stag, carrying antlers with thirteen points) the first thing that happened was the fracture of the leg-bone. This allowed the animal to fall on his back, from which position, of course, he could not rise. Terribly alarmed at what had happened to him, the poor stag then began to pull and tug at his captive leg, assisting himself to do so by means of his horns. In his frantic exertions to get free the stag a second time broke his leg, then the skin gave way, and lastly the large tendons. If his strength had lasted long enough to have ruptured the two small tendons it is possible that he might have escaped, leaving his leg in the fork of the tree. The head of the poor beast was a little further round the tree than represented in the drawing, so that it would seem the unfortunate creature had tried to use the butt of the tree as a lever to wrench off the fractured part of his leg, and so escape with his life. He did not, unfortunately, succeed in the attempt.

His Royal Highness, having been informed of the accident, judiciously ordered the **portion** of the tree which held the foot to be sawn off bodily. He then kindly sent the whole thing to me, with the request that the foot should be preserved for him without being removed from the fork in which it had been so tightly jammed by the animal itself.

This being a very difficult problem in the art of taxidermy, I first of all had a drawing made of it by Mr. Berjeau, and then sent for Mr. Keilich, whose name is well known as a talented stuffer of deers' heads, lions, tigers, and, in fact, all the larger animals. By a most ingenious plan Mr. Keilich managed to prepare the stag's foot, keeping it exactly in the position in which it was found; it was then set up in a case and was forwarded to his Royal Highness at Cumberland Lodge, Windsor Park, as a unique specimen.

I have been unable either by search or by questioning to find any record whatever of a similar accident having been known to occur to a red deer, or in fact any other kind of deer. The nearest approach to it is the case of ' locked horns,' which are not so very uncommon. Red deer in the fall of the year, as we know, are great fighters, and at that time their horns are more or less elastic. When the deer are fencing at each other the branches of the antlers are apt to slip and get fast knotted, as it were. In 1866 I examined a very fine pair of locked horns of the common American deer at Mr. Leadbeater's establishment, then in Brewer Street. In the Royal College of Surgeons there are a pair of locked horns of the Canadian elk, found just as they are, the wolves having eaten up the elks themselves. An instance of locked horns occurred at Up Park, Petersfield, in 1866, when two deer were found with their brow-antlers forcibly wedged together, hooking on as tightly as steel springs. The keeper was sent for, and one of the hooked brow-antlers was sawn off, and the deer liberated. There is a preparation of this kind of locked horns in the new museum of the University of Oxford, and similar cases are not unknown to deer-stalkers and foresters in Scotland. If I recollect rightly, the late Lord of Lovat had a fine specimen in his collection.

I have received several notes from correspondents on the above curious accident. One writes :—

' I am sure many others have seen, as I have done, a fallow buck jumping a considerable height up into the boughs of a whitethorn bush, and tossing his antlers about among them, thereby bringing to the ground a lot of haws, on which he makes a pleasant repast ; it seems almost certain that the poor stag was going through the same performance, and as he could jump higher than the fallow buck, his leg might be caught in his descent. without much blame to his sagacity or to the activity of his nature.'

Another tells me of a somewhat similar accident to a dingo at a station in Port Phillip, Australia. One of the shepherds killed a kangaroo at some distance from his hut, and to secure the carcass deposited it across the boughs of a gum tree, some six or seven feet from the ground. From the base of this tree, and at a slight angle from the trunk, a good stiff sapling had sprung up. On visiting the spot the next day the shepherd was surprised to find a wild dog jammed between the sapling and the tree, and quite dead. It had evidently made a spring for the dead kangaroo, missed its aim, and slipped into the angle, the elasticity of the sapling holding it tightly by the middle. Neither of its feet touched the ground, but the bark of both tree and sapling had been gnawed away in every direction within reach of its ugly tusks.

I have also been told of a curious accident to a pony in a park. In attempting to leap a wire fence, its foot became fixed between the upper and second wires, causing it to turn a complete somersault. Its neck was quite doubled, and death ensued in a few minutes, either from suffocation or a broken neck.

A strange accident happened to old Fanny, the fishing mare (mentioned in a previous article), when she was a three-year-old. In the field where she then was, two trees grew very close to each other. She got her head fast between them about eight feet from the ground, and was very nearly strangled before she was got out; the blocks from the mill had to be fetched to hoist her out bodily. She was fast for about an hour, the field being half a mile from the mill. No one saw how she got fast, but it was supposed she had been trying to reach the leaves, or playing.

A somewhat similar accident not unfrequently happens to birds. Blackbirds and thrushes are sometimes found caught by the head in the forks of bramble bushes, the accident having occurred when the birds were fighting. At the Surrey Gardens a fine ostrich was once killed in the following curious way:—The bird got his head into the space between two wooden oak palings; finding himself entangled, he gave a sudden kick, the effect of which was to pull his head right off.

No man would have sympathised with me more in the examination of this singular accident to a royal stag than my late friend John Keast Lord, F.Z.S., Naturalist to the British North American Boundary Commission, who wrote one of the best books in the English language on the art of travel, namely, ' At Home in the Wilderness ' (Hardwicke, 1867). Lord had twenty years' experience as trapper, hunter, and naturalist, east and west of the Rocky Mountains. He tells a terrible story of a lumberer or woodcutter having been caught by the foot in a tree which he was splitting with wedges. The lumberer was standing on the log driving in wooden and iron wedges with his ponderous mallet.

Lord writes :—' Soon a yawning crack opened along the log, and in a brief space it would have been in two, but by some mischance the man slipped, the wedge sprung instantly, and allowed the crack to close upon his foot. Having tried every means available to free himself, but in vain—shouting he knew to be useless, as there was no one within hail, and night was coming on, and he was well aware that the bitter cold of a northern winter must end his life long before any help could be reasonably anticipated—in his agony of mind and intensity of bodily suffering, with mad despair the poor fellow seized the axe, and at a single chop severed his leg from the imprisoned foot.' He managed to crawl home, but unfortunately the accident proved fatal, as in the case of the deer.

LECOMPTE, THE SEALS' FRIEND.

FRANÇOIS LECOMPTE, the late 'keeper of the seals' at the Zoological Gardens, was quite a noted character in his way. My first introduction to Lecompte was at Cremorne Gardens in 1866, where he had been engaged to exhibit a sea-bear which he had captured in South America.

The district along the east coast of South America, especially the coast of Patagonia, seems to be the head-quarters of the seal family, many of these being of gigantic size.

The following is the history of the capture of this celebrated seal, and of Lecompte's *début* as tamer of sea-bears and sea-lions :—

In 1862 some French sailors, wandering about the desolate and bleak shores near Cape Horn, came across the seal, or sea-bear, whose portrait I now give. After a great deal of manœuvring, one of the men, Lecompte, managed to get behind the seal, and catch hold of his hind flippers. The seal, of course, tried to turn and bite ; but his captor, by turning to the right or to the left, kept out of the way of his teeth.

When the beast was a bit tired, the other sailors managed to get a stick into his mouth, and to tie it tightly

FIG. 1.—THE SEA-BEAR AT THE ZOOLOGICAL GARDENS.

behind his head, so as to gag him. They then bound him up tightly with ropes, and slinging him between two oars, Lecompte and the sailors carried him to their ship, and then to Buenos Ayres. Lecompte conceived the idea of taming his captive, and for two whole years devoted himself entirely to this object, in which he at last perfectly succeeded, not, however, without great difficulty, for he bore to his grave marks of the seal's teeth on almost every limb, and his right hand was quite crippled by a bite, in which the seal almost severed the muscles of the fore-arm; in fact, the wound was so severe that the South American doctors wanted to amputate his hand altogether.

Notwithstanding the ferocity of his pet, Lecompte cultivated his intelligence, and the creature soon performed tricks which Lecompte, with true nationality, worked up into a little military episode. The sea-bear volunteered to go as a soldier to Mexico. He then passed through the forms of enlistment and drill, and finally fired a cannon. The sea-bear was exhibited in Belgium before he went to Cremorne. His dinner consisted of twenty-five pounds' weight of fish daily. His habit was to sleep all night, and during the day when his master was not with him. He awoke at the slightest noise. He did not object to visitors, but was annoyed with ladies wearing white ribbons.

Lecompte was next engaged by a travelling menagerie. The affair did not pay, so they turned out Lecompte and his sea-bear into a field by the road-side. Here he was discovered by Mr. Bartlett, who purchased his sea-bear for the society, while he himself was made the keeper.

When the sea-bear died, Lecompte was sent to the Falkland Islands, and he returned with another in August 1868. This was a female captured by Lecompte himself.

Lecompte's great triumph was his taming the sea-bear. The *pas de deux* with Lecompte and the sea-bear, which took place on the chair in the middle of the pond at the end of the platform, is well known to the public, and the photographs of these performances will now become historical.

If ever there was affection between animals and men, it was the mutual love that existed between the seals at the Gardens and Lecompte; nor do I think it was entirely cupboard love, though undoubtedly the basket of fish more or less influenced their ideas. He had names for his seals at the Gardens, and the seals knew their names—at least Kate and Fanny did.

Lecompte was most careful about fish-hooks; the fishermen who catch whiting, haddocks, &c., often cut off the snood and leave the hook in the fish, and unless he opened the fish to remove the hook, the seals would swallow hook and all, and would be nearly sure to die when the fish was digested, and the hook remained in the stomach.

Lecompte's abode was in a little house by the zebras. I frequently had lunch with him. He was a splendid cook. He once gave me a portion of a most savoury pie which he assured me was a *spécialité*. It was very good, and I ate it; but when I came to know what the *spécialité* was, I vowed I never would lunch with Lecompte again without seeing the *menu* first.

He took the greatest care of the little baby bladder-nose seals, and also of the larger specimens of the bladder-nose which Captain Gray caught and presented to the Society.

In May 1873 I received a message that two seals had arrived from Dundee for the Brighton Aquarium. I sent for Mr. Lawler from Brighton, and we both went to the docks to meet them. We called at Jamrach's on the road, to ask him to lend us a den to put them in. We found the seals on board the steamship 'Anglia' in the docks used by the Dundee ships. They were simply on deck, and only kept from going about the deck by two boards. They were pretty little things, very fat and chubby, probably about six weeks old. They had been caught in the Arctic regions, and brought to Dundee by Captain Greville, of the ship 'Camperdown;' there they were then transferred to the 'Anglia' and brought to London. We put them into a box, having cut holes in the top, and took them on a cab to London Bridge. I stopped at Billingsgate and bought 20 lbs. of live eels for them. They arrived at Brighton quite safely, and soon got accustomed to their new home; but there was some difficulty at first about their food, as they would not eat the eels or anything else. Mr. Bartlett, however, with his usual readiness, suggested a mode of feeding them which eventually proved a success.

I had scarcely got these seals all right at Brighton, when I received a telegram from Captain Gray that he had caught a young bladder-nose seal for me, and that it would arrive in London at nine o'clock the next morning. Punctual to the time the van arrived from the railway. I found the little animal was in a kind of crate, evidently put together by a ship's carpenter.

The seal looked very seedy, tired, and cold, so I took him upstairs and put him before the fire, covered him over, and let him have a sleep for two hours. He would not, however, eat or drink, although I tried him with live eels, milk, and water.

In the course of the day Mr. Bartlett called, and offered to take charge of him; so I sent him up to the Gardens, where he was placed under the care of Lecompte. Finding he would not eat, Lecompte caught him by the flippers and attempted to get a portion of eel down his throat, but did not succeed. While Lecompte was holding him he made a terrible noise, something between the cry of a child and the growling of a dog.

He was only a baby, I should say about six weeks old: the teeth were not very large, but rather formidable; the eyes, which were black, were deeply sunk into the head; the bladder on the top of his nose was just visible; his colour was a yellowish buff. He stayed a very long time under water, though so young; and when he brought his head to the surface of the water his countenance was very human, not unlike the face of a chubby-faced baby; and I can easily understand the origin of the story that seals were once human beings, namely, the Egyptians that were drowned in the Red Sea, and who were for further punishment converted into seals.

The last long interview I had with Lecompte was when the sea-lions for the Brighton Aquarium arrived at Deptford, in October 1875. Lecompte assisted to pack

the seals at London Bridge Station. It was very interesting to hear Lecompte talk to the animals. They
were very frightened and very travel-worn. 'Vous ne
connaissez pas encore votre papa, mon petit. Restez tran-
quille, mon cher. Vous avez faim? Je vous donnerai un
poisson, voilà.' Lecompte on this occasion did not look a
bit like Lecompte. When on duty in the Gardens, he was
generally dressed in a blue serge sailor's dress. When he
went with us to Brighton he had got himself up quite a
swell; his handsome face and white beard made him look
quite a gentleman, which he really was by nature. He
was one of the best talkers I ever knew; he would say
the commonest things in the most funny manner. During
the journey down, the sea-lions cried nearly the whole way,
and Lecompte tried to pacify them by paternal exhortations
in French: 'Ah! vous criez après votre papa, mes chers
phoques.' Lecompte remained two or three days at the
Brighton Aquarium, in order to reconcile the seals to
their new home, where they long flourished. The sea-
lions of the species exhibited at Brighton inhabit islands
off the coast of San Francisco; their characteristic form is
shown in the engraving on the next page.

Lecompte originally was a French man-o'-war's-man.
He gained, by his welcome 'Bon jour, Monsieur,' and his
polite conduct, the respect of all visitors to the Gardens.
His loss was greatly felt, not only by 'mes pauvres bêtes,'
but also by the public in general. So anxious was he
for the welfare of his seals, that he requested when
very ill to be taken to see them once more. During his
illness he received his full pay, and was attended by the
first medical men in London. Peace to the memory of

X

FIG. 5.—THE SEA-LIONS AT THE BRIGHTON AQUARIUM.

this faithful servant and sincere friend of dumb animals—
dumb in the ordinary sense of the word to most people,
but possessing a voice and language well understood by
their much-lamented master, François Lecompte.

I received from the Rev. Mr. Lory, of the Falkland
Islands, the skull of a large sea-lion, now in my museum.
It weighs eleven pounds, and measures from nose to the
end of the skull fifteen inches: it has evidently been exposed to the action of the weather for a considerable time
—may be for many years. The skin remains over the
anterior half of the skull; the rest of the bone is bleached
by the weather. The teeth are exceedingly beautiful,
the largest being larger than the canine teeth of a lion,
only not so pointed. Mr. Lory wrote me thus:—'The
sea-lion's head I have sent to you for your museum
is from Port Stephens, in the West Falkland Islands.
The sea-lion is one of the hair seals (the male); his mane
is thick and bushy, and his roar terrific. He measures
from twelve feet to thirteen feet in length, and sometimes
more. During the breeding season he is exceedingly
fierce, and will attack a man; at other times he avoids
him. A parishioner of mine named White had his thigh
severely lacerated by one. The wound bled profusely, but
from good attention he recovered, only to meet with a
watery grave afterwards. They breed on the north coast
of the East Falkland Islands, and in the Jasons; and during
the season the lions keep jealous guard over the females,
which are quiet, inoffensive animals. The captain of a
schooner in the Falklands told me that he and his men
suddenly came upon from eighty to a hundred of these
monsters in the Jasons, which immediately made for the

water; and as the men intercepted their path they were
obliged to defend themselves as well as they could with
their clubs. The rush was tremendous, but the lions were
more frightened than the men, who, as you may suppose,
were rather taken aback by such an unlooked-for reception
on a desolate island. Sea-lions are not easily killed by a
club; indeed, I believe the usual way of killing them is to
shoot them with ball cartridge.'

Dr. Murie, author of the most scientific monograph on
sea-lions that has ever been published, wrote me as to
this specimen :—' Your specimen is undoubtedly an old
male; the changes in appearance from the younger to
the older stages, and the differences between the male
and the female, are very curious. There are, so to say, five
grades of development. First, the brain region in the
baby is preponderant. Second, the face begins to
lengthen. Third, the teeth acquire importance ; and in
this stage sexual distinction becomes evident in the skull,
although there is still a considerable resemblance between
them. Fourth, notably differs from the preceding, the
bones becoming more massive and rugose, sexual characteristics being marked ; crests then rise. Fifth, as the
skull ripens to old age, particularly in the male, all the
characteristic points of the fourth stage are carried out by
excessive growth of processes, crests, and other superficial
developments of bony lines, spicules, and nodules. The
cavity of the eye looks forwards ; the space behind for the
temporal and other jaw muscles enlarging as fleshy bulk
preponderates over brain character.

' It follows that all the aforesaid changes are an exact
counterpart of what obtains in the gorilla. In early

youth the brain is functionally predominant. The teeth
assume importance, with a corresponding facial accession.
Lastly, whereas brain enlargement is apparently arrested,
the muscles of mastication, those of the throat and neck,
indeed, all connected with the head, and therefore
involved in the organs of offence and defence, paramountly
swell in bulk and strength; nerves and blood-vessels
augment proportionally. Thus, from the featureless skull
of the young is evolved the rugged, immense, brutal and
terrible-looking sea carnivore, peculiar to the male of this
and certain other genera of the eared seals.

'The animal to which your skull belonged is not the
elephant seal (*Morunga*), and is a very different animal
from those exhibiting at Brighton, but belongs to the
same species (*Otaria Jubata*) as the earlier specimen and
some of the later ones which the Zoological Society
possess.'

In 1875 Mr. John Willis Clarke gave a lecture at the
Zoological Gardens on Sea-lions.[1] He says concerning
the species to which this skull belongs:—'The canines
are of enormous size, and the two outermost incisors
of the upper jaw only a trifle smaller, so that when the
jaw is closed, and the lower canines fall between these two
enormous teeth, anything that may happen to come
between them is held as in a vice. The molar teeth are
so solid that sailors have mistaken them for flints. A
quantity of pebbles are always found in their stomachs.
The sea-lion is covered all over with coarse stiff hair.
Under the lower jaw and on the back of the head and
neck it is rough and shaggy. Beneath this hair is a crop

[1] *Contemporary Review*, December 1875

of under fur, distributed in delicate, short, fine hairs. Old males develop a mane. The skulls, which are picked up on the shore of the Falklands, are sometimes half as large again as those of the largest living sea-lion. The male does not attain his size until he is about six years old. There are nine well-authenticated species of sea-lions. In the North Pacific three, viz. *Otaria ursina*, *O. Gillespii*, and *O. Stelleri*. In the South Pacific two—*O. Jubata* and *O. Falklandica*. At the Cape of Good Hope, *O. Pusilla* or *Antarctica*. On the coasts of Australia and New Zealand, *O. Hookeri* and *O. Lobata*. At Kerguelen's Island, *O. Gazella*.'

The sea-lion, to which when alive the skull sent me by the Rev. Mr. Lory belonged, must have been indeed a gigantic creature, possibly as big as a moderate-sized horse.

Allied to these huge seals, but excelling nearly all of them in bulk, is the walrus (*Trichecus rosmarus*), a denizen of the Arctic regions, remarkable for its great tusks and bristly whiskers. The males are twelve to fifteen feet in length. The illustration of the walrus, and those of the sea-bear and sea-lion, show three of the most characteristic of the seal tribe.

It is not often that the walrus comes down so far south as the coast of Scotland. The following notice from a correspondent, therefore, is worthy of record :—' I have heard, to my great surprise, that a gentleman of undoubted credibility and intelligence had during last summer seen off the west coast of the Isle of Skye a large walrus. Having occasion to visit the island, I was fortunate enough to meet the gentleman who (with two friends) saw the animal, and had the account direct from himself.

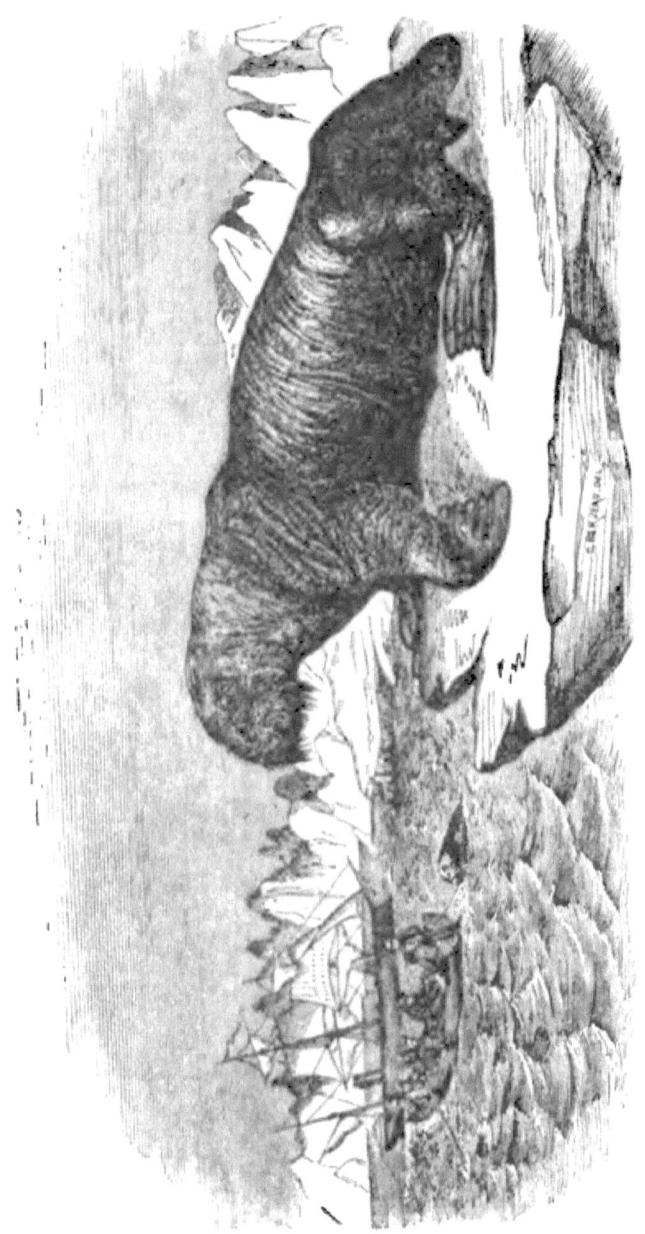

Fig. 6.—THE WALRUS.

The date .of the walrus's visit to Skye was, so far as my friend could remember, about the 20th of June 1878. He was seen lying on a rock near the shore on a fine calm evening, and my informant and his friends were able to get near enough to remove all doubt as to the identity of the animal, with which they were familiar from plates or stuffed specimens. The huge tusks were quite easily distinguished, and the length of the animal was estimated at about seven feet. On being disturbed he rolled over into the sea, swam a short distance to another rock, and clambered on to it, apparently using his tusks to aid him in doing so. After some little time he took the water again and was seen no more.'

STRUCTURE AND HABITS OF WHALES.

THERE is something very attractive to the human mind, whether educated or not, about the word 'Whale.' It may be that man, knowing his own inferiority of size and strength as compared to many gigantic animals living either on the earth or in the water, and also on the *omne ignotum pro magnifico* principle, looks upon the whale as the very embodiment of size and strength. Again, it is not impossible that our earlier impressions of Divine power may have been obtained from whales being so frequently mentioned in the Bible, especially in Gen. i., in which whales are the first created animals mentioned by name, thus—'And God created great whales.' Then, again, everybody knows the story of Jonah :—'Now the Lord had prepared a great fish to swallow up Jonah, and Jonah was in the belly of the fish three days and three nights.' On turning to Johnson's Dictionary we find evidence that in his day the science of natural history had not very much advanced, for the learned lexicographer defines a whale as 'The largest of *fish*; the largest of animals that inhabit this globe.'

Whales are of the highest interest to the public—not only in a scientific point of view, but also because their value is of commercial importance to this nation. In former times, with the exception of the celebrated Scoresby, but few persons placed on record anything relating to the structure and habits of these huge oceanic mammalia; and even now a great field of inquiry is open to those whose duty it is to hunt the leviathan of the deep amid the icebergs and frozen seas of the Arctic Ocean.

I am proud of the friendship of a gentleman who has of late years done more than any other person to give the public information relative to the fauna of the far-distant North—the whales and the seals. This gentleman has spent twenty-two whaling seasons at the North Pole, and each time he has returned from his perilous voyages he has brought us back some interesting news from his hunting grounds. I need hardly say that I refer to Captain David Gray, of the steam whaling-ship 'Eclipse,' of Peterhead, Aberdeenshire. In the course of one of his recent voyages Captain Gray has made a discovery relative to the structure of the baleen or whalebone whale (*Balæna mysticetus*), and to its mode of feeding, which to the best of my belief has hitherto been entirely unknown, and which will doubtless excite great interest among all naturalists.

The following is Captain Gray's description of the head of a Greenland whale, with sketches and measurements taken during his voyage in 1876, showing the manner in which the whalebone is arranged in the head:—

'Fig. 7 shows the mouth open, and the position of the whalebone when the animal is feeding; it is drawn to scale, and is a good representation of its appearance. It will be noticed that I have not filled in the correct number of slips of whalebone, which amount to about 300 on each

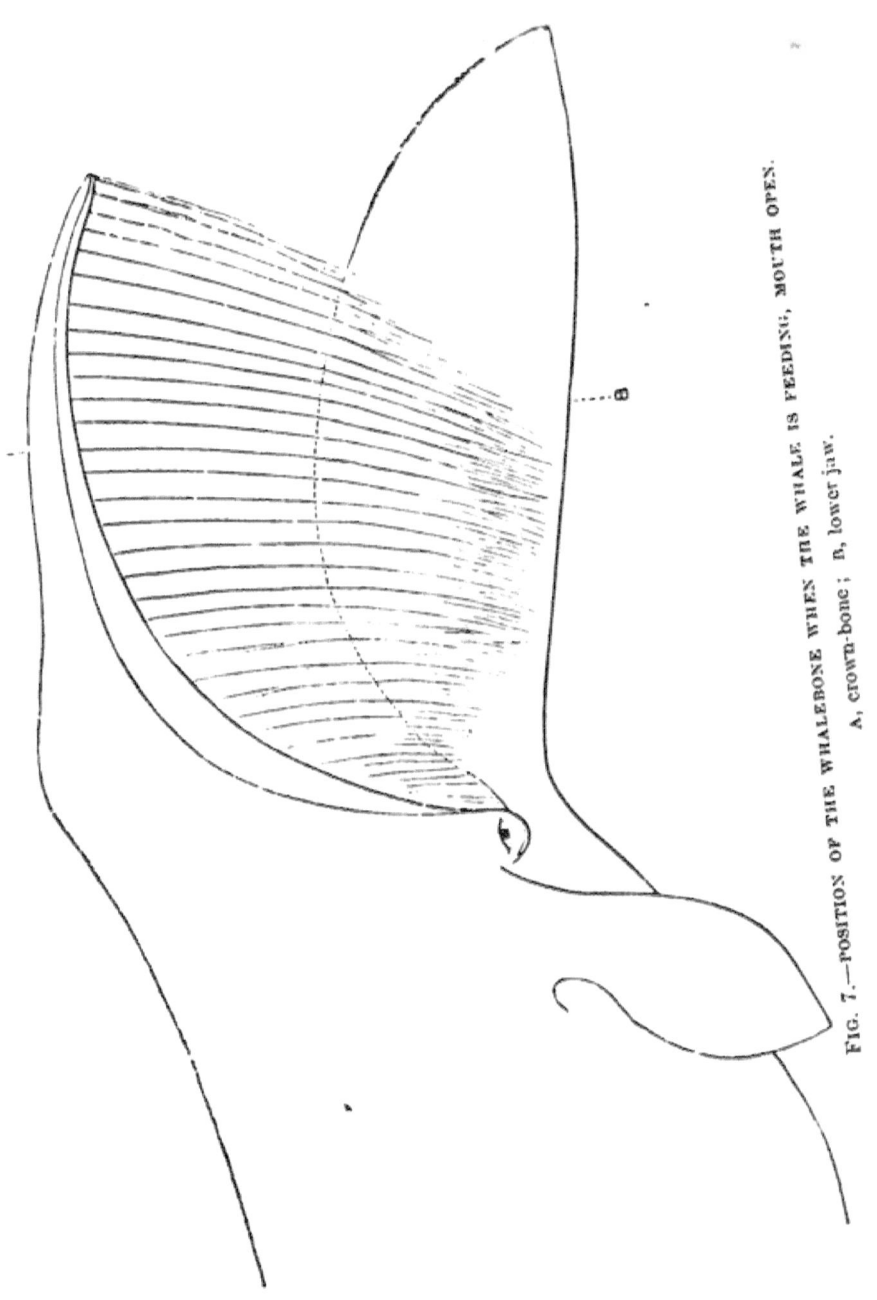

FIG. 7.—POSITION OF THE WHALEBONE WHEN THE WHALE IS FEEDING, MOUTH OPEN.

A, crown-bone ; B, lower jaw.

side of the head, but have only drawn a few lines showing
the direction they take towards the lower jaw when the
mouth is open.   I counted the number of blades of whalebone in a whale's head last voyage, and found 286 on the
left and 289 on the right side of the head.

'Along the middle of the crown-bone the blades of
whalebone are separated from each other by three-quarters
of an inch of gum, but the interval decreases, towards the
nose and throat, to a quarter of an inch.   The gum is
always white; in substance it resembles the hoof of a
horse, but is softer.   It is easily cut with a knife, or
broken by the hand, and is tasteless.

'The whalebone representing the palate is lined inside
with hair, for the purpose of covering the spaces between
the slips and preventing the food on which the whale
subsists from escaping; this hair is short at the roof of
the mouth, but is from twelve to twenty inches long at
the points of the whalebone.   The reason of this is that
when the mouth is opened the bone springs forward, and
the spaces between the slips are greatest at the points.

'Hitherto it was believed that the whalebone had room
to hang perpendicularly from the roof of the mouth to
the lower jaw when the mouth was shut, but such is not
the case.   The whalebone is arranged, as will be seen
from the sketch, to reach from the upper to the lower
jaw when the mouth is open; were it otherwise, the
whale would not be able to catch its food; it would all
escape underneath the points of the whalebone.

'Fig. 8 shows the position of the whalebone when the
mouth is shut.   The dotted lines show the jaw-bone, and
the black lines show the whalebone curving towards the

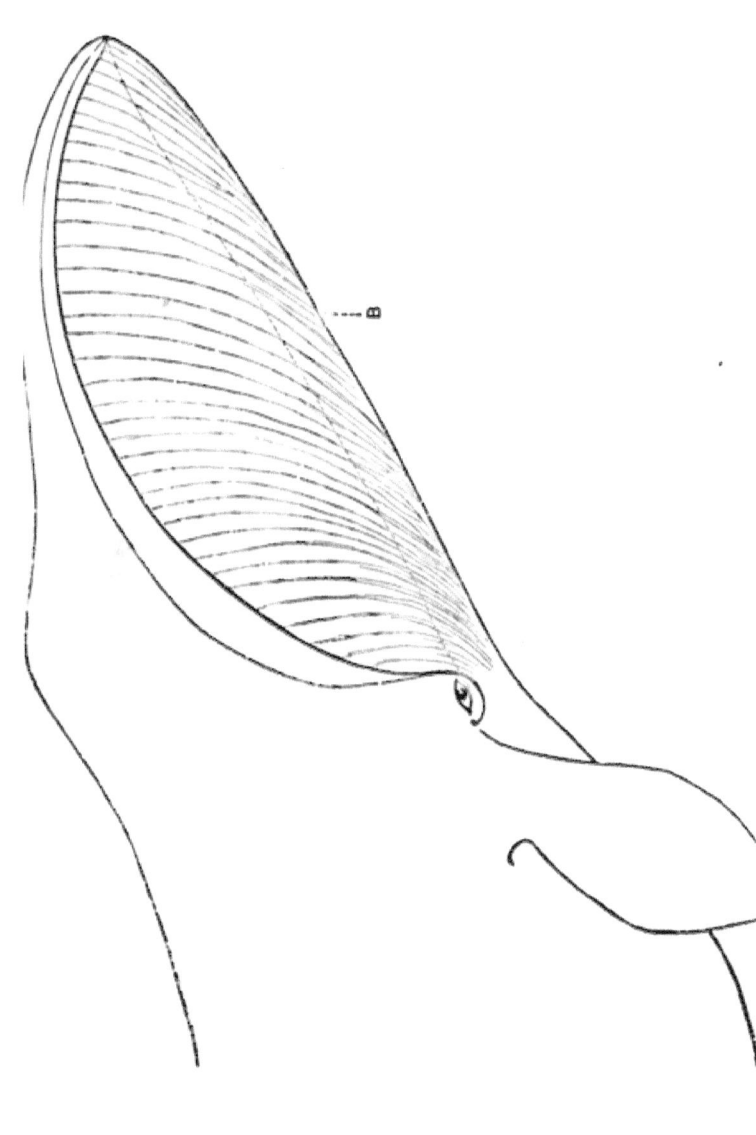

FIG. 8.—MOUTH OF WHALE SHUT; THE PLATES OF WHALEBONE FACED AWAY BY THE ACTION OF THE LOWER JAW

A, crown-bone; B, lower jaw.

throat.   It is not very correctly drawn, but it will be
sufficient to show the arrangement which allows room in
a cavity or hollow in the lower jaw for the points of the
whalebone to lie in when the mouth is shut.   The whale
has no muscular power over its whalebone, any more
than other animals have over their teeth.   When the
animal opens its mouth to feed, the whalebone springs
forward and downward, so as to fill the mouth entirely;
when in the act of ·shutting it again, the whalebone being

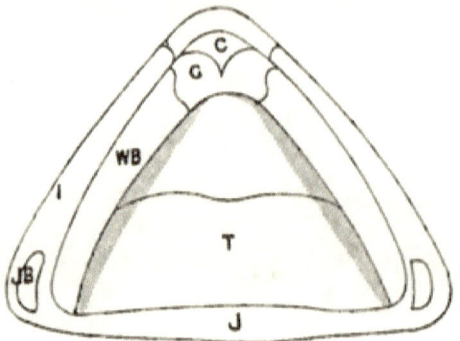

FIG. 9.-- SECTION OF WHALE'S MOUTH SHUT.

C, crown-bone ; G, gum ; WB, whalebone ; T, tongue ; L, lips
JB, jaw-bone ; J, lower jaw.

pointed slightly towards the throat, the lower jaw catches
it and carries it up into the hollow before described.

'Fig. ·9 is a cross section cut halfway between the
blow-holes and the nose along the line AB, showing the
mouth shut, and the arrangement of the lips, jaw-bones,
tongue, and whalebone.   It will be best understood by
looking at the explanation given with the drawing.

'Fig. 10 is the same section showing the mouth open.
It conveys a good idea of the great capacity of the mouth

when open compared with the comparatively small space
it has to hold the whalebone in when the mouth is shut.

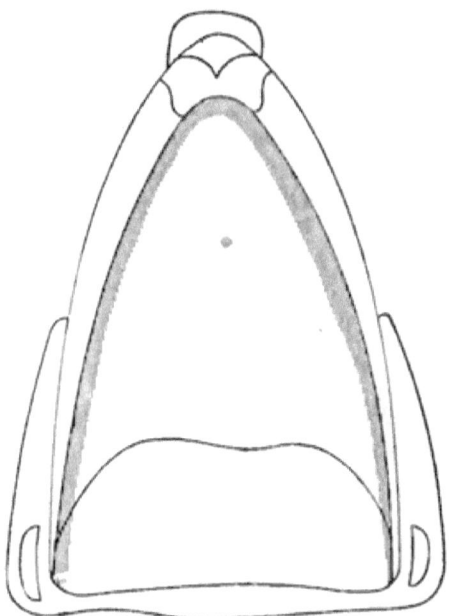

FIG. 10.—SECTION OF WHALE'S MOUTH WHEN OPEN.

'Fig. 11 is the whale that these measurements were
taken from, drawn by a lady, and is the best representation of the *Balæna mysticetus* that I have ever seen.'

The dimensions were as follows :—

	ft.	in.
Length from nose to tail	47	0
Length of head from nose to eye	17	8
Breadth of body between the fins	11	0
Breadth of head across the jaw-bones	9	3
Breadth of lip, including jaw-bone	5	5
Gape	10	8
Breadth of tail	20	0
Length of whalebone	10	1

FIG. 11.—WHALEBONE WHALE (*Balæna mysticetus*) OF THE GREENLAND SEAS.
Killed by Captain David Gray, of the ship, 'Eclipse,' Peterhead.

The problem hitherto unsolved has been the exact manner in which the whale works his plates of baleen. The result was known, but not the *modus operandi*. This is the discovery made by Captain Gray. From his paper and diagrams it will become evident that when the whale is at work catching his food in the sieve-like, hair-lined mouth, the baleen is extended to its full length along the whole row of the plates. In pictures of whales, the beast is always depicted with an open mouth, but surely the whale does not always keep his mouth open! But then the question comes, how does he shut it? and when he shuts it, what does he do with his baleen? How does he pack it away? Gray, after careful examination of many whales, has found out how this is done. When the whale closes his lower jaw, he first gently pushes backwards and upwards towards the palate the anterior plates of baleen; the posterior plates go back under pressure in succession, till all the plates of baleen lie back in the mouth, packed beautifully in regular order, one over the other, over the angle of the eye. The bundle of hairs from the tips of the plates of baleen fit into a hollow at the edge of the jaws.

I have not the least hesitation in stating that the description of the mode in which the whale packs away his baleen when he wishes to close his mouth is entirely new to the scientific world; and I challenge all comers to account for this wondrous mechanism by the doctrine of development or self-evolution. No; it is a proof—a new proof, at the head of a long catalogue of other evidences, absolutely unerring and true—that the structures of animals are not due to the causes which this doctrine would assign

Y

to them, but to the omniscience of Him who on the fifth day of the Creation completed a wondrous work :—' And God created great whales, and every living creature that moveth, which the waters brought forth abundantly, after their kind : and God saw that it was good.'

On hearing of this discovery Professor **Flower wrote** as follows :—

'Captain David Gray's observations upon the position of the whalebone in the mouth of the Greenland whale are quite novel, and of great interest. They arose, as the captain tells me in a letter just received, in consequence of a conversation which we had together a few years ago, while looking at the skeleton of the large whale mounted in the Museum of the College of Surgeons. I asked if he could explain what had always been to me, as to others who have never had Captain Gray's opportunities of observation, a great puzzle, viz. how it was that the whalebone was so much longer than the space which it occupied in the animal's mouth, supposing the blades to be placed, as usually represented, at right angles with the long axis of the jaws. This difficulty occurred in looking at all the authentic figures, such as Scoresby's, in which the height of the head is far too small for the length assigned to the whalebone on the supposition stated above, and equally in looking at the actual bony framework of the head. Captain Gray's explanation that the slender ends of the whalebone blades fold backwards when the mouth is shut, the longer ones from the middle of the jaw falling into the hollow formed by the shortness of the blades behind them, as seen in the side view, is perfectly clear and satisfactory. It shows, moreover, how, whether the mouth is shut or open, or in any intermediate position, the lateral spaces between the upper and lower jaw are always kept filled up by the marvellously constructed hair-sieve or strainer, which thus adapts itself to the varying condition of the parts between which it is, as it were, stretched across. If the whalebone had been rigid, and depending perpendicularly from the upper jaw, when the mouth was open a space would have been left between the tips of the whalebone forming the lower edge of the strainer, which, as Captain Gray justly remarks, would completely interfere with its use, although the stiff wall-like lower lip, closing in the sides of the mouth below, might have the effect of remedying such a contingency to a certain extent; at least, it would do so if the whalebone were short and firm as in the Finners. The function of this great lip in supporting the slender and flexible lower ends of the blades of the Greenland whale, and preventing them being driven outwards by the flow of water from within when the animal is closing its mouth, is evident from Captain Gray's drawings and explanation. The whole apparatus is a most perfect piece of animal mechanism.

‘ Captain Gray's evidently truthful drawing of the Greenland right whale is an acquisition to science. What is, however, really wanted to convey an impressive idea of the huge size and extraordinary conformation of this animal is an accurately prepared model of life size, constructed under the direction of one as conversant with its appearance as Captain Gray. Mr. Buckland has shown by his invaluable casts of the smaller Cetacea the best way of exhibiting the external appearance of such animals. It is greatly to be wished that they, or similar specimens, may some day find their way into the National Museum of Natural History, and may be supplemented by the more colossal species, as the sperm, Greenland, and great fin-backed whales. We have done all that we can with the space at our disposal at the College of Surgeons, in exhibiting skeletons of them and many of the smaller species of this most interesting order of animals; we must look to the new museum at South Kensington to do the rest.'

The mechanism of the whale is admirably suited for the conditions in which he is destined by the Creator to live. He wears a great-coat several inches thick—literally *in* his skin; that is to say, the cuticle, or scarf-skin, is very thin and highly polished, like a well-polished boot; the skin itself consists of cells, which are filled up with fat.

This fat, unfortunately for Mr. Whale, is very valuable, not only for burning purposes, but also for dressing jute, a flax-like material, which, when dressed with oil, assumes a lustre not unlike silk. With this jute are made carpets, curtains, and ladies' chignons. Jute is also used in the adulteration of black silk dresses. Ladies who are purchasing black silk dresses can detect the presence of jute by burning. If the fibre is true silk, being animal, the smell will be of burning animal substance; if it be vegetable, the scent of the burning material will be something like that of burning cotton.

The whale has apparently neither arms nor legs: but his two front fins are not fins, they are hands; if the skin be dissected off they will be found to contain five regular fingers, all in one case—imagine the human hand in a hedge-cutter's glove, and you have the model of the whale's paw.   He does not use these paws for prehension or touch, nor, I believe, at all for swimming ; they simply act to balance his weight in the water, and assist him in steering himself.

We now come to his tail.   Among nature's beautiful works three mechanical forces may be said to take pre-eminence : firstly, the stroke of a lion's paw ; secondly, the kick of a giraffe ; and thirdly, the stroke of a whale's tail.   The whale's tail is not only its sole weapon for defence, but is its chief organ of motion.   It is stated that whales can go through the water at the pace of twenty-five to thirty miles to the hour.   The least of these speeds would send them six hundred miles a day, or from 60° north lat. to 60° south lat. in twelve days.

Though the usual colour of the whale on the upper part is shiny black, the fore-part of the body underneath and part of the lower lip are pure white, and the under part towards the tail, slate or lead coloured.   I do not quite understand why the right whale should wear a black coat when he has to bear a temperature of such intense cold.   His cousin, the beluga, wears a white coat.   Here, then, is a problem to be solved ; but depend upon it there is a good reason for the diversity of colour in these two whales' coats.

The whale is a capital diver, but the time occupied in his diving depends upon his business, whether feeding, playing, or travelling.   He is said seldom to remain at the surface to blow longer than ten minutes, during which period he blows eight or nine times ; he then descends for five to ten minutes ; sometimes, when getting his dinner, for fifteen or twenty minutes ; when harpooned he will stay under water fifty minutes.

' When whales are harpooned,' Captain Gray writes,
' and there is no close ice in the immediate neighbourhood
that they can go to for protection, their usual custom is
to dive until they reach the bottom. They seldom go
beyond a depth of seven hundred fathoms, and remain
under water on an average fifty minutes, appearing again
near the same place where they were harpooned. They
then fall an easy prey to their pursuers, being so much
exhausted from dragging such a weight of line, and by the
great pressure they have been subjected to so far below
the surface.

' Should a whale escape, and be again harpooned, it
never commits the same mistake, no matter how many
years may have elapsed ; it always sets off as fast as it can
go along the surface, and is very difficult to take, often
tearing the harpoon out of the blubber, or breaking the
lines. Scoresby says that "a whale's brain is only equal
in proportion to the three-thousandth part of its body," but
they have a very good memory nevertheless.'

Constituted as are the lungs of human beings, it is impossible for men to stay with impunity very long under water,
but in a lung-breathing animal, such as the whale, we find
a wonderful provision for the storing of the blood. At
the back of the lungs, between them and the ribs, is a vast
plexus of blood-vessels, which retain the blood when the
beast is under water, and cannot or is afraid to come up
to breathe. In our own veins there are very complicated
and beautiful valves, well worthy the attention of engineers
who have hydraulic works to manage. Professor Owen
first pointed out that the veins in the whale are remarkable not only for their capacity, but above all *for the*

almost total absence of valves. **The fact is of** the utmost importance to whalers, inasmuch as it enables them, with such comparatively small **weapons** as the harpoon and lance, to kill such **an** enormously large animal as **a** whale. 'The non-valvular structure of the veins in the Cetacea,' says Professor Owen, 'and the pressure of sea-water at the depths to which they retreat when harpooned, explain the profuse and deadly hæmorrhage that follows a wound, which in other Mammalia would be by no means fatal.'

As an instance of the ease with which whales are sometimes **killed,** Captain Gray **thus** relates **the** capture of one :—' It was struck close to the ship during a **thick** fog with a strong gale of wind blowing, and surrounded by a close and heavy pack; a more unfavourable state of matters could hardly be. The whale took **out seven lines,** or eight hundred and forty fathoms, **and stopped** taking any more. The lines **were made fast on board, and** allowed to hang for ten hours before **commencing** to haul them **in. At the end of them** was a whale of the largest size, and **all that was holding** her was a single wire, one-eighth of **an inch in** diameter.'

On the other hand, the immense **power of the whale** is sometimes exerted with fearful effect. To show the **great** strength of a full-grown **whale,** I will quote **the** following description **of the capture of a** big whale by Captain Gray and one of his crews :—

'We were at the time **nearly close** beset, there being only **a small space of water at the floe edge;** many whales were passing through it. One of them **was** harpooned, and went off so **fast** that the harpooner failed to get a turn of the lines round the bullet-head before the boat's lines were all run out. The bullet-head is an **oak post** placed in the bow of the boat, on to which three or more turns of the line are put to help to drag the whale. The second boat's lines soon followed, but a very heavy strain was kept upon them. Two boats' lines were then attached to the end of the lines run out, so as to hang a heavier strain. They were also taken out, and other two boats bent on their lines, and the boats' bows lashed up to the ice to prevent them from being dragged under. One more line was taken out from each of the last boats, equal to two and a half miles.

'The whale by this time had reached the other side of the floe. Men were sent over the ice with lances, and succeeded in killing him; but before he gave in he broke the lines in the dying struggle. Fortunately for us, it was the line nearest the whale that gave way. He proved a valuable prize; his blubber measured twenty-two inches thick along the back.'

The bones of the whale are very peculiar. They are neither hollow, as birds' bones, nor marrow-containing, as our own bones, but composed of a series of cells. These cells are very porous, and contain more or less oil. In a section which I have lately made of a whale's arm-bone, the structure is well demonstrated, especially the binding up, as it were, of this cellular bone structure with an external coating of bone as solid as that forming the leg-bone of an ox. I understand from Captain Gray that the bones from the whales killed are in no way utilised, the reason being, I suppose, want of space on board ship.

There is one bone, however, in the whale which is of exceeding hardness; this is the ear-bone. Now, it is a very remarkable thing that the whale should be in all senses so strictly mammalian except as to one point, and that is the **ear.** The reader should look in the head of the next cod, haddock, or other fish he has for dinner, and he will find two very hard ivory-like bones. These bones are the hearing bones of the fish. **The** fish hear by means of vibration in the water. The whale also lives in the water, **and** therefore, **by** a most beautiful adaptation of means to ends, though purely mammalian, he has, under the special conditions **of** his existence, the ear-bones of a **fish.** These ear-bones **are** not unfrequently found fossil **in Suffolk.** They are called ceteolites.

When a huntsman goes in pursuit of an animal, he must of necessity acquaint himself with the machinery of offence, defence, or escape, with which the animal he is in pursuit of is endowed. The whale, as I have mentioned, has great powers of hearing. These poor persecuted brutes doubtless by this time have found out that whaling-ships are their deadly enemies, and keep a sharp look-out. The vibrations caused by the screw of a steamer would of necessity be heard through water by the whale at a great distance; therefore it is advisable, if it is desired to get near the whales, to take up the screw and use the sails only.

It is the law of nature that all Mammalia should have seven vertebræ in the neck. A giraffe has a very long neck, to enable him to pull down the lower branches of the palmtrees on which he feeds, but he has only seven cervical vertebræ. The whale is also mammalian, therefore he must have seven cervical vertebræ, and so we find he has. When seen in the carcass the whale seems to have no neck; he has not the same necessity as land animals for moving the neck, but, for all that, he requires neck-bones of some kind. We find, therefore, that the seven cervical vertebræ are flattened—in porpoises very much flattened—and appear like seven penny pieces soldered together. I have a beautiful preparation in my museum to show this.

The question now arises, what is to form the food of this marine monster? The problem is difficult, because not only must the animal feed, but he must actually lay up fat; therefore his food must of necessity be abundant; but think what kind of food is likely to be abundant in the frozen or freezing seas. We find, in fact, the largest animal in creation preying, it may be almost said, on the smallest animal in creation. The sea in these parts is sometimes so filled with immense multitudes of small animalcula dispersed through it, that they colour the water of a greenish or brown hue. The principal food of the Greenland whale consists of a small crustacean not larger than the common house-fly, which lives on these animalcula, and which is found in greatest abundance when the temperature of the sea is from 34° to 35°. The ordinary temperature of the sea amongst ice is 29°. The colour of the water varies from dark brown to olive-green and clear blue, the blue water being the coldest.

These little Crustacea are transparent, and the contents of their stomachs can easily be seen to be dark brown or green, as the case may be, giving the like colour to the sea.

Captain Gray tells me that oil can be extracted by properly treating this whale's food. Is it not wonderful that the oil should be as it were already in minute animated drops, so that the whale can easily assimilate them, and fill up the cells of his skin with a vast quantity of oil? a good whale of fifty-two feet being capable of yielding, when boiled down, twenty tons of oil. We have already seen how the whale is to catch these animated oil globules which form its food. Teeth would not be of the least use to him. The only thing to be of use would be a sieve. Aristotle first remarked this fact. '*Mysticetus etiam pilos in ore intus habet vice dentium suis setis similes*'—'The whale has hairs in his mouth instead of teeth, like the hairs of a pig.' On this Professor Owen remarks :—'To a person looking into the mouth of a stranded whale, the concavity of the palates would appear to be beset with coarse hair. The species of Balænoptera which frequents the Mediterranean might have afforded to the father of natural history the subject of his philosophical comparison.'

Captain Gray thus describes the movements of whales when feeding :—' When the food is near the surface, they usually choose a space between two pieces of ice, from three to four hundred yards apart, which whalers term their beat, and swim backwards and forwards until they are satisfied, or the food is exhausted. They often go with the point of their nose so near the surface that the water can be seen running over it, just as it does over a stone in a shallow stream ; they turn round before coming to the surface to blow, and lie for a short time to swallow the food before going away for another mouthful. They often continue feeding in this way for hours, on and off, afterwards disappearing under the nearest floe, sleeping probably under the ice, and coming out again when ready for another meal. In no other way can their sudden reappearance at the same place be accounted for.

'Very often the food lies from ten to fifteen fathoms below the surface of the water. In this case the whales movements are quite different. After feeding, they come to the surface to breathe and lie still for a minute. One can easily see the effort they make when swallowing. They then raise their heads partially out of the water, and dive down again, throwing their tails up in the air every time they disappear. Their course below the water can often be traced from their eddy. This is caused by the movement of the tail, which has the effect of smoothing the water in circles immediately behind them.

'More whales have been caught when feeding in this way than in any other; they lie longer on the surface, and generally head the same way every time they appear. This is very important to whale-fishers, because whales must be approached tail-on to give any certainty of getting near enough to have a chance of harpooning them, and the harpooner has a better idea where to place his boat to be in readiness to pull on to them whenever they come to the surface.

'Like all the other inhabitants of the sea, whales are affected by the tides, being most numerous at the full and new moon, beginning to appear three days before, and disappearing entirely three days after, the change. Often this will go on for months with the utmost regularity, unless some great change in the ice takes place, such as the floes breaking up or the ice being driven off the ground; in either case they will at once disappear.

'No doubt whales are seen and often taken at any time

of the tides; but if a herd is hunted systematically, and they are attached to a particular feeding bank, this is their usual habit. This peculiarity in their habits cannot be easily accounted for; their food is as abundant during the neap as it is in the spring tides.'

I have some very fine specimens, showing the structure of the baleen, in my museum at South Kensington. The longest slip of baleen is no less than 13 ft. 2 in. in length and 9 in. in width. This must have been taken from a magnificent animal. Two other very fine slips of baleen measure respectively 9 ft. 3 in. by 8½ in. The mode of the progressive growth of the baleen is a modification of the design adopted in the tooth of the rabbit or the tusk of the elephant. The baleen is wrongly called whalebone. It certainly comes out of the whale, but there is no bone whatever in its composition. It is composed of hardened hair. The horn of the rhinoceros is also composed of hairs matted, as it were, together into a solid horn. The hairs of the baleen are united one to the other by a kind of animal glue. By boiling and hammering I find the baleen can be reduced to a state of hair.

The great anatomist and founder of the Royal College of Surgeons was the first to describe the wonderful mechanism of the growth of the baleen. I shall quote the words of this great man :—' The plates of the baleen are formed upon a vascular substance not immediately adhering to the lower jaw-bone, but having a more dense substance between, which is also vascular. This substance, which may be called the nidus of the whalebone, sends out thin, broad prongs answering to each plate, on which the plate is formed, as the cock's spur or the bull's horn on the bony core, or a tooth on its pulp, so that each plate is necessarily hollow at its growing end, and the first part of the growth taking place on the inside of the hollow, &c.' The whole passage is too long to quote, but the process of growth may be thus illustrated :—Take an envelope, gum it up, place it on one end, cut off the other edge with scissors, gently squeeze it till it opens a little, imagine the open part of the envelope to be filled with a soft gluey material, and that this material gradually hardens into baleen as it descends, till at last it is a solid plate of baleen, *i.e.* the uncut edge of the envelope.

When at Peterhead I inspected Captain Gray's storehouse of whalebone. The whalebone, as taken from the whale, is piled up against the wall; it is then placed in a large vat containing hot water, and the rough outside is cleaned off by women. I was much struck to find how very soft and elastic whalebone is when wet. I expect that when it is in the whale's mouth it is very pliable, and, in fact, little more than hardened gum. Rats are very fond of whalebone. We pulled down the stacks of whalebone, and Gray was much annoyed to find the rats had gnawed at and spoiled some of the very best pieces. Gray tells me that a whale's age can be ascertained by the growth on the bone each year being shown by a well-marked succession of growth, somewhat like the rings in timber.

The eye of a living whale has a very comical look about it; it has eyelids which open and shut. It is placed very low down in the body (see illustration, p. 320). Captain Gray has seen a whale come up from the bottom, turn on his side, take a good look at the ship, and then go down again. He thinks the whales go under the ice to sleep.

The following are the dimensions of two of the whales of the last voyage :—A bull whale forty-eight feet from nose to tail ; nose to the eye, seventeen feet ; breadth across the head, eight feet ten inches ; gape, nine feet. Another bull whale : total length, forty-seven feet ; head, seventeen feet eight inches ; body between the fins, eleven feet ; breadth of head, nine feet three inches.

At the Peterhead Museum there is a lovely specimen of a fœtal whale about thirty inches long ; this little baby whale is the prettiest thing I have seen for many a day. From examining the specimens at Peterhead I think I discovered an indentation on the nose that proved that sucking whales have whiskers. In a porpoise just born I discovered three hairs on one side of the snout and two on the other. They were very slightly attached to the skin, and of a pinkish colour. The whales suckle their young with milk. Whale's milk sounds very like pigeon's milk. I well recollect my father, the Dean, telling a story of old Mr. Clift, of the College of Surgeons, going down to dissect a whale somewhere at the mouth of the Thames, and coming back with a quantity of whale's milk, from which he obtained cream, and subsequently butter. John Hunter (my great ideal) never tasted whale's milk, but he writes : ‘ Whale's milk is probably very rich, for in that caught near Berkeley with its young, the milk, which was tasted by Mr. Jenner and Mr. Ludlow, surgeon at Sodbury, was rich, like a cow's milk to which cream had been added.’ He then goes on to describe the milk-secreting glands, ‘ situated on each side of the middle line of the abdomen at the lower part ; they are flat bodies lying between the external layer of fat and abdominal muscles. They are there that they may not vary the external shape of the animal, and the trunk is large and appears to act as a reservoir for the milk.'

The young whales are said to suck for at least a year. The mother is very affectionate to them. The yearling whales are called 'shortheads,' because the plates of baleen are almost rudimental. I imagine that as he is sucking he does not require to feed on the ordinary food, just in the same way as a sucking human baby has no teeth, the baby teeth gradually appearing as the time for its requiring solid food progresses. When two years old, and weaned, young whales are naturally thin. They are then called 'stunts.' A great many charity children are stunts (who ever saw a fat charity child?). When they have attained their full size they are called 'schull-fish.'

The following extract regarding the size of the whales is from Scoresby's 'Voyage to Greenland,' chap. vi., page 49 :—

'This whale, though a " sucker," was 19 feet in length, and 14 feet 5 inches in circumference at the thickest part of the body. The external skin on the body was an inch and three-quarters thick, being about twice the thickness of the same membranes in a full-grown animal. The blubber was, on an average, five inches in thickness; the largest of the whalebone measured only twelve inches, about one-half of which was imbedded in the gums. The external part of these fringes, not exceeding six inches in length, did not seem sufficient to enable the little whale yet to catch, by filtration out of the sea, the shrimps and other insects on which the animal in a more advanced stage is dependent for its nourishment. Maternal assistance and protection appeared, therefore, to have been essential for its support.

'The muscles about the neck, appropriated to the movements of the jaws, formed a bed, if extended, of nearly five feet broad, and a foot thick. The central part of the diaphragm was two inches in thickness. The two principal arteries in the neck were so large as to admit a man's hand and arm. The general appearance of the brain is not unlike that of other Mammalia; but its smallness is remarkable. In this whale, of 11,200 pounds, or seventy times the weight of a man, the brain was only three pounds twelve ounces. Large as the whale is in bulk, the throat is but narrow. In this animal the diameter of the œsophagus, when fully distended, was scarcely 2½ inches, with difficulty admitting my hand. The foregoing measurements and weight all refer to a sucking whale that at the time of capture was under maternal protection.'

In the Peterhead Museum there are some very interesting specimens of harpoons. There we see a harpoon taken from the back of a whale by the ship 'Active,' June 30, 1863, supposed to have been in the whale's back thirty-three years; and a harpoon with line attached, taken out of the back of a whale by the crew of the steamship 'Eclipse,' July 1872; this harpoon had been in this whale since 1870.

I have received (among several valuable specimens from the Arctic Seas) some very fine 'whale-lice.' The Latin name of these curious parasites is *Cyamus ceti*, or *Pou de la baleine* of the French. When turned out

of the spirits of wine they dry up immediately, and show
that they are of a horny substance: they are horrid-
looking wretches, buff coloured. The largest is three-
quarters of an inch long, and about the same in width.
There are three legs on each side, and two legs which project from behind, like steering-oars. All these legs are
armed with a claw. The two hind legs have the longest
and strongest grappling-hooks. On placing a big claw
under the microscope, I find it is crooked, at about the
angle of a fish-hook half unbent. The lower third of the claw
is transparent, and has a point sharper than the sharpest
sewing-needle ever turned out at Redditch. So sharp are
these needle-pointed claws that I find if I apply the dead
whale-louse to my cheek, the sharp claws take a firm hold
on to the flesh. Even picked up they will stick firmly to
the fingers. Each beast has two very minute black
eyes, like specks, and the back appears armour-plated, not
unlike the back of an armadillo. There are three females
among the lot. They carry their eggs, the size of a large
egg of an ant, in a sac under the posterior third of the
body. Why do all these parasites breed so fast? These
specimens were taken from a fair-sized whale; the place
where they were found was behind the pectoral fins, just
where they join the body. It frequently happens that the
lice congregate in patches as big as a plate all over the
whale's body, eating great holes into the skin of the unfortunate beast. The whale seems to suffer much from the
persecution of these terrible sharp-clawed parasites, for he
is often seen to jump clean out of the water, as though
attempting to get rid of them. No jumping out of the
water would unseat these sure-seated jockeys, for they

must be cut out of the skin with a knife before a man can get them off. It is stated (but not by Captain Gray) that the whale-lice are occasionally seen in such numbers upon the whales that the individuals so infested are recognised at a considerable distance by the peculiar colour imparted to them by the mass of parasites.

It is very difficult to form a theory as to what may be the use of these parasites to the whale. There may possibly be a reason, but I doubt whether the wretches can afford much domestic pleasure and comfort to the persecutee. It may be possible that it is nature's ordained means for keeping the species in check, and not allowing the whales to increase too rapidly in the seas which they inhabit. I will illustrate my meaning thus :—

In the vast forests of Africa live elephants. Now, these animals are so large and strong that there is nothing bigger than they to beat them. From the elephant we go downwards in the scale of creation, and we will stop at the point of flies. All along this great series we find one kind of animal preying upon another, in obedience to the law, ' Eat and be eaten.' The reader will ask, what is to kill and eat the elephant? My answer is, the flies, of course; and I believe it is a positive fact that a great many elephants are killed by flies. These gigantic animals get wounded. In the hot climates where they live the wounds immediately attract swarms of flies; these flies lay their eggs, and when the young are hatched out they eat great holes into the elephant's body. Pain, irritation, and fever are caused by the attacks of these flies, and I am informed that it not unfrequently happens that elephants are found dead, the cause of death being fly-blows. It may be possible, therefore, that these whale-lice, minute as they are in comparison to the gigantic size of the whale on which they live, may sometimes cause the death of the whale. The death of the whale would be a great boon to the sharks, sea-birds, shrimps, and other sea creatures, to which his flesh is as a Greenwich dinner to hungry Londoners; but yet these comparatively small beasts are not of themselves sufficiently powerful to kill a whale.

A man may fight single-handed a lion, an elephant, or other wild beast, and will probably be victorious; but place this same victorious man in a bed previously occupied by a colony of fleas or Norfolk Howards, and he would soon run, despite a well-stocked armament of rifles, shot-guns, and other sporting paraphernalia. The same inability in man to fight numbers of minute things has often been proved by salmon-anglers, who have been forced to retreat from the river-bank by clouds of mosquitoes, when they did not care a bit for half a dozen water-bailiffs, even though armed with the new clauses of the Salmon Bill of 1873.

It may be possible that these whale-lice, insignificant and unimportant as individuals, may by numbers and constant irritation kill a whale fifty-seven feet long and weighing over a hundred tons, this being about the largest right whale Captain Gray has ever killed.

Whales are also subject to another kind of parasite; it is a barnacle which buries itself deep in the skin of the head. It is called *Coronula balænearis*, or the 'whale's barnacle.' A specimen sent me from Golspie was figured and described in *Land and Water*, May 19, 1866. The specimen itself is in my museum.

THE WHITE WHALE AT WESTMINSTER AQUARIUM.

IT will be well recollected that a whale was on view in the Westminster Aquarium in October 1877. This whale did not survive very long. Farini, then the manager, with great pluck said to his agent, Mr. Zach Coop, ' Zach, he is dead. Go and fetch me another whale; be off directly.' So off goes Mr. Zach up to Lerwick, Shetland, to see whether, by the assistance of the Lerwick fishermen, he could not fill up the vacancy in the whale tank in the Westminster Aquarium. Mr. Coop was, however, a little too late in the season for the Lerwick whales, so he returned whaleless. So said Farini, ' Well, if you cannot catch a whale this side of the Atlantic, we must go to the other side for him.' The telegraph was set to work, and a whale-trap was prepared in St. Paul's Bay, which is situated in the Gulf of St. Lawrence, to the westward of Newfoundland. In the spring of the year the whales come into the estuary of the St. Lawrence River, probably in search of food. So it came to pass that directly the school of whales in the year 1878 entered the River St. Lawrence, they swam straight into the most ingenious trap awaiting them, and were caught, or rather made to strand themselves.

A whale ashore is as helpless a thing as a ship ashore.
There he must stay, floundering on the sand, rock, or mud,
till either the water comes to his assistance, or else he is
picked up by the hands of man. Previously to the whales
coming to St. Paul's Bay their travelling carriages were
prepared to bring them to London. These consisted of
immense boxes or packing-cases, the lids being formed of
loose canvas. Zach Coop managed to pack four of these
gentlemen—one for Westminster, one for Manchester, and
one for Blackpool. The other, the fourth, probably dis-
gusted at the whole proceeding, maliciously departed this
life in the middle of the Atlantic.

The authorities of the Westminster Aquarium tele-
graphed me that the whale would probably arrive about
six o'clock. I had not long to wait when a cab drove up,
out of which jumped Farini, looking very pale and travel-
worn. In the transport of the whales from Liverpool
various misadventures and difficulties, requiring great
management, had taken place. But, however, all's well
that ends well, and the first words that Farini said to me
were, 'He is all right.' Having gone through many such
expeditions in carrying water beasts long distances, I fully
sympathised with Farini's joyous exclamation.

The box was brought to the Aquarium in a van. They
slid it out of the van gently on to the shoulders of a small
army of men. After a considerable amount of shuffling
of feet, and orders promptly obeyed, the whale's box was
placed upon trestles alongside of his future home, the
covering of the canvas was taken off, and I had the first
look at him. He was lying on his stomach in the box,
and was securely packed round with seaweed so that he

could not flop about. I could not see his face, only his blow-hole, which I was delighted to find was acting smoothly and well. The general appearance made one query whether he was alive or dead, but the action of the blow-hole on the top of the head gave one an idea that the creature was a gigantic white human baby with black lips, snoring in its sleep.

The whale is said to weigh about a ton and a half. We did not attempt to lift him out of the box, but simply ordered the carpenters to knock away the boards from one side of it, and to clear away the seaweed as much as possible. This done, all hands were piped to tilt the box —'One, two, three,' and the whale gradually turned over on his side like a man in a restless sleep. Another inch more up, and Mr. Whale rolled off into the water with a terrific splash and bang, sending the spray flying all over the place.

At first he sank right to the bottom, and remained there some little time. We watched him with great anxiety. So numerous had been his adventures for the last five weeks, that no doubt he did not quite know where he was, whether back home in the Gulf of St. Lawrence, or still in his box. Nor had he probably quite made up his mind whether he ought to adapt his blow-hole to breathing air pure and simple, or whether he would have to take the usual precautions to prevent the air getting down into his nose when in the water.

After a while the whale began to realise his position; he gently got up steam with his tail, and gradually ascended to the surface. Arrived there he gave us a specimen of his first blow, which sounded not unlike the splutter made by a man when he first reaches the air after a dive. Then he went down again, being probably somewhat nervous at the assembled company. Finding that he was not molested or bothered by anything, he then began to enjoy himself in his bath, and mightily pleased he seemed to be with the lavations of cold water once more.

I was sorry to see that during his five weeks' journey his cuticle, or scarf-skin, had got loose and was peeling off; but as a set-off to this, he had no cold in his head. When the last whale arrived he certainly had threatening inflammation of the lungs. This present fellow had no symptoms whatever of this.

I picked out of the box a bit of the whale's cuticle; it is very thin, and about the consistency and feel of oiled silk or gutta-percha sheeting. On one side it is very smooth, and looks as though it had been highly polished with furniture polish; it is very transparent, and exhibits numerous specks, reminding us of the appearance of the insertion of the hairs—always in threes—into a pigskin saddle. I was pleased to see that the bath seemed to refresh the whale very much, and to relieve him of much of the skin hanging loose about him. To my mind, the fear was that fungus might grow upon him.

After the whale had been in the bath about an hour I again examined him. By this time the beast seemed to have made himself quite at home. He did not seem the least frightened, but was gently swimming up and down the tank. It was a curious thing that not once did he go near the sides of the tank. He kept in the middle, swimming backwards and forwards

within a given distance. He went to the ends of his beat,
turned round, and came back again, sometimes swimming
in an oval. When he came to the end of his beat he
went 'threes about.' In performing this movement, he
turned his side up to the top of the water, so that one
could see his funny little bead-like black eye. That
whales do this when they look to the top of the water—
the natural position of the eyes enabling them to see
only sideways—is a fact, as I know from Captain David
Gray, for he has seen more than once a whale come up
from deep water, and inspect the ship, swimming round
and round it, just as did the Westminster whale. When
the whale had been in his whalery about three hours,
he had quite recovered himself both in mind and body.
He was swimming very leisurely, very easily, and very
gracefully, and blowing about three times in two minutes ;
his blow-hole is situated a comparatively long distance
from the point of his nose. The first thing to be observed was the point of his nose; instantly followed the
blow-hole, and you could hear the sharp quick puff, which
can be imitated by saying the word 'puff' with open
lips. Then came his arched back, which appeared
for a moment on the surface of the water like a crescent.
Many of our friends have doubtless seen porpoises rolling
at sea, and what a curious appearance their black backs
have in the distance.

> Upon the swelling waves the dolphins show
> Their bending backs, then, swiftly darting, go,
> And in a thousand wreaths their bodies throw.

I was at once reminded of pictures on old china, &c.,

of Arion, who made his escape by mounting a dolphin and
riding him across the ocean, a fact thus chronicled by
Ovid :—

> But past belief, a dolphin's archèd back,
> Preserved Arion from his destined wreck ;
> Secure he sits, and with harmonious strains
> Requites the bearer for his friendly pains.

How Arion managed to stick on the slippery back of a
dolphin, a considerable 'buck jumper,' I know not, but
poets and painters are very wonderful fellows, and can
make impossibilities look like possibilities.

The arrival of this whale was important in two senses.
Firstly, as a sight pure and simple, to the younger minds
certainly educational. I observed two little children gazing
most attentively at the whale, and that a new idea was at
that moment being photographed on their infant minds I
have no doubt. Secondly, the whale may enable naturalists to discover many points in the history of Cetacea
hitherto unexplained, to wit, the action of the blow-hole.
The problem solved by this wonderful piece of mechanism
is very marvellous.

The first unaided idea, of course, is that an animal
destined to live in water must be a fish, and, of course,
breathe by gills. I once terribly offended an old salt by
telling him a whale was not a fish. ' Hang it, man !' he
said, ' I've been at sea man and boy for forty years, and
now you tell me a whale is not a fish !' A whale, however, is pure mammalian like ourselves. The young are
born alive and suck milk ; their blood is warm ; they have
a four-cavitied heart ; their bones, muscles, and nervous
system resemble in structure those of other Mammalia.

But the orders are that these great Mammalia are to live all their lives in the waters without ever coming out. Other creatures, notably the hippopotamus, the walrus, and seals, come out of the water when they choose, but get their food in the water; how then is the breathing of these animals to be managed? In the seal we find self-acting valves that close the apertures in the nostrils as tightly as a cork in a wine-bottle when the creature descends beneath the waves.

In the whale we find altogether a different kind of self-acting breathing-valve. The windpipe does not communicate with the mouth; a hole is, as it were, bored right through the back of the head. Engineers would do well to copy the action of the valve of the whale's blow-hole; a more perfect piece of structure it is impossible to imagine. Day and night, asleep or awake, the whale works his breathing apparatus in such a manner that not a drop of water ever gets down into the lungs. Again, the whale must of necessity stay a much longer period of time under water than seals; this alone might possibly drown him, inasmuch as the lungs cannot have access to fresh air. We find that this difficulty has been anticipated and obviated by a peculiar reservoir in the venous system, which reservoir is situated at the back of the lungs.

The white whale is the *Beluga delphinapterus*. His home is in the Arctic seas, especially the great bays and straits which so properly record the names of Davis and Hudson, and which may be generally said to separate Greenland (lat. 60° to 80° N.) from the north-east coast of British North America. What they do or whither they go all the winter, no human being knows. Their structure is such that their fat, which surrounds their body like a great-coat, preserves them during the awful cold they have to bear. In habits these animals are gentle, and not fierce like the great cachalot. They are fond of company, and go in herds. I am informed that they will seek rather than avoid the company of man, and that when a vessel is in sight they will come and play round the bows as a sort of welcome to their kingdom in the vast deep. It is also stated that Mr. Beluga forms a sort of advanced guard of the valuable whalebone whale; and when the beluga is seen, harpooners begin to look up their whale lances. Like the right or whalebone whale, the attachment of the mother to its calf is very great. The calf, when first born, is said to be of a dazzling whiteness; as it gets bigger it becomes milk-white. Beluga's food is cod, flat-fish, such as plaice, flounders, &c., and possibly salmon. At the Aquarium he was fed with eels. One of these eels managed to creep inside a fold of the whale's skin, and seemed inclined to eat the whale instead of the whale eating him; the whale had to be caught with a great sheet of canvas, and taken out of the water before this eel could be removed. Tench were also tried, as the eels seemed a little too active for Beluga, and tench are slug-gish. It was curious to remark how the eels seemed to know he was their enemy, for they kept up in a corner quite clear of his track. Roach also were placed in his tank; it was very remarkable to see how the roach seemed likewise to know that the whale was their enemy. As he came near them the shoals broke up immediately, and dispersed right and left as quickly as they could.

Beluga's mouth was not very wide; he had nine or ten small teeth in it. His pectoral fins were oval, broad, and thick, and he generally used them for balancing purposes. Every now and then he took a stroke with them to assist his forward movement.

Those who wish for a nearer view of the beluga should examine the cast which I took of him, now in my museum, which contains a very fair collection of casts of the whale kind. Casting is the only possible way of preserving the exact outline of whales. The plaster takes accurately the impression of every fold in the skin, and the exact dimensions of the tail, mouth, eyes, lips, &c. No stuffing skeletons or drawings will do this. The drawback to casting is that it is very expensive and exceedingly laborious.

NATURAL HISTORY OF THE ARCTIC NARWHAL.

WHEN at Peterhead, during the herring inquiry, I observed on board the whaler 'Eclipse,'[1] a very fine specimen of the narwhal's skull, with the horn still resting in it. This specimen Captain Gray most kindly gave me for my fish museum, South Kensington. The total length of this horn projecting from the skull was 4 ft. 1 in. and the portion of the horn inside the skull 10 inches; the weight of the horn ten and a half pounds. The beauty of this specimen is that it is quite in the rough. One-half of it presents a dark reddish appearance, as if it had been touched over with paint. Captain Gray tells me this is a natural colour, and is frequently seen in narwhal horn. The twist of the horn goes from right to left. The horn grows from the left side of the skull. It seldom if ever grows from the right side of the skull, never from the centre. Occasionally narwhals' skulls are found with two horns; in this case the right horn is always very small. Captain Gray has been kind enough to send me the following interesting account of the narwhals that have come under his notice. It will be seen from this what huge creatures these narwhals really are :—

[1] I have given a full description of the 'Eclipse' in my *Log-book of a Fisherman and Zoologist*, p. 295.

' I herewith send you all the measurements of narwhals that I have recorded.

'1st. Female; length, 12 ft. 6 in.; girth, 7 ft. 6 in.; horn, 3 ft. 10 in. long, very rare in the female.

'2nd. Male; length, 13 ft.; girth, 8 ft.; horn, 5 ft. 4½ in.

'3rd. Male; length, 14 ft. 3 in.; girth, 8 ft. 4 in.; horn, 6 ft. 4½ in.

'4th. Male; length, 14 ft. 4 in.; girth, 9 ft. 1 in.; had a broken horn, which I sent you lately.

'5th. Male; length, 15 ft. 1 in.; girth, 9 ft. 5 in.; horn, 7 ft. 6 in.

'6th. Male; length, 15 ft. 4 in.; girth, 10 ft.; horn, 7 ft. 8 in. You have this horn in your museum.

'The narwhal whose head and horn I gave you lately, was caught in latitude 78° 45' N.; longitude 0° 30' W. I do not know what might have been the length of the longest horn I have seen, but I have measured one 8 ft. 4 in., and I do not think they often exceed that length.

' I am not sure what use the narwhal has for its horn. It is only the males who usually have them. We see them often striking them against each other, and they are nearly always broken at the point.

'The narwhal is a very peaceful creature; they are like their big brothers the whales. The male and female go in different herds. They are very subject to colds, if one may judge from the hoarse way some of them blow; you would fancy sometimes you had got amongst a herd of cattle. I examine the stomach of every narwhal taken, and find that their staple food in Greenland is cuttlefish.

The inner skin of the narwhal is used for making shoe-leather.

'Narwhals are only taken by whale-fishers as a pastime. I have heard of vessels in Davis Straits taking 100 of them. I do not know any particular use for narwhal horns. There was a great demand for them some years since. Their value at that time was from 20s. to 30s. per pound. It was said they were sent to Japan to ornament religious houses or churches, but I do not know the truth of this.'

Captain Gray is quite right about the use of narwhal horns in Japanese temples. A friend of mine sent two hundred pounds' worth of narwhal horns to the Chinese and Japanese markets, but unfortunately the ship was taken by pirates. The Chinese Ambassador not long ago examined at my house the specimen Captain Gray gave me, and was so much struck with its appearance that I do not think it possible he could have seen a narwhal horn before. He was most anxious to get a specimen to take back with him to China. I fancy that the narwhal horns are used in some form of worship in the Buddhist temples in China.

As regards the question of the female narwhal carrying a horn, Captain Gray captured in June 1872, as above mentioned, a female narwhal carrying a horn 3 ft. 10 in. in length. The only other instance I have met with of a female narwhal having a horn is mentioned by Scoresby. In the account of his voyage to Greenland in 1822, he says :—' Besides the whale now captured we killed during our stay near the same place two female narwhals, one of which, a case most extraordinary if not unprecedented in this sex, had an external horn. This horn was 4 ft. 3 in. in length, of which 12 inches were embedded in the skull. It had also a milk tusk, as is common in others of the sex, 9 inches long, of a conical form, and obliquely truncated at the thicker end, without the knot found in many of the milk tusks. The horn, as in the male, was on the left side of the head. The length of the animal was 13 ft. 6 in. It was beautifully variegated with bluish black or grey spots. It differed in no respect from other females of the same age excepting with regard to the horn.'

The ivory of the weapon is valuable ; it is more compact, harder, and more susceptible of a good polish than that of the elephant's tusk. There is shown to visitors at the Versailles Library a walking-stick formed of a narwhal's tusk, ornamented with mother-of-pearl. The throne of the Kings of Denmark, once—and perhaps still—to be seen in the Castle of Rosenberg, is of the same material.

Some years ago there was a remarkable collection of narwhal tusks on sale at Mr. Wareham's, Castle Street, Leicester Square. There were upwards of forty of these tusks, varying in length from 2 ft. 6 in. to 9 feet. I do not recollect ever having seen so many or such fine tusks in one series.

When Captain Gray returned from his whaling voyage in 1879, he gave me the following most interesting account of a fight between a narwhal and a walrus :—

Extract from the Log of the S.S. 'Eclipse,' July 6, 1879.
' Running north through floes and loose ice this forenoon I noticed some distance ahead what I at first took to be the stock of a hand harpoon, standing out of very greasy water, and a number of birds sitting round it. This I at

first thought might be a dead whale, just rising to the surface, but I soon saw that it was a narwhal horn. As we came nearer I observed something brown-looking, and was puzzled for some time before I made this out to be a walrus, evidently holding the narwhal.

'As soon as we were near enough, I sent two boats away with orders to strike a hand harpoon into the narwhal, and fire a gun harpoon into the walrus, both of which they did. The first harpooner struck the narwhal close past the walrus's nose, whereupon he looked very savage, and let go his hold of the narwhal, which immediately began to sink. The walrus being unwilling to part with his prey upon such easy terms, dived underneath the narwhal and raised him to the surface, again renewing his hold with his teeth, and clasping him round the body with his flippers.

' The second boat now came up, and the harpooner fired his gun harpoon through the walrus's neck. He then let go his hold of the narwhal, and dragged the boat a considerable distance to windward, when a rifle bullet in the back of the head finished him.

' On examination, after getting them on board, we found the narwhal disembowelled, and a great part of the belly eaten away or torn into shreds by the walrus, who had been very particular as to the parts he ate, and had been taking plenty of time to feed. He had eaten the blubber as clean off the skin as if it had been flinched with a knife. The narwhal was quite fresh, and newly killed, and in the death-struggle had been all scored with the walrus's tusks from nose to tail in every direction, although the inner skin was not cut.

' The walrus was in prime condition. The blubber upon him was three inches thick : his stomach was quite full of pieces of sealskin and the part of the narwhal which he had eaten.   He had, at a moderate estimate, one hundred and fifty gallons of oil and blubber in his stomach.

' The length of the narwhal was fourteen feet, exclusive of horn, by nine feet in circumference. The length of horn was five feet.

' The walrus measured eleven feet long, and nine feet ten inches in circumference.

' The question is, How did the walrus manage to hold a powerful animal like the narwhal ? certainly more in his element than the walrus, and who can spin out a hundred fathoms of whale line very smartly, even with a big gun harpoon through and through him.

' The only way I can think of is that he had found the narwhal asleep, gone underneath him, dug his tusks into his belly, and clasped him round the body with his flippers, in which position we found them, with this difference, that the walrus was uppermost.

' This is only the third walrus I have seen off on the deep-water whaling banks during the last fourteen years. Their natural home being near the land, where their ordinary food is, all kinds of shellfish, I could never before understand how they got their living so far from the shore, not knowing that they would eat seals and narwhals, or that they could catch them.   . . .

' I expect that those we see out in deep water are like rogue elephants driven out of the herd, or like the man-eating tigers we hear of in India.'

UNCLE TOM, THE ALLIGATOR, AT THE SOUTHPORT AQUARIUM.

I WAS much pleased to be able to pay a short visit to the
Southport Aquarium on my way home from the north in
November 1876. The most remarkable novelty was a
splendid alligator about eight feet long. He had a nice
spacious glass cage all to himself, the two ends of the cage
containing gravel stones, and in the centre was a pond in
which he could bathe when so inclined. When first
bought, Mr. Alligator was in a very seedy condition
indeed, terribly thin and wan-looking—in fact, half
starved. His skin was all in cracks, and his coat of mail
had to be oiled every morning by means of a flannel on
the end of a stick. This acted like a Turkish bath to our
friend, and did his constitution good. For many days,
even weeks, he sulkily refused to eat and lay quiet and
still like a stuffed thing. At last he took—all of a gulp—
a live pigeon, and ever afterwards he fed well. The secret
of getting him to eat was temperature—temperature the
old story, the key to so many fishery problems, whether of
salmon, oysters, or alligators. Hot-water pipes were introduced under the floor of his den, and Mr. Alligator,
feeling the agreeable heat to his gouty toes and elegant
figure, fancied, I suppose, he was back again in the tropics,

so he woke up and began to eat; and what more tasteful beginning could there be than a nice live pigeon with feather sauce? This ogre now feeds capitally on pigeons; in fact, he is getting expensive to keep; he will eat beef, fish, and almost anything. They don't stand live pigeon dinners every day.

Anxious to show me his pet feeding, the curator offered to give the alligator more supper; he had already devoured his proper supper. The curator got on to the top of the cage and touched him gently with an iron rod. I was surprised to see the activity of the rascal; he opened his eyes with a jerk, up went his head like a run-away hansom cab horse, he gave an indignant whisk with his tail like a lady picking up her skirts when a clumsy fellow puts his foot on the pet lace, and, to my surprise, began to puff himself up. Gradually he became larger, larger, and larger, like the blowing up of a football; his armour glittered, and the bony studs stood well out from the soft intermediate skin. I confess, when at his full I longed to run a pin into him to save his life, as I saw he had a chance of meeting with the same fate as the foolish frog in Æsop's Fables, who vainly puffed himself up trying to become as big as the ox, with whom he was having an argument. Just, however, as he came to the bursting point, *Alligatorus Rex alligatorum* suddenly relaxed himself, and his steam escaped, I suppose, through his larynx and nose. Anyhow, he began a most sonorous hiss. 'H-i-s-s, h-i-s-s;' I can hear it now—just the noise a dragon ought to make. It was like no hiss I ever heard before, much deeper and louder sounding than any snake. As he continued his hissing he became thinner and thinner, till he looked quite the skeleton of his former pretty self. Then he began to blow himself up again, for (I could see it) the iron rod was getting up the monkey of Mr. Alligator.

A chicken's head and neck were then suddenly thrown into the bath; in an instant Leviathan forgot his rage. (Mem.: when a *homo bipes implumes,* one of our own noble species, loses his temper, give him a dinner, and he will be all right, showing once again that 'the nearest way to the heart is down the mouth.') However, hearing the chicken's head fall splash into the water, the alligator —he should be called Uncle Tom—was after it in an instant, and seized it just as a dog catches up a running rat in his mouth. He first of all bit it spitefully as though to kill it, if it happened to be a live thing; and then—one, two, three, and away—chump; back went his head, down his throat went the chicken's head in a moment. Reader, hold your nose and swallow a pill before the looking-glass, and you will understand how Uncle Tom swallowed the chicken's head. His blackship then gave a gulp, and, like the 'Oh the poor workhouse boy' in the song, asked for more. Three chickens' heads and a bit of beef, extra rations, did Uncle Tom get that evening, and all on my account. Supper over, he crawled on to his warm bed of shingle, and as the door over his head closed, he lazily shut his eyes, as much as to say, 'Thank ye, my boy, you may come as often as you like. Now don't bother me, I'm going to sleep; good night, my hearties.' 'Here, hie! please give me a nice live pike for my breakfast to-morrow morning. I like pike; I shall dream of pike, for I like (just as you like) a bit of sport as well as a bit of grub, and if I can combine the two, why, so much the better.'

Really, 'Uncle Tom' is a grand beast; he is growing so fast that he is to have a new drawing-room and dining-room, and then he will have space to swish his tail; he has not much room for his tail just now. I wonder how it is that in the 'struggle for existence' his tail has not begun to curl; may be his descendants in one hundred thousand years will have their tails curled up like a pug-dog's. By the way, why do some pigs wear straight tails, some curly tails? There's a problem for you.

Besides big Uncle Tom, there are a number of smaller alligators. Close to the end of the Uncle's cage is a charming family of baby alligators, from ten inches to one foot long. These little boys and girls have a nice hot nursery, heated from underneath, and a flannel blanket over their dear little heads. They are as active as blackbeetles, and when their counterpane is taken off, scuttle away in all directions. If I reckoned right, there were twenty or thirty of these little fellows. Several of the ladies in Southport have purchased pets from among them, and it may be that no Southport lady will consider her establishment perfect without a baby alligator to bask on the hearth-rug, and go out for a walk on the promenade with her. When the pet defuncts, he can be stuffed, gilt, and put in the hat for an ornament, don't you know?

However, those in the Aquarium are growing fast; they gorge like charity children at a 'tea and bun' festival. The keeper cuts up fish into small bits, and throws them into the cage; they scramble for them famously, and apparently love each other in that disinterested, charitable, and unselfish manner which may be seen by a careful observer who throws down handfuls of coppers among the London *gamins* and street Arabs in the crowd when waiting for the Lord Mayor to pass through Fleet Street on ' All Sprats' Day, November 9.

But there are yet more of Uncle Tom's relations at Southport. A huge box, looking like a gigantic coal-scuttle, stands near the boilers in the engine-room. Open *sesame!* and lo and behold a nest of young alligators of all sizes and shapes, like the ladies' bonnets and hats in a Regent Street shop! The curator dives his hand in and picks them out one by one, holding them aloft like an old fishwife in the Edinburgh market selling Scotch haddies. The lot are not yet presentable. They have not yet received the certificates of the School Board, and their tempers and appetites are not sufficiently mollified by the furnace fire to go into the glass apartments which are getting ready for them, so they remain at their ease, toast themselves before the engine-room fire, while the engine-driver consoles their minds by whistling to them ' Tommy, make room for your uncle,' and feeds them with bread and cheese, which they will not eat.

*

THE WAXWORKS IN WESTMINSTER ABBEY.

In all ages and in all times there has been a natural desire among the human race to perpetuate the memory of themselves, their ancestors, and of illustrious persons, both men and women. The modes adopted of preserving the memory of deceased people have been, first, by preserving the actual bodies; second, by making likenesses of these bodies; or third, by erecting monuments with the name engraved upon them. In the earliest ages of mankind the ancient Egyptians, who had attained to a high state of civilisation, attempted to preserve the remains of their friends by means of embalming.

My dear old friend Herodotus, born B.C. 484, who, some two thousand three hundred years ago, note-book in hand, 'inspected' the manners and customs of the Egyptians, obtained from the priests—I wonder how he got the information?—a detailed account of how to make mummies. This is the sum and substance of Herodotus's official report. Mummy-making was probably a profession, and these mummy-makers charged pretty high for their labours. To make a person into a first-class mummy cost a talent of silver (about equal to 225*l.* of English money), the second cost twenty minæ (or 75*l.*), the third a much smaller sum. The Egyptian mummy-makers knew quite

well that the dry climate of Egypt would greatly assist in
the preservation of their work   Those of my readers who
wish to see a first-class mummy should examine, in the
Royal College of Surgeons, Lincoln's Inn Fields, the remains of the priest of the god Ammon.   The name of this
dignitary of the Egyptian Church was Horsiensi of Thebes.
He was the son of Naspihiniegori, another priest, and he
held the office of thurifer, or incense-bearer—there was no
Lord Penzance in those days.   Now the Rev. Horsiensi has
in his mummy state attained a good old age.   Thebes, also
called Hecatompylos, on account of its hundred gates, was
in its splendour 1600–800 B.C., so that the mummied
priest we can go and see any day is about three thousand
years old.

The first form of monument was simplicity itself—it
consisted simply of throwing a stone or earth upon the
deceased person.   We find this idea conveyed to us very
neatly by Horace (Odes, i. 28) in the request made by the
deceased sailor, Archytas, to throw an earthen veil over his
shipwrecked body :—

> At tu, nauta, vagæ ne parce malignus arenæ
>   Ossibus et capiti inhumato
> Particulam dare. .   .   .   .   .
> Quamquam festinas (non est mora longa), licebit
>   Injecto ter pulvere curras.

> Nor thou, my friend, refuse with impious hand
> A little portion of this wandering sand
> To these my poor remains.
> Whate'er thy haste, oh ! let my prayer prevail,
> Thrice throw the sand, then hoist the flying sail.

The urgent request of poor Archytas was probably due

to the idea which prevailed among the good people of those days, that an unburied person wandered about after death one hundred years. Here is the evidence of the belief. Virgil writes (Æneid) :—

> Hæc omnis, quam cernis, inops inhumataque turba est ;
> Portitor ille Charon ; hi, quos vehit unda, sepulti.
> Nec ripas datur horrendas et rauca fluenta
> Transportare prius, quam sedibus ossa quierunt.
> Centum errant annos, volitantque hæc littora circum.

'All that crowd which you see consists of unburied persons. The ferryman is Charon ; these whom the stream carries are interred, for it is not permitted to transport them over the horrid banks and hoarse resounding waves before their bones are lodged in urns. They wander a hundred years, and flutter about these shores.'

The loose stones thrown on a body out of respect were probably after a while replaced by one stone. The body was buried, and the stone placed above the body as a memorial of its resting-place. The best example of this, to my idea, is conveyed by the Pyramids of Egypt, which are sepulchral monuments to the memory of kings. When the Radcliffe Library was first built at Oxford, it was spitefully remarked that this learned physician simply wished to erect a huge monument to himself.

The modern form of monument is a stone placed either over the grave, or else in some place where the deceased was personally known. Such a monument may be said to represent the separate stones thrown on Archytas, consolidated into one block, with the name subsequently inscribed thereon.

Another kind of monument is the actual representation

of the person when alive. The figure was represented either as a whole figure such as a life-sized statue, or as a bust; and the figure or bust we find either erected in public places, such as the Duke of Wellington at Hyde Park Corner, Lord Nelson at Charing Cross, Jenner at Kensington Gardens; or placed in a consecrated edifice. Hence probably the origin of conserving these memorials of the illustrious departed at Westminster Abbey, that tomb of kings; or, as the eloquent Dean Stanley so aptly called it, the 'home of the people of England, and the most venerated fabric of the English Church.'

These monuments are made sometimes of stone, generally of the most imperishable stone, viz. marble. They are also sometimes made of metal, highly gilt, and ornamented; seldom of wood. There is, however, another kind of material which claims favour to be utilised for monumental purposes; that material is wax. Wax in itself is about as imperishable a substance as can be found among animal or vegetable substances; but it has the disadvantage of being easily melted, and very friable, hence it has not been used very much for monuments. Wax was sometimes used in embalming, and it was a capital material for making the wrinkles in the bandages of mummies air-tight; even in the present day a form of wax is used for the tops of pickle-bottles. The body of King Agesilaus was enveloped in wax, and conveyed to Lacedemon. The Persians also used it for sepulchral purposes— *Persæ jam cera circumlitos condiunt ut quam maxime permaneant diuturna corpora.* In the days of our ancestors, it appears that wax was put on its trial for monumental purposes, and I propose in this article to make some remarks on the use of **wax** for effigies, commonly known as waxworks.

Waxen images of persons seem somehow or another to have fallen into disrepute. For my own part, if wax can be used to preserve the likeness of a person, I do not see why it should not be as highly esteemed as marble. I suppose it is not much thought of because of the waxen heads of ladies with long hair we see in the barbers' shops. Waxen babies, pigs, ears, hands, arms, eyes, noses, &c., are hung up as *ex-votos* at the present day in churches in France.

I have lately examined very carefully the oldest waxworks in England. These, I need hardly say, are the waxworks now in Westminster Abbey, and which to my mind are national relics worthy of the greatest respect and reverence. The following account is given in a description of the Abbey, its monuments and curiosities, printed by ' J. Newbery, at the Bible and Sun, in St. Paul's Churchyard, 1754.' In this curious pamphlet, the Westminster Abbey waxworks are called the ' Play of the Dead Volks ' (*sic*) and the ' Ragged Regiment.'

The following is the account of the condition of these waxworks one hundred and twenty years ago :—

' Over this chapel (Islip, otherwise St. Erasmus) is a chantry, in which are two large wainscot-presses, full of the effigies of princes and others of high quality buried in the Abbey. These effigies resembled the deceased as nearly as possible, and were wont to be exposed at the funerals of our princes and other great personages in open chariots, with their proper ensigns of royalty or honour appended. Those that are here laid up are in a sad

mangled condition; some stripped and others in tattered
robes, but all maimed or broken. The most ancient are
the least injured, by which it would seem as if the cost-
liness of their clothes had occasioned the ravage; for
the robes of Edward VI., which were once of crimson
velvet, but now appear like leather, are left entire; but
those of Queen Elizabeth and King James I. are entirely
stripped, as are all the rest of everything of value. In
two handsome wainscot-presses are the effigies of King
William and Queen Mary and Queen Anne in good condition, and greatly admired by every eye that beholds
them.'

The figure of Cromwell is not here mentioned, but in
the account of his lying in state the effigy is described as
made to the life in wax, apparelled in velvet, gold lace,
and ermine. 'This effigies (sic) was laid upon the bed of
state, and carried upon the hearse in funeral procession;
both were then deposited in Westminster Abbey; but at
the Restoration the hearse was broken in pieces, and the
effigies was destroyed after hanging from a window at
Whitehall.'

When my father was Dean of Westminster, somehow
or other he seldom used to show visitors to the Abbey
into this curious room, and it is now only to be seen by
special order from the Dean. The visitor ascends through
a time-worn staircase into the chapel, and a most curious
sight then meets his eye. Set up against the wall are
very large, massive cases, not unlike big clock cases.
There are glasses in front of these, so that the figures
inside can well be seen. As far as I could see, they are not
labelled except with chalk superscriptions.

Dr. Stanley, Dean of Westminster, has, in his most interesting 'Memorials of Westminster Abbey,' p 340 (Murray, 1868), the following able observations on these waxworks :—

'Amongst the various accompaniments of great funerals—the body lying in state, guarded by the nobles of the realm ; the torchlight procession ; the banners and arms of the deceased hung over the tomb—there was one so peculiarly dear to the English public as to require a short notice.

'This was the *herse*—not, as now, the car which conveys the coffin, but a platform highly decorated with black hangings, and containing a *waxen effigy* of the deceased person. It usually remained for a month in the Abbey, near the grave, but in the case of sovereigns for a much longer time. It was the main object of attraction, sometimes even in the funeral sermon. Laudatory verses were attached to it with pins, wax, or paste. Of this kind probably was Ben Jonson's epitaph on Lady Pembroke :—

> Underneath *this sable herse*
> Lies the subject of all verse,
> Sidney's sister,' &c.

They were ever highly esteemed as works of art.

'Mr. Emanuel Decretz (Sergeant-painter to King Charles I.) told me [1] in 1649 that the catafalco of King James at his *funerall* (which is a kind of bed of state erected in Westminster Abbey, as Robert, Earl of Essex had, Oliver Cromwell, and General Monke) was very ingeniously designed by Inigo Jones, and that he made

[1] Aubrey's *Letters and Lives*, ii. 412.

the four heads of the caryatides of plaster of Paris, and
made the drapery of them of white callico, which was very
handsome and very cheap, and showed as well as if they
had been cutt out of white marble.

'These temporary erections, planted here and there in
different parts of the Abbey, must of themselves have
formed a singular feature in its appearance. But the
most interesting portion of them was the "lively effigy,"
which was there placed after having been carried in a
chariot before the body. This was a practice which has
its precedent, if not its origin, in the funerals of the great
men of the Roman Commonwealth. The one distinguishing mark of a Roman noble was the right of having
figures with waxen masks, representing his ancestors,
carried at his obsequies and placed in his hall.

'In England the royal funerals were, till the time of
Henry V., distinguished by the exhibition of the corpse
itself of the deceased sovereign. But even before that
time the practice of effigies had been adopted.

'These wax figures were detached from the herses and
kept in the Abbey, generally near the graves of the
deceased, but were gradually drafted off into wainscot
presses above the Islip Chapel. Here they were seen in
Dryden's time—

> And now the presses open stand,
> And you may see them all a-row.

'In 1658 the following were the waxen figures thus
exhibited:—

> Henry the Seventh and his fair Queen,
> Edward the First and his Queen,

Henry the Fifth here stands upright,
And his fair Queen was this Queen,
The noble Prince, Prince Henry,
King James's eldest son,
King James, Queen Anne, Queen Elizabeth.
And so this chapel's done.

'With this agrees the curious notice of them in 1708 :—

'And so we went on to see the ruins of majesty in the women (*sic*, waxen?) figures placed there by authority. As soon as we had ascended half a score stone steps in a dirty, cobweb hole, and in old, worm-eaten presses, whose doors flew open at our approach, here stood Edward III. as they told us, which was a broken piece of waxwork, a battered head, and a straw-stuffed body, not one-quarter covered with rags. His beautiful queen stood by, not better in repair; and so, the number of half a score kings and queens, not near so good figures as the King of the Beggars make, and all the begging crew would be ashamed of their company. The rear was brought up with Good Queen Bess, with the remnants of an old dirty ruff, and nothing else to cover her.

'Stow also describes the effigies of Edward III. and Philippa, Henry IV. and Catherine, Henry VII. and Elizabeth of York, Henry, Prince of Wales, Elizabeth, James I., and Queen Anne as shown in the chamber close to Islip Chapel. Of these the wooden blocks, entirely denuded of any ornament, still remain.

'But there are eleven figures in a tolerable state of preservation. That of Queen Elizabeth was, as we have seen, already worn out in 1708, and the existing figure is,

B B

doubtless, the one made by order of the chapter to commemorate the bicentenary of the foundation of the Colle-
giate Church in 1760.   As late as 1783 it stood in Henry
VII.'s Chapel.   The effigy of Charles II. used to stand over
his grave, and close beside him that of General Monk.
The former is tolerably perfect, and seems to have early
attracted attention from the contrast with his battered
predecessors.   Monk used to stand beside his monument
by Charles II.'s grave.   The effigy is in too dilapidated a
condition to be shown, but the remnants of his armour
exist still.   The famous cap, in which the contributions
for the showmen were collected, is gone.'

The first effigy to which I made my bow was King
Charles II., dressed in magnificent raiment.   The wax of
the face is somewhat bleached by the sun, but I should
imagine from the pictures that the portrait is exceedingly
good.   The robes once must have been very grand ; the
lace on the king's breast is of the finest Venetian point.
The king has long black hair ; he was evidently a dark-
looking man, but one expects that any moment his features will break out into a jovial smile.   King Charles II.
died A.D. 1685—nearly two hundred years ago.   If this is
the original effigy used at his funeral, it has lasted very
well indeed.   Immediately opposite King Charles II.
stands, also in a large case like a clock case, the Duchess
of Buckinghamshire, with one son as a child.   She was
the daughter of James II. ; she died in 1743, and the
waxen effigies of herself and her son were prepared for
her funeral.   It is difficult, on account of the bad light,
exactly to make out her dress, but it appeared to be very
magnificent, though dust-covered, and in excellent pre-

servation, although nearly one hundred and forty years old. The other surviving effigies are those of William and Mary, Queen Anne, the beautiful Duchess of Richmond, of Charles II.'s time, the Earl of Chatham, and Lord Nelson; the last two figures not being genuine funeral effigies, but added as attractions to the collection.

THE JEWS' FISH-MARKET IN LONDON.

PASSOVER CUSTOMS OF LONDON JEWS.

HAVING heard that a great number of small fry of fresh-water fish were being sent to the Jews' fish-markets in London, between Bishopsgate and Whitechapel, in the spring of 1878, I made time, during the sitting of the Committee on Mr. Mundella's Fresh-Water Fishery Bill, now a most useful Act of Parliament, to inspect for myself, in order to see how far the proposed provisions of this Act might interfere with the food supply of those wonderful people the Jews. My visit was paid just before the Feast of the Passover was about to commence.

This part of London is simply a Jewish colony, and the general appearance of the place and people gave me the idea of a strange foreign town. I seldom heard English spoken at all, in the streets or between buyer and seller, but a language was used in conversation quite strange to me. I wondered if it might be Hebrew. The streets were very narrow and very dirty; the shops also had a strange look about them; the advertisements in the windows appeared to be in Hebrew, not in English. The bakers seemed very busy; their shop windows were filled with round thin cakes, about twelve inches across; these are the Passover cakes. Several men were packing

these cakes in half-hundredweights, probably to send to
Jews in other parts of England.

Another species of food I observed was quite new to
me, namely, cucumbers, apparently boiled and placed in
salt and water, selling at a penny or halfpenny a slice ; I
cannot think how any one can eat them.   The fried fish
shops were very abundant ; the fish was sold cold, and
looked excellent : of course I tasted this ; it was plaice,
cut into junks, and sold for a penny and twopence a junk.
This fish is, I believe, first dipped in batter, and then fried
in boiling oil ; but this cannot be quite all, because the
fish had a nice delicate taste of almonds ; perhaps it may
be almond oil that is used, or essence of almonds with
salad oil.   Halibut, as well as plaice, seems to be a very
favourite fish with the Jews, but it is more expensive.
Halibut is considered by very many people to be superior
to any other sea fish.

Some of the shops sold fowls.   I observed that all the
fowls sold were very old, many of the hens having long
spurs ; I understand that a Jew or Jewess will always buy
fat fowls, no matter what their age may be ; they buy for
weight, if for nothing else.   The same rule applies to old
ducks and geese—they must have weight : they probably
have some peculiar way of cooking these old fowls.   When
they buy live fowls, they take them to their butcher, and
pay a penny or twopence to have them killed : there are
persons employed purposely to kill the beasts and other
animals.   The bullock is not slaughtered in the same way
that is usual in ordinary slaughterhouses ; according to
the Jewish religion, the beast must die from its throat
being cut, instead of being knocked on the head.   The

slaughterer of the cattle must be a Jew. 'London Labour and London Poor' tells us, 'Two slaughterers are appointed by the Jewish authorities of the synagogue, and they can employ others, who must likewise be Jews: if there is any trace of disease in the animal, the meat is pronounced unfit for the food of the Jews, and is sold to the Christians. To the parts exposed for sale, when the slaughtering has been according to the Jewish law, there is attached a leaden seal, stamped in Hebrew characters with the name of the examining party sealing. The meat killed by a Christian is called *tryfer*; that killed by the Jews is called *kosher*. On a Saturday there is cold fish for breakfast and supper; indeed, a Jew would pawn his shirt off his back rather than go without fish then, and in holiday time he will have it; it is not considered a holiday unless there is fish.

The thing that struck me most was the custom of the Jewish women wearing wigs. When standing at the corner I counted no less than nine Jewesses wearing wigs. Some of these wigs were brown and some black. They were apparently not worn for show purposes; some were low down on the forehead, some all awry, and some at the back of the head. I cannot conceive how the Jewesses can wear these hideous wigs. I believe this custom of wearing wigs is not confined to the poorer classes.

Statistics inform us that thirty-five thousand Jews reside in England; of these about eighteen thousand live in London. Of all curious places in London commend me to the Jewish fish-market in Petticoat Lane.

My learned friend Dr. Adler, the eminent Jewish Minister, and son of the chief Rabbi, wrote me to the

following effect:—' We Jews eat fresh-water fish simply
because we like them, and because the poor can afford
to buy them better than meat, which is more expensive.
We eat cucumbers simply because we regard them as a
delicacy, and most of our poor come from Holland and
Germany, where everybody eats cucumbers.

'The origin of eating fresh-water fish and cucumbers
may possibly be derived from the fifth verse of the
eleventh chapter of Numbers : "We remember the fish,
which we did eat in Egypt freely; the cucumbers,
and the melons, and the leeks, and the onions, and the
garlick."

'With reference to the wigs worn by the Jewish
women, these wigs are only worn by married women,
mostly Polish. The object is to cover the hair so as not
to be so attractive as before marriage.

'Our Passover is the eating of unleavened bread, but
the Paschal lamb is not offered any more, as the Temple
is destroyed.

'The language you heard in the market was not
Hebrew ; Hebrew is not spoken any more as a living
language. The conversations you heard were carried on
in a kind of German or Dutch mixed up with a few
Hebrew words. The advertisements in the shop windows
were not Hebrew, but German in Hebrew letters. A few
Hebrew words are used, such as *kosher*, "that which is
lawful to eat." Meat of an animal that has died without
being properly slaughtered, or suffering from any disease,
is called *tryfer*.'

THE MANATEE.

IT is very satisfactory to find that the science of natural history gets more and more popular year by year. This fact, I think, is obvious, inasmuch as it now pays to bring to this country, for purely show purposes, rare and valuable creatures from even the most distant parts of the world.

Five manatees have been exhibited in this country. The first was caught in 1866 in the Maroni River, Surinam, and Mr. Clarence Bartlett went out on purpose to bring it over. This animal was called by the familiar name of Patcheley, and he became by handling quite tame. Mr. Bartlett was in the habit of going into the water to feed him from a bottle containing milk, of which he was very fond. With a great deal of trouble Mr. Bartlett brought the animal to this country, but, unfortunately, not alive.

The name manatee has been given to this animal on account of the hand-like shape of the swimming paws, hence manatee. This curious creature is found in the great waters of South America, especially in the Amazon, and in Africa. It is also called *Vacca marina*, or seacow. I have consulted my old friend Gesner's *Icones*

Animalium (Heidelberg, 1606). He gives a wonderful picture of the sea-cow—meer-ochs in German. Of course Gesner had never seen a manatee or sea-cow; but what easier than to make one from imagination? We find, therefore, a very rude drawing of a cow's head projecting out of the water. The cow has the mouth open, as if in the act of bellowing, and has a splendid beard and dilated nostrils.

The next manatee came to the Zoological Gardens in August 1875. This animal was sent over by Mr. R. Swain, from Pin Point, Demerara, South America. The small seal pond was prepared for her reception by filling it with fresh water warmed to a proper temperature. The poor manatee seemed to much enjoy her bath after such a long sea voyage.

I do not recollect ever having seen a more interesting animal. The manatee belongs to the class *Sirenia*, but it is very puzzling to know what she is, whether a pachyderm or a cetacean. I think she may be said to be a little of both. She is purely an aquatic animal, and when seen in the water her head reminds one of something between a mole and a pig. Her body is terminated by a large tail, the shape of a lady's fan. She swims with it, moving it up and down, with the same action as a porpoise, and not sideways like a fish. Take a pig, tie his hind legs and curly tail, and flatten them into a broad, flat appendage, like a beaver's tail; turn his fore-feet into paddles like a turtle's flippers; cut off his ears, give him valvular nostrils like a seal, reduce his eyes to one-fourth, and then you will have a manatee. The people in Demerara call it the 'sea-pig.'

The eyelids are very peculiar; they are formed of circular muscular rings, like india-rubber rings. The hairy-eared rhinoceros has the same peculiar formation of eyelids. The manatee's eyes are very minute, and of a dull blue colour.

Mr. Bartlett was much pleased to find the manatee feed so well; she would eat lettuces and vegetable marrows all day. She got quite tame like a sheep, and would follow Mr. Bartlett round the pond and eat from his hand. It was very interesting to remark the extreme quiet with which this animal, one can hardly say swims, but rather gently glides through the water. Its skin is covered with two kinds of hair, soft and bristly. The appearance of the back reminds one of a prickly pear. The nostrils are most peculiar; they are situated at the extreme end of the nose, and the two valves seem to rise from the inside, with exactly the same quiet motion as does the hydraulic lift when it rises level with the platform at the Great Western station; or, again, its action may be likened to the working of the lid of the nest of the trap-door spider. She was supposed to be about half grown. The length of a full-grown manatee is from fourteen to sixteen feet, and the weight would average about 1,500 lbs. This manatee at the Gardens was seven feet two inches long, and weighed about 4 cwt.

The price asked for the manatee was 400l.

The tail contains a considerable quantity of oil; the natives chop it up and expose it to the sun, they then boil it and get oil, which is pure and not rancid. The old pharmacists prescribed this to cool the blood. It is said to taste like oil of almonds. Dr. Murie weighed the fat of this animal for dissection, and found it weigh twenty-four lbs. ten ounces, about one-nineteenth of the total weight of the animal.

Another manatee was exhibited at the Westminster Aquarium in 1878. It was captured off an island at the mouth of the Essequibo River, British Guiana. Since then two young manatees have been exhibited at the Brighton Aquarium.

The flesh of the manatee is considered a great delicacy; when roasted it has the taste of pork with a flavour of veal. It is said to retain its freshness much longer than other meat in a tropical climate, where meat generally putrefies in twenty-eight hours, and to be therefore well adapted for salting or pickling, as the salt has time to penetrate the meat before it is spoiled. The Indians hunt the manatee with harpoons. The cry, Mr. Bates reports, is something like the bellowing of an ox. The natives look upon the manatee as a supernatural animal, because it suckles its young as a human mother does her baby. The Indians say the milk is good.

The manatees are said to be whale-like in habit, and when at home to leap out of the water in a whale-like manner; and they were formerly abundant in the entrances of the Orinoco and the Amazon. They also ascend the rivers and take up their abode in the fresh-water lakes. Formerly they were very abundant in Cayenne, where the flesh was sold for 3d. per pound; but this caused them to be nearly exterminated, like the unhappy dodo.

The anatomy of the manatee is another instance of the adaptation of structure to the physical conditions under which the animal has to pass its existence. As a writer remarks, 'The power of swimming which these animals possess not only renders them quite safe from those casualties to which ruminant animals would be subject when the rains and inundations come, but it gives them a facility and a range in their migrations in quest of food which not even the fleetest of the antelopes, or any of the Mammalia which walk upon the earth, can possess. These last are hemmed in by the mountain ridges, by the deserts, and even by the larger rivers, and their march is laborious, and their food is often scanty. The manatee, on the other hand, launched upon the water, buoyant, and at home in that element, can, without any fatigue, migrate for thousands of miles whenever such migrations become necessary. In these extended marches they are not restrained even by the sea; for although it is not very probable that vegetable feeders will range the breadth of the ocean, yet it is certain that these animals often pass along the shores to very considerable distances.

'They also have this advantage, that they are far more certain of provisions by the way than the walking animals which migrate on land. In tropical countries there is never any barrenness if there is water, whether that water be a lake, a stream, or the sea; and thus the animals in question can always approach the bank and feed whenever a supply is required.'

In that admirable book, 'The Naturalist on the Amazons,' Mr. Bates gives us the following account :—

'They harpooned a manatee, or *Vacca marina*. On this last-mentioned occasion we made quite a holiday ;

the canoe was stopped for six or seven hours, and all
turned out into the forest to help to skin and cook the
animal. The meat was cut into cubical slabs, and each
person skewered a dozen or so of those on a long stick.
Fires were made, and the spits stuck in the ground, and
slanted over the flames to roast. A drizzling rain fell all
the time, and the ground around the fires swarmed with
stinging ants, attracted by the entrails and slime which
were scattered about. The meat had somewhat the
taste of very coarse pork ; but the fat, which lies in thick
layers between the lean parts, is of a greenish colour,
and of a disagreeable, fishy flavour. The animal was a
large one, measuring nearly ten feet in length and
nine in girth at the broadest part. The manatee is
one of the few objects which excite the dull wonder
and curiosity of the Indians, notwithstanding its com-
monness.

'The fact of its suckling its young at the breast,
although an aquatic animal resembling a fish, seems to
strike them as something very strange. The animal,
as it lay on its back, with its broad rounded head and
muzzle, tapering body, and smooth, thick, lead-coloured
skin, reminded me of those Egyptian tombs which are
made of dark, smooth stone, and shaped to the human
figure.'

I learn from Kirby's 'Bridgewater Treatise' that
Roupell, a traveller in Africa, discovered a species of
dugong (the dugong closely resembles the manatee) in
the Red Sea, and he is of opinion that it was the skin of
this animal with which the Jews were commanded to
cover the Tabernacle.

In the 'Proceedings of the Zoological Society,' vol. viii. p. 127, is a paper by Dr. Murie on the 'Anatomy of the Manatee,' which I consider one of the best he ever published. The skin, says Dr. Murie, claims for the manatee a kindred with the pachyderms. The anterior face, and particularly the under side, has a very warty surface and pitted structure. This skin is excessively thick and strong.

The Rev. J. G. Wood writes: 'So thick and strong is it that the wretched steel of which the native weapons are composed—namely, the machetes, or sword knives—are quite unable to penetrate the hide. Nothing is so effectual a weapon for this service as a common English three-cornered file, which is fastened to a spear-shaft, and pierces through the tough hide with the greatest ease. The skin of the manatee is so thick that it can be cut into strips like the too-celebrated "cow-hide" of America, which is manufactured from the skin of the hippopotamus.'

The upper lip of the manatee is full and cleft in the middle. It is covered inside with tufts of stiff bristles. Dr. Murie considers that these bristles inside the mouth correspond to and are the homologues of the whalebone in the mouth of the whale. These bristles are prehensile, as they will, I find, gently clasp one's fingers when the manatee can be persuaded to take a lettuce from the hand. I have not had an opportunity of examining the skull of a manatee. Professor Owen in his 'Odontology' has figured the teeth. He says they are thirty-six in number, nine on each side of both jaws. They are all implanted by two fangs, which enlarge as they descend and bifurcate at the extremity. The professor continues, 'The shape, structure, and mode of implantation of the molars of the manatee quite accord with the pachydermal type, and herein more especially with the tapir and dinotherium,' a very curious extinct animal, about whose habits very little is known.

THE GREAT SEA-SERPENT.

In June 1877 the Lords Commissioners of the Admiralty received official reports from the officers of the royal yacht 'Osborne,' relative to a large marine animal seen off Sicily; the documents were forwarded to the Right Hon. R. A. Cross, Secretary of State for the Home Department, who did me the honour to request my opinion on the matter. This subject being of so much interest and importance as bearing on the question of the existence or non-existence of the great sea-snake, I obtained the opinions of Professor Owen, Mr. A. D. Bartlett, of the Zoological Gardens, Captain David Gray, of the whaling ship 'Eclipse,' Peterhead, and Mr. Henry Lee. These papers, together with my own opinion, were forwarded to the Lords of the Admiralty, who kindly gave me permission in the interests of science to publish them, together with the evidence of the officers of H.M. yacht 'Osborne.

Commander Pearson, of the royal yacht 'Osborne,' in forwarding the accounts of the three officers of that yacht, who saw the sea monster off the coast of Sicily on June 2, 1877, writes:—'I myself saw the fish through a telescope, but at too great a distance (about 400 yards) to be able to give a detailed description; but I distinctly saw the seal-shaped head, of immense size, large flappers, and part of a huge body.'

Lieutenant Haynes writes, under date, ' Royal Yacht " Osborne," Gibraltar, June 6 : '—' On the evening of June 2, the sea being perfectly smooth, my attention was first called by seeing a ridge of fins above the surface of the water, extending about thirty feet, and varying from five to six feet in height. On inspecting it by means of a telescope, at about one and a half cables' distance,[1] I distinctly saw a head, two flappers, and about thirty feet of an animal's shoulder. The head, as nearly as I could judge, was about six feet thick, the neck narrower, about four to five feet, the shoulder about fifteen feet across, and the flappers each about fifteen feet in length. The movements of the flappers were those of a turtle, and the animal resembled a huge seal, the resemblance being strongest about the back of the head. I could not see the length of the head, but from its crown or top to just below the shoulder (where it became immersed) I should reckon about fifty feet. The tail end I did not see, it being under water—unless the ridge of fins to which my attention was first attracted, and which had disappeared by the time I got a telescope, was really the continuation of the shoulder to the end of the body. The animal's head was not always above water, but was thrown upwards, remaining above for a few seconds at a time, and then disappearing. There was an entire absence of " blowing " or " spouting." I herewith enclose a sketch (A) showing the view of the " ridge of fins," and (B) of the animal in the act of propelling itself by its two fins.'

Lieutenant Douglas M. Forsyth writes, under date, ' Royal Yacht " Osborne," at sea, June 4, 1877 : '—' At five

---

[1] A cable's length is 240 yards.

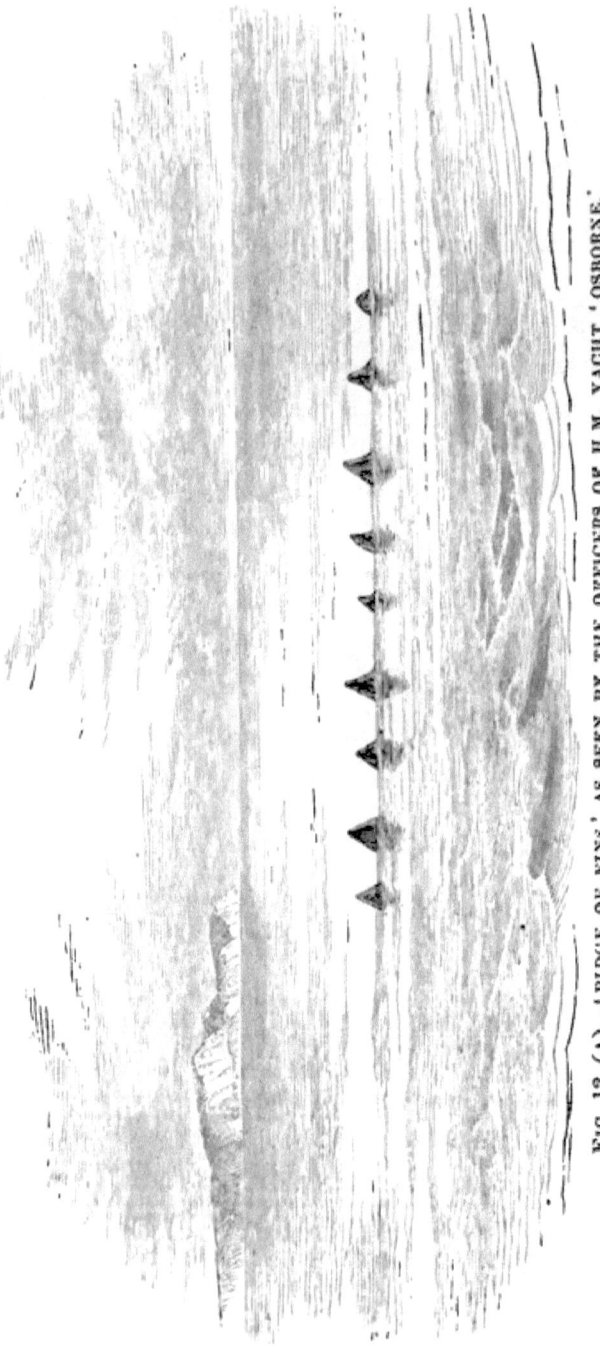

FIG. 12. (A) —'RIDGE OF FINS' AS SEEN BY THE OFFICERS OF H.M. YACHT 'OSBORNE.'

Fig. 13. (B)—ANIMAL SEEN THROUGH A TELESCOPE, IN THE ACT OF SWIMMING AWAY.

p.m. on the 2nd inst., while passing Cape St. Vito, north
coast of Sicily, I observed a large, black-looking object on
the starboard quarter, distant about two cables; and on
examining it with a telescope, I found it to be a huge
monster, having a head about fifteen to twenty feet in
length. The breadth I could not observe. The head
was round, and full at the crown. The animal was slowly
swimming in a south-easterly direction, propelling itself
by means of two large flappers or fins, somewhat in the
manner of a seal. I also saw a portion of the body of the
animal, and that part was certainly not under forty-five
or fifty feet in length.'

Mr. Moore, engineer of the royal yacht 'Osborne,'
writes:—' When looking over the starboard quarter of
the ship, my attention was called by observing an uneven
ridge of what appeared to me to be the fins of a fish above
the surface of the water, about a cable's length distance
from the ship. They varied in height, as near as I can
judge, from seven to eight feet above water, and extended
about forty feet along the surface. Not having a telescope
with me, I regret I am unable to give a further description.'

I submitted these reports to Professor Owen, who sent
me the following as his opinion on the matter:—' I have
carefully perused and considered the documents from the
Admiralty and Home Office which you submitted to me.
First as to Captain Pearson's letter. The objects or phenomena may have been of a nature unknown to the observers, but were not necessarily caused by a monster.
The appearances may not have been caused by a "fish."
The expression " seal-shaped head," " flappers," &c., denote

rather a cetacean than a " fish " or " monster ; " but, viewed
at the distance given, the ideas thereby excited and expressed are of no help or value to the naturalist. Secondly,
as to Lieutenant Haynes' letter :—Phenomena noted
through a telescope, at the distance given, by one not
conversant with natural history, are very seldom available
to one who is ; the present case is no exception. The
period during which the object was watched, or during
which uninterrupted observation of the phenomena was
made, should have been noted, in order to found an
opinion of the bearing of Lieutenant Haynes' remark as
to the motion of the animal's head. Thirdly, as to Lieutenant Forsyth's letter :—A seal propels itself chiefly by
its hind pair of flippers, which stretch backward beyond
the tail, to part of which they are attached. Fourthly,
as to Mr. Moore's letter :—Compare this with Lieutenant
Forsyth's statement, and with Lieutenant Haynes' statement.

'The discrepancies in the records of the watchers of
the same phenomena show the difficulty of exact observation at the distances and under the circumstances of
the case, both ship and object or objects being on the
move ; and remarks thereon by observers not conversant
with natural history, and so situated, preclude the formation of any opinion worth recording of the nature of the
object or objects causing the phenomena as interpreted
by the foregoing witnesses.

'But although the statements and terms applied may
be insufficient to enable the naturalist to recognise the
subject thereof, they by no means afford ground for concluding that what was seen was afforded by an object

unknown and unrecorded in natural history. There are
no grounds for calling it a "sea monster." I beg to call
attention to the paragraph concluding the Manual of
Zoology in the Admiralty Manual of Scientific Enquiry,
12mo, 3rd ed., 1859 :—"When an object is seen afloat,
and attracts notice by its magnitude or other peculiarity,
and is not captured, its nearest approach to the ship, its
mode, course, and rate of progression, and the parts
actually recognisable should be noted at the time with
the utmost accuracy. If practicable, a boat should be put
off for close observation and possible capture. If the observer has not the zoological knowledge, or the opportunity for exact inspection, requisite for determining the
species from the phenomena, he should abstain from
giving the object any special name. Supposing it to be
an animal, a shot fired, if even it do not hit, may so
alarm the creature as to cause some sudden movement
which may reveal more of its true nature." '

Mr. Bartlett's opinion is as follows :—

'In undertaking to write my opinion upon the statements made in this report, I must endeavour as far as possible to divest myself of the knowledge of all previous
accounts that have from time to time been published upon
this subject.

'Firstly, I think few men holding themselves as
honourable and trustworthy officers in Her Majesty's Service would risk their high position by any false or fabricated story of this nature. I will, therefore, take it for
granted that they described to the best of their ability
what they saw.

'Secondly, I have now to consider what appears to me

one very simple matter. All persons, by continual practice in the use of their eyes on land and at sea, acquire a great power in distinguishing and recognising the objects they have constantly under observation, and persons accustomed to the sea are most remarkable in this, to them, most important matter; men always on the look-out notice the smallest as well as more important objects, during the long periods they pass watching for something to turn up, and are not likely to mistake the ordinary and common occurrence of the appearance of seals, porpoises, sharks, or whales, for some previously unseen or unknown monster of the deep.

'I am therefore willing to admit and believe that some large animal or animals have presented themselves within sight of the officers of the "Osborne."

'My difficulty is to offer some explanation, and ascribe to some kind of animal the description laid before me. It is evidently not a serpent. According to all known species of serpent, none of them have fins or flippers or any external organs used for swimming, nor does the description agree with any of the seals or sea-lions, as no animal of this kind has fins on the back, nor do they use the flippers in front while swimming.

'Sketch (B) at first looks like a monster turtle, but sketch (A) at once dispels this idea.

'I have now to consider in what respect it resembles the whales and porpoises, and find it quite impossible to believe that men who must be well acquainted with the movements and frequent appearance of these creatures could so distort and magnify any of the known kinds into the object they have described.

'Lastly, I come to the sharks. The largest specimens known fail, however, to give me any hope of satisfying myself or any one else that any number of sharks could have led to the report furnished by the officers of the "Osborne."

'The description fails entirely in so many important points, that one cannot help being struck with the dissimilar appearances presented.

'I may remark that the fins upon the back give strength to the idea that sharks were the nearest approach to the creature or creatures seen ; but the head and neck described at once dispel the thought that any kind of shark could, by any possibility, be mistaken for what was seen.

'That the sketch (A) represents a number of fins like the back fins of sharks, supposing two or three sharks to be in company, would easily be concluded, did not the great height (six or eight feet out of the water) at once dispose of the probability of any known shark having fins of these dimensions.[1]

'I now feel called upon to answer the question, What was it ?

'I must, in reply, admit that I am unable to identify the figures and description with any known animal. With the dimensions given, it is most conclusive—in fact, proof positive—that no known species of animal was seen, the dimensions being so extraordinary that they admit of no doubt but that the creature is entirely unknown to

---

[1] There are Finner whales and large grampuses with a dorsal fin from four to six feet high. See Dewhurst, *Cetacea.* The *Selache,* or basking shark, also has a back fin between five and six feet high, corresponding with the dimensions given by Lieutenant Haynes.

naturalists. But I fully believe in the existence of animals in the deep at present unknown either by specimens or by perfect descriptions ; not only do I accept as true the statements made to the best of the judgment and belief of the parties who have made them, but doubtless from time to time other wonderful sights have presented themselves, and have remained unrecorded from fear of derision and misbelief ; but this, as seen at 400 yards on a clear day, appears so perfectly easy of observation that I cannot doubt the correctness of the statement in sketch (B).

'When we consider the vast extent of the ocean, its great depth, the rocky, cavernous nature of the bottom—of many parts of which we know really nothing,—who can say what may have been hidden for ages, and may still remain a mystery for generations yet to come ? for we have evidence on land that there exist some of the largest mammals, probably by thousands, of which only one solitary individual has been caught or brought to notice. I allude to the hairy-eared two-horned rhinoceros (*R. lasiotis*), captured in 1868 at Chittagong (where it was found stranded in the mud), and now known as an inhabitant of the Zoological Gardens.

'I could find other instances, but content myself by stating that this animal remains unique, and no part or portion was previously known to exist in any museum at home or abroad. We have here an instance of the existence of a species of rhinoceros, as large nearly as the hippopotamus, found on the continent of India, of which country we in England are supposed to know so much, where for many years collectors and naturalists have worked and published lists of all the animals met with, and here they have hitherto failed to meet with or obtain any knowledge of this great beast.

'May I not, therefore, presume that, in the vast and mighty ocean, animals, perhaps of nocturnal habits (and therefore never, except by some extraordinary accident, forced into sight), may exist, whose form may resemble the extinct reptiles whose fossil remains we find in such abundance?

'The form indicated and described strongly resembles some of the extinct reptilian characters, and reminds one of the models of fish-lizards and other animals described and constructed by Waterhouse Hawkins, under the direction of Professor Owen, and exhibited in the grounds of the Crystal Palace at Sydenham; and, as far as I am able to judge from the evidence before me, I have reason to believe that aquatic reptiles of vast size have been seen and described by those persons who have endeavoured to explain what they have witnessed.

'One thing is certain, that many well-known reptiles have the power of remaining for long periods (months, in fact) at the bottom, under water or imbedded in soft mud, being so provided with organs of circulation and respiration that they need not come to the surface to breathe. The large crocodiles, alligators, and turtles have this power, and I see no valid reason to doubt but that there may and do exist, in the unknown regions of the ocean, creatures so constructed.

'It may be argued that, if such animals still live, they must from time to time die, and their bodies would float, and their carcases would be found, or parts of them would wash on shore. To this I say, however reasonable such arguments may appear, that with most animals that die or are killed in the water, they sink at first to the bottom, where they are likely to have the flesh and soft parts devoured by other animals, such as crustacea, fishes, &c., &c.; and sinking in the deep, the bones, being heavier than the other parts, may soon become imbedded, and thus concealed from sight.

'In conclusion, I cannot shut my eyes to the many reports and statements made from time immemorial by persons far above suspicion of fraud or deception, and whose lives have been, for the most part, spent at sea, and whose knowledge of the appearances of all marine animals commonly seen entitles them to our most serious consideration.

'These more recent instances recorded by honest and trustworthy persons satisfy me that it is not only unfair, but unwise, and a great mistake, to disregard and throw overboard, as it were, the evidence brought by these different observers, simply because we cannot at present define exactly, by specimens or otherwise, the exact nature of the creatures that have been observed.'

The following is Mr. Henry Lee's opinion :—

'The evidence of "great sea-serpents," or other so-called "marine monsters," having been occasionally seen, is such as would be regarded as valid and cogent in any court of justice. The witnesses are trustworthy as to character, and competent by training and experience. The officers of Her Majesty's Navy are incapable of combining together to officially and intentionally promulgate falsehood; and they and the seamen under their command are too much accustomed to the sights of the sea to be easily misled, either to greatly exaggerate the dimensions of an animal in view, or to be so entirely deceived by appearances as not to recognise one already known to them. It appears to me, therefore, that, with such testimony before us, incredulity (which is more frequently than credence the result of want of knowledge) is unjustifiable; and that the statements and descriptions of such witnesses ought to be frankly accepted and carefully considered, with a view to satisfactory explanation, if that be possible.

'It should be remembered that the existence of gigantic cuttle-fishes was popularly disbelieved until within the past five or six years, during which period several specimens—some of them fifty feet in total length—have been taken, and all doubts upon that subject have been removed.

'In more than one case the appearance of the "sea monsters" described by masters of merchant vessels almost exactly accords with that of these great squids. These decapods are pelagic in their habits, and must not be confounded, as they too often are, with the octopods, which are rock-dwellers.

'In another case I agree with Professor Owen and Captain Gray, that the appearance of a whale attacked by a sea-serpent as seen by the crew of the barque " Pauline," on July 8, 1875, in lat. 5° 13' S., long. 35° W., may possibly be attributed to the movements of two whales rolling over and over. But the animal described by Commander Pearson and the officers of the Royal yacht " Osborne," and that seen by Captain McQuhae of H.M.S.

" Dædalus" in 1848, do not come within the scope of either of these suppositions. Lieutenant Haynes and Mr. Forsyth report that the former had flappers fifteen feet long, the movements of which were like those of a turtle; and Captain McQuhae says of the latter that it kept its head, which was, " without any doubt," that of a snake, constantly about four feet above the surface of the sea; that there was, at the very least, sixty feet of the animal *à fleur d'eau*, and that it passed so near to the vessel's quarter that, although it was swimming at the rate of from twelve to fifteen miles an hour, if it had been a man of his acquaintance he could easily have recognised his features with the naked eye. Neither whales nor sharks use their pectoral fins, or flippers, to swim with—their sole organ of propulsion is the tail; neither do they uplift out of water a head like that of a snake. I believe, therefore, that in both of these instances an animal has been seen which is either totally unknown to science, or which has hitherto been believed to be extinct.

'Other appearances described cannot be explained away as having been produced by sharks, whales, seals, cuttles, ribbon-fish, or logs of wood covered with barnacles and seaweed; and to insist on attributing them to one of these, or some other familiar object, is to assume that the stay-at-home naturalist has perfect cognizance of every existing marine animal of large size, and that the sea-going eye-witness is so inexperienced and uninstructed that his assertion that what he saw was none of these is worthless. I cannot regard such an assumption in either case as warrantable.

'During the deep-sea dredgings of H.M.S. "Lightning," "Porcupine," and "Challenger," many new species of Mollusca, and others which had been supposed to have been extinct ever since the Chalk epoch, were brought to light; and by the deep-sea trawlings of the last-mentioned ship there were drawn up from great depths fishes of unknown species, and which could not exist near the surface, owing to the distention and rupture of their air-bladder when removed from the pressure of deep water.

'I therefore think it by no means impossible—first, that there may be gigantic marine animals unknown to science, having their ordinary *habitat* in the great depths of the sea, only occasionally coming to the surface, and perhaps avoiding habitually the light of day; and, second, that there may still exist, though supposed to have been long since extinct, some of the old sea-reptiles whose fossil remains tell of their magnitude and habits, or others of species unknown even to palæontologists.

'The evidence is, to my mind, conclusive that enormous animals, with which zoologists are at present unacquainted, exist in the "great and wide sea;" and I look forward hopefully to the capture of one or more of them, and the settlement of this vexed question.'

Such were the opinions I received. For many years past I have taken the greatest interest in the reports of so-called sea-snakes. There are certainly snakes in the sea. These are generally very poisonous. They can be known from land snakes by having a flat tail for the purpose of swimming. I am, however, myself by no means a believer in the so-called 'great sea-snake.'

If such an animal existed, upon what can it subsist?

Where does it live? How does it multiply? and above all, how is it that the remains, especially the bones, are never found? Dead whales and whales' bones are often found, why not also the remains of the 'sea-snakes' (so called) if they had any existence?

According to Professor Owen's lectures, which I attended years ago, unknown monsters at sea have, when boats have been lowered to examine them, turned out to be—First, small whales or porpoises; second, seals; third, turtles, swimming respectively in Indian file one after the other, probably in the act of migrating. Congers or a line of congers may also have given origin to the story.

Some 'sea-snakes' have turned out to be logs of wood, more or less covered with seaweed and barnacles, or else trees floating with the roots uppermost. These objects moving with the rise and fall of the waves would give the appearance of a living animal with a mane.

The *Gymnetrus*, or 'Banks's oar-fish,' as well as the ribbon-fish, is also liable to be taken for a sea-snake. A bone, supposed to be that of a great sea-snake, was found in Bermuda. It turned out to be the body spine of a *gymnetrus*.

I have received from Nice a specimen of a ribbon-fish. A coloured cast, as well as the specimen itself, can be inspected in my 'Museum of Economic Fish Culture,' South Kensington.

In June 1877 a lady at Tenby saw an object which she took to be a kind of sea-serpent. In course of conversation with this lady, I came to the conclusion that what she saw was a very large octopus or cuttle-fish, swimming as it generally does, viz. with the pear-shaped body going front, the long tentacles following on behind. In my Museum of Fish Culture, South Kensington, is a model of a huge cuttle cut out in wood, quite large enough to give the appearance seen by this lady.

In September 1872 I received, through the Duke of Marlborough, an account of a 'sea-serpent' seen in Loch Hourn, Scotland, on the 20th and 21st August 1872, by the Rev. David Twopeny, late vicar of Stockbury, Kent, and by the Rev. John Macrae, late minister of Glenelg, Invernesshire, and his two daughters.

In describing this monster Mr. Twopeny says :—

'We saw it repeatedly for two days together in the Sound of Sleat, between Skye and the mainland, and in the opening of Loch Hourn. The weather was still and hot, and the sea like glass, and it is in such hot still days in August that it is described as being seen in the large Norwegian fiords, not often in the open sea. The head always appeared first, then the part next to the head, and then the rest, one bit after another, to the end. The greatest number of these convolutions, as the books call them, was eight including the head; they always appeared regularly, one after the other, beginning next the head, but when they disappeared they all sank together leaving the head visible. It appeared to be basking and often moved slowly, but sometimes with great rapidity, and when at the most rapid rate, these convolutions disappeared. We had three binocular glasses on board, and four people capable of observing.

'When first we saw it, it was going on at a very leisurely rate, and we saw it capitally, when it suddenly turned and came towards us; but when at about 100 yards (as Mr. M. computed, and he is a very accurate observer), it turned off. It was never nearer to us than this. They were getting the cutter on with sweeps both days, and it repeatedly came towards us, as if attracted by the rowing. Once on the second day it rushed along at a great rate, scarcely any of it visible, but making a tremendous rush through the water, and the noise was quite audible on board, the sea being quite still, and no wind. As to the size, it must be a good deal guesswork, but if one of the convolutions was six feet (and I can hardly think they could be less), and the intervals between the same, and six feet under water at the tail, it would be ninety-six feet. Many of the Norwegian accounts compute it to be considerably longer. They speak of its appearance being like a string of barrels, and that is just what this looked like. When I saw it the second day a good way off in the opening of Loch Hourn, I thought that if there was a vessel of that length it would be a large one. From that point it was on the second day more or less within sight of us till dusk, going on northwards, as we were going, towards the Kyle Rhea Skye Ferry; and we heard the next day that it passed the ferry with a rushing sound, which was heard by the people on shore. This creature is totally different from the animal which Captain McQuhae saw in 1848, and which he declared was a sea-serpent, but Professor Owen believed it to be a large seal. There is scarcely a probability but that this is a serpent. I imagine it raises its back to sun itself, and then straightens itself to go quickly. As it was approaching us at the nearest I plainly saw the sea running off its back and the back

D D

FIG. 14.—SEA-SERPENT AS SEEN IN THE HIGHLAND LOCH IN 1872.

of its head, as it does from a low flat rock which has been
submerged by a wave. F. M. was frightened out of her
wits, thinking it was coming down upon us; and between
that and the dangers of the sea—for she is always frightened in a boat—she insisted afterwards on being landed
at half-past two in the morning, and walked home by
herself in the moonlight, thirteen miles over wild mountain tracks.   Mr. M., who is a great naturalist, is greatly
interested about the creature. He has all his life been
going about on these seas, but never saw or heard anything of the kind before. He knew Mr. Maclean, the
minister of Eig, who saw it off Coll in June 1808, and
says he was quite a man to be believed. They well know
all the sea creatures here, whales, porpoises, seals, and
say there is not the slightest resemblance in them to this
animal; and I have seen porpoises repeatedly, and very
different they are.

  'Last summer Mr. M. heard that some unknown
animal was rushing about Loch Derich with great rapidity
for several days, and he imagines it must have been such
a one as we saw.

  'A word more about "the beast," as we call it here.
F. thought that the tumult of the water about the neck
was occasioned by a mane lashing about, and it might
well have been that, as far as the appearance of the water
went, but I saw no mane. The head appeared flattish,
and I saw distinctly under the chin, as shown in the
sketch. We could not see the eye. Mr. M. says very
truly, that I shall get the curves more accurately by drawing the whole of the curves, under water and all.   In the
sketch they are misshapen, and a little too high. These

convolutions rose easily, and not with a jerk—sometimes three, then four—always one after the other, lying next the head. The largest number I counted was six. Mr. M., who is very accurate, at one time counted eight, including the head. On the second day, in the latter part of the day, as we were going home in the Sound of Sleat, and the beast at a distance, going about and about, but still the same way, two of our party were both positive that they saw a back fin stick up, when not a very great part of the creature was visible. I did not see it, for I was perfectly tired out, and not any longer observing. If the fin exists, it must at other times have been in one of the submerged parts. I am very curious about this creature, and should much like to know what other people have seen. The first day Mr. Lillingstone's large schooner yacht was becalmed all day in the Sound with us, that is, from one to two miles off, and I think the people on board must have seen it. They had with them a steam launch, a noisy concern, with which they were always going about, and that may have kept it off.

'At the distance we saw it the colour appeared black. When the beast was first seen Kate M. said that the dark ridges were waves caused by the motion of the animal, such as might be in the wake of a steamer; but she soon abandoned this opinion, and I was satisfied, as I looked at it, that this was perfectly impossible. The creature was to the north of us, opposite to the sun, which was shining strongly at half-past twelve. No wave could have looked like that on the light side, with the sun shining upon it; nor do I believe a wave could have been nearly so black with the sun shining behind it. The moment the least fragment appeared, it looked inky black, like the head, as dark as a black slug, and totally different from anything in the water; and I was quite sure that no wave, even in shadow, could have looked like that. The next evening we had a ripple in the still sea in long dark lines between us and the sun. I was curious to see how far the creature would have been deeper in tone than these lines if he had passed among them then; but the only time he appeared just then was when he passed with an audible rush; scarcely any part of him was visible, and that had water rushing over it. Throughout, whenever he appeared, there was the same blackness, like a black slug, different from anything around. Two gentlemen have been here, from Eig, who have been cruising about the Hebrides for several weeks. One of them said that when he lived in Eig, he believed he had struck a thing of this kind; but Mr. M., on his describing it, said he had no doubt it was a basking shark, which is seen here sometimes. That creature has no power of raising its back in curved ridges like this.'[1]

A case was published in the papers in 1875 giving an account of a 'great sea-snake' attacking a whale. My friend Captain Gray tells me that this appearance of the snake curled round the whale was doubtless due to the appearance and reappearance of the fins of a large whale, rolling over and over. The hunchback whale has very long fins, ten to fifteen feet in length, and sometimes when they are playing about, they would present the same appearance as was shown in the 'Illustrated London News' some time since, in which was represented a serpent attacking a whale.

[1] An account of this appearance was also published by Rev. J. Macrae and Rev. D. Twopeny in the *Zoologist* for May 1873.

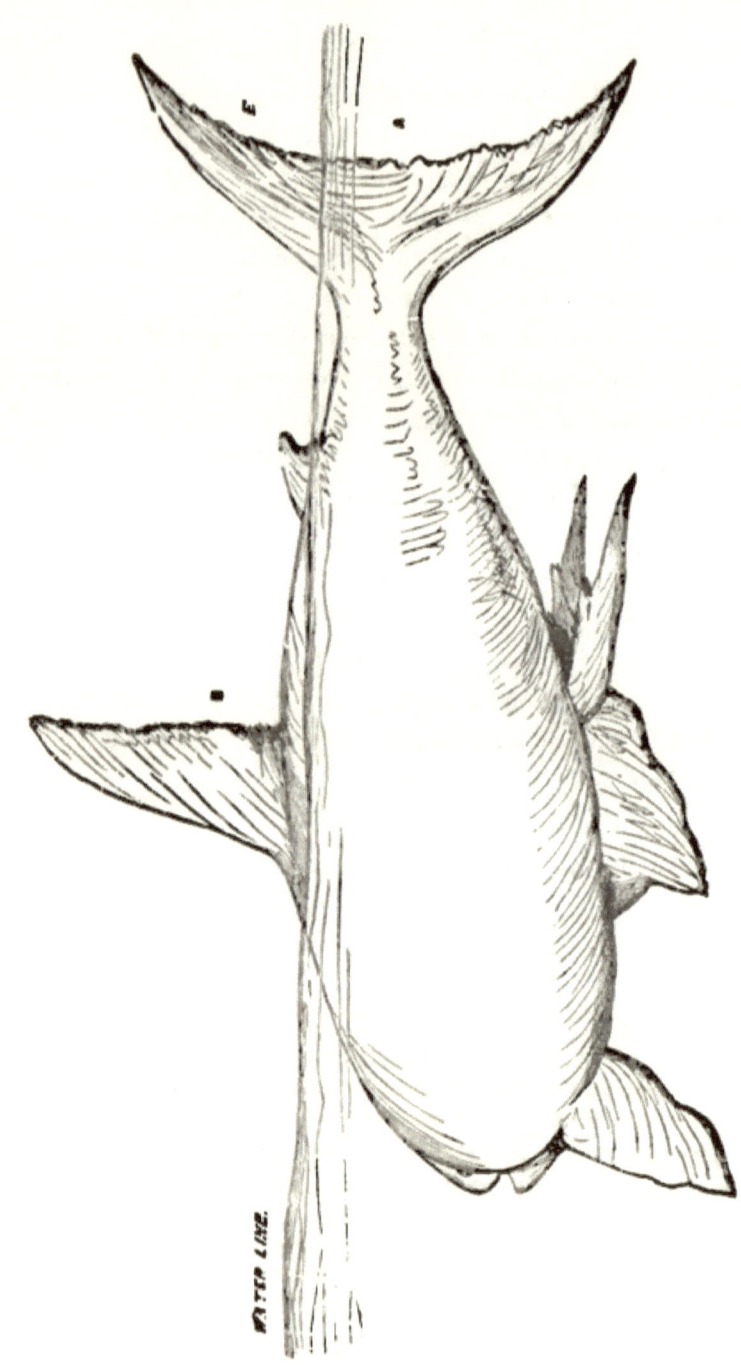

WATER LINE.

FIG. 15. — BASKING SHARK WITH FINS PROJECTING ABOVE THE WATER.

I must now give my opinion on the sea monster as seen by the officers of the yacht 'Osborne.' That they observed portions of some living creature or creatures is quite evident, but query, What was its or their true nature?

Possibly I may be wrong, but my theory is that the phenomenon was caused by *three or four basking sharks swimming in a line one behind the other*. The dorsal and caudal or tail fins of these huge fish projecting above the surface of the water might give the appearance shown in the drawing opposite, which I have had made as an illustration of my theory. It is a sketch of the basking shark, now at the British Museum. This specimen is twenty-eight feet long, and the skin weighed over one ton. The height of the dorsal fin was five feet three inches, length of upper lobe of tail five feet nine inches, length of pectoral fin along anterior margin five feet three inches.[1] I have drawn a line to show that if the fish were on the surface of the water the dorsal and tail fins B and E would project five or six feet into the air.[2]

[1] *Land and Water,* vol. xx. p. 177. The fins have now somewhat shrunk.

[2] The basking shark derives this name from its habit of remaining at the surface of the water almost motionless basking in the sun. It is sometimes called the sail-fish, from the 'sail-like aspect of its dorsal fin, which projects high out of water' (Wood's *Natural History*). It is often found in the Mediterranean. Spallanzani describes several kinds, and says they are found of great size in the summer in the Straits of Messina. Sometimes it is seen on the English coast; the British Museum specimen was cast ashore near Ventnor in March 1875. They occur frequently off the west coast of Ireland, especially on a bank about a hundred miles west of Clew Bay, Ire'and, where on sunny days in April and May they appear in great numbers, their dorsal fins being seen at a distance rising several feet out of water as they lie motionless basking in the sun (F. Buckland's *Natural History of British Fishes,* p. 216). Cuvier says they sometimes attain a length of more than

The grampus and sword-fish are not uncommon in the seas near Sicily, and a herd of either of these may possibly have given origin to the phenomenon. I agree with my friend Mr. Bartlett, that the captain and officers of the 'Osborne' deserve the thanks of naturalists and the public for giving their reports of this marine phenomenon.

When at Peterhead, on the Herring Inquiry, August 28, 1877, I had a long interview with my friend Gray. Captain Gray has had upwards of thirty years' experience in killing whales and seals in the Greenland seas and Baffin's Bay. He informs me that a full grown whalebone whale (*Balæna mysticetus*) would measure fifty to fifty-five feet in length. Scoresby, writing in 1830, mentions a whale fifty-eight feet in length. This was the longest he killed among 300 individuals. Gray says the appearance in the second figure given by the officer of the 'Osborne' closely represents a Greenland whale going away from the spectator. The whale, however, has not the power to bring up his fins as represented; neither are they of the same shape, or half the size. A whale's fin resembles a human hand with a mitten on. A whale propels himself entirely by his tail, and uses his fins only for rising to the surface by spreading them out, at other times they lie close along its sides. 'I have seen,' Captain Gray subsequently wrote, 'the movements of the Greenland whale, the Rorqual, and the Nordcaper, or Hunchback, below the water as closely and as distinctly as I could wish, and none of them use

thirty feet French, or thirty-two English feet (*Règne Animal*, vol. I. p 600). One caught at Hastings in 1808 and described by Sir E. Home (*Phil. Trans.* vol. xcix. p. 206), was thirty-six feet six inches long.

their fins in propelling themselves. **If** you have seen the porpoise in the Brighton Aquarium, you will have seen all the movements on a small scale. I have frequently seen whales show their fins, but at those times they were lying on their side, or rolling over and over. We constantly see the Nordcaper off Peterhead during the herring fishery season. I have noticed them within a quarter of a mile of the shore lying on their side, thrashing with their long fins.' As regards the distance mentioned in the report, viz. about 400 yards, he considers that a whale-boat could have performed the distance easily in three minutes in smooth water, and that **at this** distance objects could **be** clearly made out **by a good** telescope. He has, however, **known experienced seamen on board** the 'Eclipse' make mistakes in the recognition **of objects** floating in the water. Thus one officer of **the ship once** mistook a walrus for a whale, although the walrus was quite close to the ship; and **an experienced** seaman mistook a seal for a whale. Over and over again **he has** known a narwhal mistaken **for a whale.** He thinks the observers of the phenomenon **from the deck of the** 'Osborne' must have seen more animals than one going together, and showing different parts of their bodies.

No single animal, recent or **fossil, known** to science affords any analogy to the 'ridge of fins;' **while the ap-**pearance closely corresponds with **what must be a not** uncommon sight off the coast of Sicily, or elsewhere, where basking sharks **abound.**

Several kinds of whale are met with in the Mediterranean, though their appearance there **is** doubtless becoming more rare. The Spermaceti **whales, which**

attain a length of 50 to 100 feet, are found there (Cuvier, 'Règne Animal, vol. i. p. 342). Also a Rorqual, called by Cuvier 'le Rorqual de la Méditerranée.' A Rorqual 75 feet in length was stranded near St. Cyprien, Eastern Pyrenees, in 1828.

Whales are sometimes found in company with basking sharks, and also pursuing or pursued by other Cetacea.

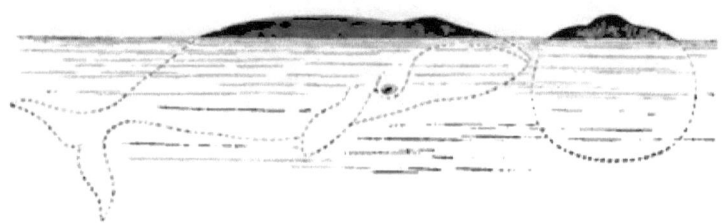

FIG. 16.—GREENLAND WHALE SWIMMING AWAY.

From a sketch supplied by Captain Gray.

Sonnini mentions a basking shark 31 feet long, caught six leagues from Boulogne in 1802, after a fight for 36 hours with a whale 85 feet long, which afterwards floated off towards England. The Spermaceti whales, especially the small-eyed Cachalot (*Physeter microps*), pursue and attack the smaller Cetacea, tearing them with their crooked teeth, while other species of whales are attacked by the grampus or sword-fish.

It is quite possible, therefore, that among a shoal of basking sharks in the Mediterranean a whale should appear rolling over and thrashing with its fins, which would afford a not improbable explanation of the phenomena observed.[1]

---

[1] Commander Macdonald, of the 'Vigilant' fishery cruiser, offered another similar explanation as follows:—'Sketch A, with its ridge of

As to the sea-serpent of Loch Hourn, I candidly confess that I am at a loss to come to any definite conclusion.

In the 'Naturalist's Library,' vol. viii., 'Marine Amphibia,' is given an engraving of a marine sea-snake by Pontoppidan, Bishop of Berg, and the drawing now before the reader is amazingly like the drawing by Pontoppidan.

In Topsel's edition of Gesner, 1658, there is a drawing of the 'sea-snake,' and in this instance again the animal is very much like the two mentioned before. Gesner says, 'There are also in the Suevian Ocean, or Baltic, sea-serpents of thirty or forty feet in length, whose picture is thus described as it was taken by Olaus Magnus, and he further writes that these do never harm any man until they be provoked.'

It is, therefore, evident to my mind that the coast of Norway and the north of Scotland are occasionally visited by a living creature, which, for want of a better name, is called 'The Great Sea Snake.' The theory that this

nine fins, said to be about thirty feet long, I take to be a fair representation of a small shoal of caing or bottle-nose whales (they are not unknown off Sicily). I have frequently seen a similar ridge of firs, and quite as uniform, extending not only thirty feet, but three hundred yards and more. With respect to sketch B, I have several times witnessed what I believe to be an explanation of it. Every variety of the whale known on the coast of the United Kingdom, when about to pair, swim slowly in pairs shoulder to shoulder for some time, and when going away from the observer the dorsal fins appear lying over at an angle of 45°, swaying slightly up and down. When in this position both whales may readily be mistaken for one of great breadth, the dorsal firs resembling side flappers; and when the head of one is slightly elevated above the other, it might fairly produce the impression conveyed by the sketch, especially on a person who saw the phenomenon for the first time.

phenomenon is caused by seals or porpoises swimming in a row seems to be fairly upset by the account given above. I think, after great consideration, it might have been a Gymnetrus, Banks's oar-fish (*Regalecus Banksii*), figured in Couch, vol. ii. p. 250. He says the largest was obtained at Kiess, near Wick; it measured fifteen feet and about a half in length, and as it had been injured much about the head, probably more. Its greatest depth was one foot two inches, its thickness three inches and a half, the weight one hundred and eighty-two pounds. There is, however, a point which must not be lost sight of in bringing this theory to bear. A gymnetrus, or a conger, when swimming would generally move its body in curves horizontally with the surface of the water, whereas in the drawing now before us, and the other two drawings above mentioned, the curves are represented with perpendicular motion.[1] Now, flat fish have this action, and it may be therefore that the living phenomenon was a ground fish. The Ichthyosaurus and Plesiosaurus, now fossil in the lias formation, must from their anatomy have swum after the manner of porpoises. We have not yet caught this Scotch sea-snake, whatever it may be; all that we can, however, deduce is that from its motion it is a ground and not a surface beast, and I do not think it could be a cetacean, because, be it well remarked, there is no record or any single account of its having blow-holes, or of its spouting. I shall

---

[1] Couch describes the Gymnetrus as rearing its head and crest above water, and moving sometimes with a lateral and sometimes with a vertical undulating motion; its size 'falling very far short indeed of the famous sea-serpent, but conveying the impression that the latter is a species of this same order of fishes.'

conclude by giving a catalogue of the sea-snakes, according to the 'Naturalist's Library,' 1839.

1. A specimen stranded on the island of Stronsay, one of the Orkneys, 1808. The bones were deposited in the Museum of the University of Edinburgh, and in the Royal College of Surgeons, and were determined by Sir E. Home to be the bones of a basking-shark. This beast is said to have measured 56 feet in length, and 12 in circumference, but Sir E. Home considered this measurement uncertain. ('Phil. Trans.' vol. xcix. p. 213.)

2. A specimen seen off the island Stonness, no date.

3. August 1817. Sea-snake seen in the harbour of Gloucester, thirty miles from Boston, America.

4. 1818. Seen by the fishermen of Sejerstad, in the Folden Fiord, Norway.

5. July 1819. It appeared off Otursun, Norway.

6. An animal with a serpent-like head raised two feet above the surface, and thirteen folds, was seen off Nahant, Boston, in August 1819.

7. In 1822. Again seen off one of the islands of Soroe, near Tinmask, Norway.

8. May 1833. One seen by three officers of Rifle Brigade off Halifax.

9. The sea-serpent again appeared off Nahant, going into Lynn Harbour, Boston, on July 14, 1833.

10. In the summer of 1837, it was reported near Storfosen, at the Kervang Islands.

Since then there is the beast seen by Captain McQuhae of the 'Dædalus,' on August 6, 1848. The sea-serpent of Loch Hourn, seen in August 1872; besides the creatures seen from the 'Pauline' in July 1875, and by the officers of the 'Osborne' in June 1877. So here we have a dozen or more so-called sea-serpents.[1]

From the above I think we may conclude that, whatever the sea-serpent may be, it generally appears in the hot months of the year from June to September, and this is all that I have to say about the great sea-snake at the present, wishing from the bottom of my heart that some one would catch it. I need not say how delighted I should be to have the job to cast and dissect it, and see how it eats.

[1] See also Sir Charles Lyell. *Second Visit to the United States*, vol. i. p. 131. London, 1849. Gosse, *Romance of Natural History*, vol. i. p. 275. London, 1880.

PRINTED BY
SPOTTISWOODE AND CO., NEW-STREET SQUARE
LONDON

With a Portrait.   Large crown 8vo. price 12s. 6d.

LIFE OF FRANK BUCKLAND.

By his Brother-in-Law, GEORGE C. BOMPAS,

Editor of 'Notes and Jottings from Animal Life.'

EXTRACTS FROM NOTICES BY THE PRESS

THE SPECTATOR.

'The charm of this book consists in the strong impression it gives us that Frank Buckland, with all his earnestness of character and scientific zeal, took his place in the animal world as a fellow-creature among fellow-creatures ; not, of course, disguising from himself for a moment the superiority of his own race to those of the creatures he studied with so much enthusiasm, but at the same time not importing into his attitude towards them any of the airs or pretensions peculiar to human nature...... In a word, it would be hard to find a volume so full of what is amusing, and yet so wholly free from any element by which one is ashamed to be amused.'

THE CONTEMPORARY REVIEW.

'The "Life of Frank Buckland" is a very delightful book. Mr. Bompas has put it together with great skill, mostly out of Mr. Buckland's own letters, journals, or articles, and gives us a very distinct picture of a man of curious but charming individuality, who lived among his beasts in an honest, brotherly way, like the people in old popular tales, and comforted himself in death by the belief that he "was going a long journey, where I think I shall see a great many curious animals." From first to last the book is readable and full of interest.'

THE GRAPHIC.

'The "Life of Frank Buckland" is from beginning to end such delightful reading that we cannot quarrel with Mr. Bompas because several of the stories have been already told. We can't have too much of Frank Buckland and Mr. Bartlett, and their sayings and doings at fairs and in shows. And besides enough of this to make his book a storehouse of delights for young people, Mr. Bompas gives us a very complete life of our late Inspector of Fisheries, whose appointment to that office was a rare instance of a man getting just the place for which nature had fitted him.'

THE TIMES.

'The fault we find with Frank Buckland's Life is that the early chapters are too delightful. The volume is full of instruction and varied entertainment for all who sympathise in Buckland's favourite pursuits ; but the story of the boy as father of the man is so piquant and original as rather to spoil us for what is to follow We can recall no equally striking example of the precocious bent of irrepressible instincts.'

LAND AND WATER.

'Charming reading from beginning to end. Frank Buckland as we knew him appears to have been the same Frank Buckland (on a miniature scale) in childhood. Keen in perception, earnest in work, genial, honourable, and clever, his life's history presents not only amusing but profitable reading. The story (which includes a great deal of most interesting extracts from his diaries and writings) gives us a well-arranged account of his journey through life, and when we have finished the volume we feel we have, so to speak, seen a photographic picture of Frank Buckland from life to death.'

THE LITERARY WORLD.

'To our thinking it would be difficult to find a biography at once more amusing, interesting, instructive, and inspiring than this of the genial, pure-minded, and enthusiastic naturalist who seemed but the other day to be among us in the full vigour of his manhood.'

THE GLOBE.

'Already a familiar household word, the name of Frank Buckland will possess new and vivid attractions for the general public from the incomparable biography of him which has just been written by his brother-in-law, Mr. George C. Bompas. Mr. Bompas could hardly have done his work better.'

London : SMITH, ELDER, & CO., 15 Waterloo Place.

SMITH, ELDER, & CO.'S PUBLICATIONS.

LIFE OF HENRY FAWCETT. By LESLIE STEPHEN, Author of '**A** History of English Thought in the Eighteenth Century,' 'Hours in a Library,' &c. Fourth Edition. Large crown 8vo. With 2 Steel Portraits. 12s. 6d.

A JOURNAL KEPT BY DICK DOYLE in the year 1840. Illustrated by several hundred Sketches by the Author With an Introduction by J. HUNGERFORD POLLEN, and a Portrait. Second Edition. Demy 4to. 21s.

. The Journal has been reproduced in fac-simile, and is printed on fine paper. It is handsomely bound in cloth, and forms a very elegant gift-book.

DON QUIXOTE. The Ingenious Gentleman, Don Quixote of La Mancha. By MIGUEL DE CERVANTES SAAVEDRA. A Translation, with Introduction and Notes, by JOHN ORMSBY, Translator of the 'Poem of the Cid.' 4 vols. 8vo. 12s. 6d. each.

ENGLISH LIFE IN CHINA. By Major HENRY KNOLLYS, Royal Artillery, Author of 'From Sedan to Saarbrück,' Editor of 'Incidents in the Sepoy War,' 'Incidents in the China War,' &c. Crown 8vo. 7s. 6d.

WITH HICKS PASHA IN THE SOUDAN. By Col. the Hon. J. COLBORNE, Special Correspondent of the *Daily News*. With Portrait Group of Hicks Pasha and Staff. Second Edition. Crown 8vo. 6s.

SOME LITERARY RECOLLECTIONS. By JAMES PAYN, Author of ' By Proxy ' &c. Fcp. 8vo. limp cloth, 2s. 6d.

MRS. DYMOND. By Miss THACKERAY (Mrs. RICHMOND RITCHIE). Large crown 8vo. 12s. 6d.

HAYTI ; or, the Black Republic. By Sir SPENSER ST. JOHN, K.C.M.G., formerly Her Majesty's Minister Resident and Consul-General in Hayti, now Her Majesty's Special Envoy to Mexico. With a Map. Large crown 8vo. 7s. 6d.

THE SCOURGE OF CHRISTENDOM : Annals of British Relations with Algiers prior to the French Conquest. With Illustrations of Ancient Algiers from 1578 to 1824. By Lieutenant-Colonel R. L. PLAYFAIR, H.B.M.'s Consul to Algiers. With Illustrations. Demy 8vo. 14s.

THE GIANT'S ROBE. By F. ANSTEY, Author of ' Vice Versâ.' Fourth Edition. Crown 8vo. 6s.

CITIES OF EGYPT. By REGINALD STUART POOLE. Crown 8vo. 5s.
' A book which does not contain a dull line from beginning to end.'—ACADEMY

LEAVES FROM THE **DIARY OF** HENRY GREVILLE. Edited by the VISCOUNTESS ENFIELD. **FIRST SERIES.** 8vo. 14s. SECOND SERIES. With Portrait. 8vo. 14s.

UNDERGROUND RUSSIA : Revolutionary Profiles and Sketches from Life. By STEPNIAK, formerly Editor of 'Zemlia i Volia' (Land and Liberty). With a Preface by PETER LAVROFF. Translated from the Italian. Second Edition. Crown 8vo. 6s.

London : SMITH, ELDER, & CO., 15 Waterloo Place.

SMITH, ELDER, & CO.'S PUBLICATIONS.

London SMITH, ELDER, & CO., 15 Waterloo Place.

E E

SMITH, ELDER, & CO.'S PUBLICATIONS.

WALKS IN FLORENCE AND ITS ENVIRONS. By SUSAN and JOANNA HORNER. New Edition, Revised and Enlarged, with numerous Illustrations. 2 vols. crown 8vo. 21s.

THE LIFE OF LORD LAWRENCE. By R. BOSWORTH SMITH, M.A., late Fellow of Trinity College, Oxford; Assistant Master at Harrow School; Author of 'Mohammed and Mohammedanism,' 'Carthage and the Carthaginians,' &c. New, Revised, and Cheaper Edition, being the Sixth Edition. 2 vols. large crown 8vo. with 2 Portraits and 2 Maps, 21s.

LIFE OF SIR HENRY LAWRENCE. By Major-General Sir HERBERT BENJAMIN EDWARDES, K.C.B., K.C.S.I., and HERMAN MERIVALE, C.B. With Two Portraits. 8vo. 12s.

LIFE OF LIEUT.-GENERAL SIR JAMES OUTRAM. By Major-General Sir FREDERIC J. GOLDSMID, C.B., K.C.S.I. Second Edition. 2 vols. demy 8vo. 32s.

MOHAMMED AND MOHAMMEDANISM : Lectures delivered at the Royal Institution of Great Britain in February and March 1874. By R. BOSWORTH SMITH, M.A. Second Edition, Revised, with considerable Additions. Crown 8vo. 8s. 6d.

THE MERV OASIS : Travels and Adventures East of the Caspian during the Years 1879-80-81, including Five Months' Residence among the Tekkes of Merv. By EDMOND O'DONOVAN, Special Correspondent of the *Daily News*. In 2 vols. demy 8vo., with Portrait, Maps, and Facsimiles of State Documents, 36s.

MERV : a Story of Adventures and Captivity. Epitomised from 'The Merv Oasis.' By EDMOND O'DONOVAN, Special Correspondent of the *Daily News*. With a Portrait. Crown 8vo. 6s.

THE LIFE OF MAHOMET. With Introductory Chapters on the Original Sources for the Biography of Mahomet, and on the Pre-Islamite History of Arabia. By Sir WILLIAM MUIR, LL.D. 4 vols. demy 8vo. 32s.

THE LIFE OF MAHOMET. From Original Sources. By Sir WILLIAM MUIR, LL.D. A New and Cheaper Edition, in one volume. With Maps. 8vo. 14s.

ANNALS OF THE EARLY CALIPHATE. By Sir WILLIAM MUIR, K.C.S.I., Author of 'The Life of Mahomet,' &c. With Map. 8vo. 16s.

ESSAYS ON THE EXTERNAL POLICY OF INDIA. By the late J. W. S. WYLLIE, C.S.I., India Civil Service, sometime Acting Foreign Secretary to the Government of India. Edited, with a brief Life, by W. W. HUNTER, B.A., LL.D. With a Portrait of the Author. 8vo. 14s.

EGYPT OF THE PHARAOHS AND OF THE KHEDIVE. By the Rev. F. BARHAM ZINCKE. Second Edition. Demy 8vo. 16s.

THE ANNALS OF RURAL BENGAL. From Official Records and the Archives of Ancient Families. By W. W. HUNTER, LL.D. Vol. I. The Ethnical Frontier. Fifth Edition. Demy 8vo. 18s.

By the same Author.

ORISSA ; or, The Vicissitudes of an Indian Province under Native and British Rule. Being the Second and Third Volumes of 'Annals of Rural Bengal.' With Illustrations. 2 vols. demy 8vo. 32s.

A LIFE OF THE EARL OF MAYO, Fourth Viceroy of India. 2 vols. Second Edition. Demy 8vo. 24s.

London : SMITH, ELDER, & CO., 15 Waterloo Place.

W. M. THACKERAY'S WORKS.

NEW 'STANDARD' EDITION. In 26 vols. large 8vo. 10s. 6d. each. This Edition contains some of Mr. Thackeray's writings not before collected, with many additional Illustrations. It has been printed from new type, on fine paper; and, with the exception of the Edition de Luxe, it is the largest and handsomest edition that has been published.

THE ÉDITION DE LUXE. Twenty-four Volumes, imperial 8vo. Containing 248 Steel Engravings, 1,473 Wood Engravings, and 88 Coloured Illustrations. The steel and wood engravings are all printed on real China paper. The NUMBER of COPIES PRINTED is LIMITED to ONE THOUSAND, each copy being numbered. The Work can only be obtained through Booksellers, who will furnish Information regarding terms, &c.

THE LIBRARY EDITION. With Illustrations by the Author, RICHARD DOYLE, and FREDERICK WALKER. Twenty-two Volumes, large crown 8vo. handsomely bound in cloth, price £8. 5s.; or half-russia, marbled edges, £12. 12s.

. *The Volumes are sold separately, in cloth, price 7s. 6d. each.*

THE POPULAR EDITION. 12 vols. crown 8vo. with Frontispiece to each volume, scarlet cloth, gilt top, price £3; and in half-morocco, price £5. 5s.

. *The Volumes are sold separately, in green cloth, price 5s. each.*

CHEAPER ILLUSTRATED EDITION. In Twenty-four Volumes, crown 8vo. price 3s. 6d. each. In Sets of Twenty-four Volumes uniformly bound in cloth, price £4. 4s.; or handsomely bound in half-morocco, price £8. Containing nearly all the small Woodcut Illustrations of the former Editions and many New Illustrations by Eminent Artists.

THIS EDITION CONTAINS ALTOGETHER 1,526 ILLUSTRATIONS

By the AUTHOR: LUKE FILDES, A.R.A.; Mrs. BUTLER (Miss Elizabeth Thompson); GEORGE DU MAURIER; RICHARD DOYLE; FREDERICK WALKER, A.R.A.; GEORGE CRUIKSHANK; JOHN LEECH; FRANK DICKSEE; LINLEY SAMBOURNE; F. BARNARD; E. J. WHEELER; F. A FRASER; CHARLES KEENE; R. B. WALLACE; J. P. ATKINSON; W. J. WEBB; T. R. MACQUOID; M. FITZGERALD; W. RALSTON; JOHN COLLIER; H. FURNISS; G. G. KILBURNE, &c., &c., &c.

BALLADS. By WILLIAM MAKEPEACE THACKERAY. With a Portrait of the Author, and 56 Illustrations by the Author; Mrs. BUTLER (Miss Elizabeth Thompson); GEORGE DU MAURIER; JOHN COLLIER; H. FURNISS; G. G. KILBURNE; M. FITZGERALD; and J. P. ATKINSON. Printed on toned paper by Clay, Sons, & Taylor; and elegantly bound in cloth, gilt edges, by Burn. Small 4to. 16s.

W. M. THACKERAY'S SKETCHES.

THE ORPHAN OF PIMLICO, and other Sketches, Fragments, and Drawings. By WILLIAM MAKEPEACE THACKERAY. Copied by a process that gives a faithful reproduction of the originals. With a Preface and Editorial Notes by Miss Thackeray. A New Edition, in a new style of binding, bevelled boards, gilt edges, royal 4to. price One Guinea.

London: SMITH, ELDER, & CO., 15 Waterloo Place.

www.ingramcontent.com/pod-product-compliance
Lightning Source LLC
Chambersburg PA
CBHW021327110726
47900CB00005B/1378